# Logic and Ontology in Heidegger

# Logic and Ontology in Heidegger

David A. White

Ohio State University Press
COLUMBUS

Portions of chapter 3 appeared in *Southwestern Journal of Philosophy* (Fall 1980):102-25; reprinted by permission.

Portions of chapter 4 appeared in *Southwestern Journal of Philosophy* (Fall 1978):51-63; reprinted by permission.

Portions of chapter 7 appeared in *Monist* (October 1981):518-33; reprinted by permission.

Portions of chapter 8 appeared in the *Tulane Studies in Philosophy* (Fall 1984); reprinted by permission.

Copyright © 1985 by the Ohio State University Press
*All Rights Reserved*

**Library of Congress Cataloging in Publication Data**

White, David A., 1942-
    Logic and ontology in Heidegger

    Bibliography: p.
    Includes index.
    1. Heidegger, Martin, 1889-1976—Contributions in logic.
 2. Heidegger, Martin, 1889-1976—Contributions in ontology.
 3. Logic.  4. Ontology.  I. Title.
 B3279.H49W45  1985        111'.092'4        85-15300
 ISBN 0-8142-0396-5

# Contents

**Preface** .............................................. vii
**Abbreviations** ...................................... xiii

### Part One  Logic and Ontology

**Introduction**
On the Possibility of Interpreting Heidegger ..... 3

**Chapter 1**
The Challenge of the Principle of Contradiction .. 22

**Chapter 2**
The Ontological Structure of Negation ........... 44

**Chapter 3**
Sameness and Difference ....................... 67

**Chapter 4**
Identity and the History of Metaphysics ......... 88

### Part Two  Ontology and Logic

**Chapter 5**
The Individuation of Things .................... 105

**Chapter 6**
The Existence and Nature of Deity .............. 128

**Chapter 7**
History and Being ............................. 149

**Chapter 8**
The Structure of Being as Presence (*Anwesen*) ... 175

**Conclusion** ........................................ 206
**Notes** ............................................. 211
**Bibliography** ...................................... 229
**Index** ............................................. 241

# Preface

THE THOUGHT OF MARTIN HEIDEGGER PRESENTLY stands as a paramount contribution to twentieth-century reflection. Whether Heidegger occupies a similar position in subsequent ages depends on many factors, one of them being the simple matter of whether there will be any subsequent ages. The possibility of a future depends on the realities of the present, and it is safe to say that the twentieth century has seen a mixed performance in the human drama, with perhaps more darkness than light as its legacy. Heidegger has not been absent from this stage—to his detractors, he looms as a key figure in the spread of a distinctively philosophical darkness; to his devotees, he has endowed our world with one of its few illuminating moments. Which critical estimate will prevail can be determined only when the future has retreated into the present. It nonetheless seems evident that how the future views Heidegger will be based, at least in part, on how Heidegger is understood in relation to the past, in particular to that past which is the history of metaphysics. This study is intended to contribute to one aspect of that understanding—the relation between Heidegger's approach to logic and the effect this approach had on his own formulation and development of problems appropriate to thinking.

Heidegger said much about logic. His quest to divine the hidden recesses of Western metaphysics compelled him to subject the so-called formal principles of rationality to frequent critical scrutiny. Heidegger pursued this phase of his quest for Being not from mere antiquarian interests, but because such an investigation bore directly on those problems that must engage the attention of thought in the present-day world. It should therefore be possible at least to indicate the direction in which Heidegger's own thinking on a given ontological region or even on Being itself depends on his position concerning the hidden metaphysical structures embedded within the principles of logic. In fact, we shall see that the structure of thought implicit in Heidegger's critique of the metaphysics in logic frequently determines the content of his own substantive contributions to thinking as Denken. If we understand why Heidegger says what he says about logic, then we will appreciate more fully why he says what he says about those matters capable of being thought. And it will become evident that various crucial questions concerning these substantive doctrines begin to take shape in the background area defined by Heidegger's prior understanding and analysis of the implicit metaphysics at work in the putatively "formal" principles of logic.

The theme of Heidegger on logic has not gone unnoticed in the secondary literature, and commentary on the more important sources will appear at suitable junctures below. I may at this point be permitted a summary evaluation of this work, with the promise to substantiate my impressions with subsequent arguments on specific points. In general, the existing studies either lack sufficient ontological scope or fail to drive Heidegger's position to the point where assessment of that position is possible. The theme of Heidegger on logic is a complex matter, requiring extensive analysis. And once analyzed, this theme produces problems and paradox. The scope and rationale of the critical stance to be employed in this study will be developed more fully in the Introduction, but it is worth noting now that my intention is not simply to interpret Heidegger, but to formulate potentially relevant criticisms of him as well.

It is also worth mentioning here at the outset how the reader should approach the word "logic" in this work. Heidegger generally refers to logic as if it were a closed and finished system, a seamless whole with little if any internal differentiation. The contemporary divisions of logic into tense logic, modal logic, epistemic logic, etc., as well as the many issues that remain under dispute by logical theorists, find no place in Heidegger's thought. Logic is simply logic, animated by a certain set of presuppositions that Heidegger has attempted to bring into the open for study and criticism. Even such a fundamental difference as that between the logic of propositions and quantificational logic is never introduced. Now I do not want to contend that Heidegger was unfamiliar with, say, the complexities and subtleties that appear in *Principia Mathematica*; the point is that Heidegger's writings do not approach logic as the varied and multiform discipline which it in fact is. The sense in which Heidegger did understand logic will become apparent as this study unfolds. And it is fair to say now that the reader with an elementary grasp of logical operations and theory will be adequately prepared for this aspect of what will follow. It must also be said, however, that the questions, inferences, and ontological positions Heidegger formulates on the basis of his treatment of logic will make a different kind of demand.

The study opens with an Introduction in which I offer arguments for certain principles of interpretation. This preliminary discussion is necessitated by the fundamental character of the present inquiry. Part 1, Logic and Ontology, is in four chapters. Chapter 1 develops Heidegger's thinking on the principle of contradiction, in many ways the cornerstone of his critique of logic. In chapter 2 the concept of negation is analyzed, particularly with respect to Heidegger's attempt to provide an ontological basis for that concept. Chapter 3 discusses the concepts of sameness and difference, and Heidegger's integration of history into these concepts. This theme is developed further in chapter 4, which emphasizes the status of the principle of identity as an historical phenomenon.

Part 2, Ontology and Logic, is also divided into four chapters. Chapter 5 discusses the individuation of beings with special attention to the concept of thing (*Ding*) as developed in Heidegger's distinctive doctrine of the fourfold. Chapter 6 details the existence and nature of one particular being, the deity, again against a backdrop of the fourfold. Chapter 7 concerns Heidegger's understanding of history in relation to the notion of the ontological difference between Being and beings. And chapter 8 attempts to describe the intricate structure of Being as presence (*Anwesen*), a position developed in Heidegger's late essay "*Zeit und Sein.*" Some final thoughts are contained in a brief conclusion.

Two notes on the general format of the work. First, in Part 1, Heidegger's various discussions of logical principles have been arranged in approximate systematic order. Heidegger frequently reflects on logic in general and on given logical principles in particular, but these analyses are not always prefigured in titles of books and essays. They are integrated into reflections on topics of apparently nonlogical nature—doubtless a carefully designed mode of exposition intended to contribute to our awareness that logic permeates all of our representational thinking on matters metaphysical, and on everything else as well. Heidegger leaves to the reader the tasks of gathering what he has said in various sources about, e.g., the principle of contradiction, then of unifying these utterances into coherent positions. Such unification is one of the goals of the presentation in Part 1. However, I attempt to base my interpretations whenever possible on a textual whole—a complete essay or extended discussion—rather than on isolated dicta collected here and there.

Second, the range of problems discussed in Part 2 is, of course, hardly a comprehensive treatment of Heidegger's later thinking, but these problems are nonetheless seminal to Heidegger and they possess, in their own right, a rich tradition within the history of metaphysics. Furthermore, these problems have been stops along Heidegger's own way, and they have been crucial stops. If, therefore, the way of Heidegger's own thinking was, as he himself said, continuous in direction and goal, then any criticism showing that some part of that way moved errantly may result in abandoning that way, or at least striking forth in a different and perhaps already trodden direction.

One final remark. All studies of Heidegger appearing prior to the completion of the *Gesamtausgabe* planned by Vittorio Klostermann are in a sense premature. Until all volumes of this edition are at hand, no work on Heidegger can lay claim to anything like comprehensiveness. This study considered every available volume of that edition, as well as all the work that Heidegger himself saw through press. Now it is possible that this latter body of writing, itself voluminous, will in the end convey whatever is significant in Heidegger's thought, with the other volumes of the *Gesamtausgabe* adding background and incidental development but little or perhaps even nothing in the way of radical revision or change of doctrine. This expectation may not be justified, of course, but here again only time will tell.

In any case it is the destiny of most secondary sources to become dated sooner or later even when the textual basis to be considered has been completed. In this instance, however, the target of Heidegger's critical thinking—the history of metaphysics and the patterns of logical thinking left by that history—are and will be with us for an extended period of time. My hope would be that this study will contribute to the reader's understanding of one important and perhaps unavoidable way to reflect on the logical and metaphysical implications of Heidegger's thought.

Some of the material of this book has already appeared elsewhere in different forms. Earlier versions of chapters 3 and 4 were published as articles—"Heidegger on Sameness and Difference" in the *Southwestern Journal of Philosophy* (1980) and "Two Premises in Heidegger's Analysis of Identity" in the *Southwestern Journal of Philosophy* (1978). Part of chapter 7 originally appeared as "On Historicism and Heidegger's Notion of Ontological Difference" in *Monist* (1981). And part of chapter 8 was published as "On Being and Unity in Heidegger" in *Tulane Studies in Philosophy* (1984). I would like to express my appreciation to the editors of these journals for permission to incorporate this material into this book. I would also like to thank Mary Jeanne Larrabee for her typically perceptive editing, both philosophical and stylistic. And a final note of gratitude to S. Davey for her careful work in typing the manuscript.

# Abbreviations of Heidegger's Works

| | |
|---|---|
| **AE** | *Aus der Erfahrung des Denkens* |
| **AM** | *Aristoteles, Metaphysik Theta 1-3 von Wesen und Wirklichkeit der Kraft* |
| **EH** | *Erläuterungen zu Hölderlins Dichtung* (4th ed.) |
| **EM** | *Einführung in die Metaphysik* |
| **FD** | *Die Frage nach dem Ding* |
| **FS** | *Frühe Schriften* |
| **G** | *Gelassenheit* |
| **GM** | *Die Grundbegriffe der Metaphysik Welt-Endlichkeit-Einsamkeit* |
| **GP** | *Die Grundprobleme der Phänomenologie* |
| **GR** | *Grundbegriffe* |
| **H** | *Heraklit Seminar Wintersemester 1966 / 67* |
| **HA** | *Hölderlins Hymne "Andenken"* |
| **HE** | *Heraklit 1. Der Anfang des abendländischen Denkens 2. Logik. Heraklits Lehre vom Logos* |
| **HG** | *Hölderlins Hymnen "Germanien" und "Der Rhein"* |
| **HH** | *Hebel der Hausfreund* |
| **HI** | *Hölderlins Hymne "Der Ister"* |
| **HO** | *Holzwege* |
| **HP** | *Hegels Phänomenologie des Geistes* |
| **ID** | *Identität und Differenz* |
| **K** | *Die Technik und die Kehre* |
| **KP** | *Kant und das Problem der Metaphysik* |
| **KR** | *Die Kunst und der Raum* |
| **L** | *Logik Die Frage nach der Wahrheit* |
| **MA** | *Metaphysische Anfangsgründe Logik im Ausgang von Leibniz* |
| **MH** | *Martin Heidegger zum 80. Geburtstag* |
| **NI** | *Nietzsche I* |
| **NII** | *Nietzsche II* |
| **P** | *Parmenides* |
| **PG** | *Prolegomenon zur Geschichte des Zeitbegriffs* |
| **PI** | *Phänomenologische Interpretation von Kants Kritik der reinen Vernunft* |
| **PT** | *Phänomenologie und Theologie* |

| | |
|---|---|
| **S** | *Schellings Abhandlung über das Wesen der menschlichen Freiheit (1809)* |
| **SD** | *Zur Sache des Denkens* |
| **SG** | *Der Satz vom Grund* |
| **SH** | *"Sprache und Heimat"* |
| **SZ** | *Sein und Zeit* |
| **US** | *Unterwegs zur Sprache* |
| **VA** | *Vorträge und Aufsätze* |
| **WD** | *Was Heisst Denken?* |
| **WM** | *Wegmarken* |
| **WP** | *Was ist Das—Die Philosophie?* |

# PART I
# Logic and Ontology

INTRODUCTION

# On the Possibility of Interpreting Heidegger

THE MODALITY IN THE TITLE OF THESE INTRODUCTORY remarks may seem out of place. After all, in one sense the possibility of interpreting Heidegger has clearly been actualized, since the existing interpretations already number in the thousands. But the fact that there are many interpretations of Heidegger does not touch the sense of possibility I wish to discuss here. This sense depends on taking into account the implications that arise when the radical character of Heidegger's mode of questioning is placed in conjunction with the attempt to reformulate Heidegger's teaching in order to evaluate that teaching according to some standards of rightness.

For Heidegger, it is axiomatic that (a) Being (*Sein*) is essentially historical, (b) the history of metaphysics has distorted the true nature of Being, and (c) we remain within the history of metaphysics even after our sensibilities have detected this distortion. It is nonetheless possible, we are told, for thinking in the sense of Heideggerian Denken to overcome the history of metaphysics represented only in truncated form. Now the way in which the student of Heidegger approaches the separation between Denken and the metaphysical tradition will play a crucial role in determining both the substance and the tone of what will be written about Heidegger. If, for example, one believes that the distance between thinking and metaphysics is wide, then one will likely stay within the spacious confines of Heidegger's own explicitly defined universe in order not to taint his teaching with metaphysical impurities. Hence the many secondary sources about Heidegger that read much the way Heidegger's prose reads. However, this approach, although laudable in terms of respect for Heidegger's uniqueness as a thinker, typically results in literature that is primarily and uninformatively repetitive.

The dense textures of Heidegger's distinctive language receive little clarification from this perspective.

At the other extreme, we find Heidegger's work approached from the outside, from some relatively secure bastion of metaphysical respectability. Interpretations originating from this perspective are, as a rule, representations of Heidegger that display a certain immediate intelligibility. But this usually desirable characteristic is paid for at the expense, perhaps, of denying Heidegger the possibility of contributing something significant to classical philosophical problems. After all, it would seem to be a category mistake to view Heidegger as little more than an extension of the metaphysical tradition from which his thought arose. Heidegger's challenge to this tradition can hardly be accorded the weight due to it if the challenge is reduced to but another moment in the history of that which is challenged.

These interpretive extremes may be contrasted as follows: (1) Heidegger's thinking is so different that it cannot be compared with anything else in the prior history of metaphysics; therefore, it can and must be analyzed only in its own terms. (2) Heidegger's thinking is basically no different from any significant moment in the prior history of metaphysics; therefore, it may be analyzed according to whatever appositions or points of tangency may appear to the informed observer. Since these extremes mark the limits of interpretive possibility, every secondary source on Heidegger will be either at one of the two end points or somewhere in between.

It should be emphasized at the outset of this study that the interpretation offered below is situated closer to the second of these two extremes. There are important reasons for adopting this procedure, and I shall develop them later in the Introduction. But by way of appreciating the need to argue this point in advance, let us consider a series of representative objections that this type of critical inquiry is bound to excite among those who believe that secondary sources on Heidegger belong at the other end of the interpretive spectrum.

Many students of Heidegger think that language borrowed from some existing metaphysical position will necessarily distort the Heideggerian intent to overcome metaphysics and its attendant features of representational thinking and truth as correctness or correspondence. But this critical approach rests on accepting a crucial premise, one that may or may not have been demonstrated in Heidegger's own work. For what if Heidegger has only attempted—and failed—to overcome truth as correctness? Should we assume that just because Heidegger says that Denken has overcome this and all other phases of metaphysics that such overcoming has come to pass? Furthermore, even if Heidegger has succeeded in so overcoming any conception of truth dependent on metaphysical notions, does it follow that Heideggerian truth is free to ignore the opposition between truth (however it may ultimately be defined) and falsity or error? If there is no provision for such opposition, then the Heideggerian can say anything about anything without fear that some standard of rightness must be met. For, in fact, there are no such standards, or at least no available standards, precisely because standards are manifestly metaphysical and metaphysics has been overcome. The practitioners of Denken may then say whatever they please.

The need to meet a standard of truth is logically preceded by the need to meet some standard of meaning. An utterance must be meaningful before it can be determined as true or false. Here again, however, the Heideggerian might contend that the contrast between meaningful and meaningless language is yet another vestige of metaphysics, a vestige that has in fact vanished with the advent of Denken. But if there is no opposition between utterances that are meaningful and those that are meaningless, then it seems, again, that Denken has the freest of all possible reins. It can say virtually anything and assert that what has been said is meaningful. But how could a given utterance ever be shown as meaningless if there is no standard to use as the ground for such an appeal? Some kind of opposition between meaningful and meaningless must surely be assumed, even (and, perhaps, especially) when Heideggerian texts are being construed. One must approach Heidegger's writings from the right direction in order to have some chance of understanding the proper meaning of what he has written. In view of the extreme diversity of opinion concerning what Heidegger "means" on almost every topic dealt with in his work, it seems clear that we must slant ourselves toward that work in the most sympathetic and informed manner.

At this point some Heideggerians might object that words such as "slant" should not be used with regard to understanding the expression of Denken since they are representional by virtue of being "metaphysically horizonal" and therefore distort Heidegger's teaching. These Heideggerians hold that an approach adopting such words would detrimentally affect whatever results are obtained from such an approach. We are, it would seem, at a serious hermeneutical impasse.

But surely the impasse is not completely impenetrable. For, first, one should recall that Heidegger's own favorite image of the "way" or "path" of thinking is no less horizonal and, if this way winds up or down a Zarathustrian-type mountain, no less slanted. And, second, even the most concrete language is not without a certain abstract penumbra, especially when the language involved is employed in a secondary source. As a result we must wonder whether there is a significant difference between asserting that we must "dwell" with Heidegger's thinking rather than get the right "slant" on this thinking. If so, then whoever insists both that there is such a difference and that this difference matters must demonstrate how it affects the point of any interpretive claim in which this and similar words may appear.[1]

One is tempted to overlook complaints of this sort as an unfortunate scholastic quibble. After all, a secondary source on Heidegger is *about* Heidegger; surely we need not and perhaps should not attempt to *imitate* Heidegger's unique mode of linguistic expression while purporting to clarify the significance of that expression. But such summary dismissal would be premature. For embedded in this critical reaction to "metaphysical" language about Heidegger is an attitude concerning secondary discourse that must be brought into the open and examined.

In general, a secondary source is written in order to increase understanding of the meaning and implications of a primary source. The secondary source may have a commendatory or critical purpose as well but these are usually derivative concerns. Now the intention to clarify presupposes that the primary source is, by itself, difficult to understand to some degree. If the primary source were not difficult to understand, then a secondary source would be otiose. A primary source is in many cases difficult to understand because its terminology is either newly minted or traditional but with newly assigned meanings. An effective secondary source must confront such terminology and attempt to render it more accessible. If a secondary source relies too heavily on employing the terminology of the primary source while putatively explicating that source, then it merely repeats the difficulties present in the original work. Therefore, it seems that in order to be effective, a secondary source must introduce terms that differ from those contained in the source to be clarified.

However, at precisely this point many Heideggerians would object to this line of reasoning. For them, the introduction of a second-order vocabulary doubtless derived from some metaphysical orientation *necessarily* distorts whatever aspect of Heidegger is to be analyzed by means of that vocabulary. For these students of Heidegger, the very presence of language other than and possibly even in opposition to Heidegger's own—quite apart from whatever interpretation results from the implementation of that language—disfigures the intention of that thinking.

But the upshot of this conviction is, surely, a dilemma, and one with particularly disconcerting consequences: If the secondary study is predominantly faithful to the language of Denken, then the secondary source is a virtual repetition of the original text and thus fails to illuminate that Denken; and if the secondary study introduces different terminology for purposes of clarification, then the residual metaphysics animating that terminology invevitably distorts Heidegger's meaning in the very process of attempting to clarify it. If we attempt to clarify, then we inadvertently but necessarily distort; yet if we preserve the letter of the original in order not to distort, then we fail to clarify.

This problem does not arise from a spirit of willful isolationism on the part of Heidegger's more perfervid admirers. The problem originates with Heidegger himself, particularly in his attitude toward the limitations inherent in the relevant forms of language at his disposal. Thus, in the important essay "*Zeit und Sein*," Heidegger concludes the brief introduction by affirming that the reader should not "listen to a series of propositions," but rather should "follow the movement of showing" (*SD*, 2). The suggestion is that the intended meaning can be gleaned from the ensuing language only by attending to that language in something other than the way one attends to language presented in a connected series of propositions. Furthermore, the essay concludes by stating forthrightly that to say what Heidegger wanted to say, an obstacle had to be overcome. The obstacle—and this is the concluding proposition of the essay—"The lecture has spoken merely in propositional statements" (*SD*, 25). The problem of choosing discourse appropriate to Heidegger's train of thought thus goes much deeper than whether or not critical terminology should be similar to or other than that found in Heidegger's original texts. For here, in the absolutely ultimate matter of attempting to think Being, Heidegger maintains that the very form of a proposition necessarily hinders what must be said. But how then does a thinker express what is to be thought?

It has been said of the attempt to write about Heidegger that the interpreter must face the question of the possibility of reformulating in propositions what is only accessible nonpropositionally.[2] Let us then face this question. What does it mean to assert that something is "only accessible nonpropositionally"?

Now it should be noted immediately that the negational element in "nonpropositionally" is ambiguous. It could mean either nonpropositionally in the sense of referring to an activity completely other than language as normally understood—e.g., gesture—or it could mean nonpropositionally as referring to a linguistic utterance that somehow escapes the formal considerations usually pertaining to propositions. The first alternative, i.e., something completely other than propositions, may be illustrated by the brief but seemingly pregnant discussion of gesturing in the dialogue between the Heideggerian questioner and the Japanese in Heidegger's *Unterwegs zur Sprache*.[3] Although the suggestion in this context is that gestures can be powerfully evocative, it seems certain that they can hardly replace vocalized or written language; it might therefore be preferable to interpret "nonpropositionally" according to the second alternative, i.e., as some form of language. But what kind of language? Mysticism and poetry, each in it own way, admit of meaningful discourse via nonpropositional linguistic forms. But Heidegger has denied that his own Denken is or can be read as a form of mysticism.[4] And as for poetry, although it is often placed on a par with thinking (e.g., the many references to *Denken* and *Dichten* in Heidegger) it is nonetheless still distinct from thinking. Therefore, even if Heidegger's own language is as much Denken as Dichten, that language cannot simply be reduced to a species of poetry, for then it could no longer maintain its status as an exemplar of, or at least a guidepost to, authentic thinking.[5]

The inference is that nonpropositional linguistic forms cannot include either mystical language or poetical language. Now already in *Sein und Zeit*, Heidegger spoke of the need to liberate grammar from logic (*SZ*, 165), although at that time, and in later works when the same point was pressed,[6] Heidegger did not specify precisely how such liberation was to be accomplished, nor what the results would look like by comparison with traditional logico-grammatical language. Perhaps a language free of logical constraints is the desideratum. But the point that must be made at this juncture is that whatever the form of language that is compatible with Heideggerian Denken may assume, some consideration must be made for the opposition between (what, in metaphysical parlance, have been referred to as) truth and falsity. Call it authentic language and inauthentic langauge—for present purposes the designating terms as such do not matter. The preservation of the opposition is the crucial point,[7] and I suggest that however radically innovative or creatively reactionary nonpropositional language may become, it still must retain a fixed contrast between saying something "true" and saying something "false."

Heidegger frequently described the products of his own thinking as incomplete and provisional (*SZ*, 17). His thinking remained only a questioning, and it inhabited areas of speculation so rarified and without available supports that while exploring their confines one can never prove anything—one can only point out or recommend (*ID*, 84). On occasion, Heidegger even abjured having a philosophy at all (*PG*, 417). Whatever else it may be, such self-effacement is intended to emphasize the fact that Heidegger's way is one on which he and all his companions are still moving. How then, it might be asked, can an external observer viewing the way being traversed halt this thoughtful motion by attempting to evaluate the results by assuming that some measure of finality has been secured?

A response to this question can be initiated by noting Heidegger's own assertion—answers to the questions raised by his mode of fundamental questioning were indeed to be had (*WM*, 100). The element of process inherent in Heidegger's approach to these issues thus does not altogether preclude the establishment of something like a final statement. And for our purposes, all that is required is the admission that Heidegger's own positive responses are, if not finalized, then at least limited to some determinable position. If, therefore, Heidegger's way is one that does not go everywhere at once, then it is possibile that this way might in some respect be on the wrong track. Assume that we, prospective thinkers, are lost in a forest. Given this situation, we know from common experience that some ways to escape are better than others. And while wandering within that forest, it is vital for our well-being to realize that some ways go absolutely nowhere. If we persist in following one of these ways, then it can be argued that we simply want to stay lost. Heidegger's own way may lead into darkness, shadows, or light. We can determine whether either of the first two alternatives will be the case only if we cling to a belief in some standards while following the implications of Denken.

For the language of traditional metaphysics, logic provides a formal measure for this standard. Thus, a proposition may be true or it may be false, but a proposition cannot be both true and false at the same time and in the same respect. It would not be completely beyond the realm of propriety to expect that logic will perform the same or similar function for Denken—whatever the linguistic form Denken may finally assume. But this expectation may be premature. And to substantiate this suspicion, we shall now briefly consider an approximation of Heidegger's position on logic, and also respond to yet another set of possible objections against the line of inquiry developed in the study proper.

Here is a passage from the conclusion of Heidegger's "Letter on Humanism:" "The fittingness of the saying of Being, as of the destiny of truth, is the first law of thinking—not the rules of logic which can become rules only on the basis of the law of Being" (*WM*, 193-94). This passage is obviously crucial for the scope of our study, and we shall return to its significance in more detail later in the body of the work. For now, let us consider the claim that "the first law of thinking" is the "fittingness of the saying of Being"—*not* "the rules of logic."

In his book, *Heidegger: The Critique of Logic*, Thomas A. Fay offers the following remarks on the confrontation between Heidegger and logic: "If by logic one understands a reflection on *logos*, then of course it is perfectly compatible with his *Denkweg*. If, however, one takes logic as it has traditionally been understood and practiced, then one is forced to say that it is incompatible with Heidegger's way of thought."[8] On the next page, Fay adds that "as far as Heidegger himself is concerned in his own quest after Being, logic by its very nature could not have any useful role to play."[9] Finally, Fay describes the strategy in Heidegger's approach to logic: "At a time in the history of philosophy when modern linguistics, an outgrowth of the spirit of technicity as Heidegger sees it, is tending to establish itself as the *only* legitimate way of philosophizing, he has felt compelled to show its limitation and assert the lawful rights of another way."[10]

According to Fay the nature of logic as traditionally understood does not permit it to play any role in Heidegger's quest to determine the meaning of Being. Now in one sense, this claim is unexceptional, since logic has generally been considered to be purely formal, i.e., independent of content. On this understanding of logic, whatever Heidegger could discover and state to be proper to Being would remain apart from the formal character of the logical principles that govern the utterance of these discoveries. But in another and far stronger sense, Fay seems to be contending that the traditional understanding and practice of logic render it "incompatible" with Heidegger's way of thought. But in what does this incompatibility consist?

Upon reflection, there are two senses of "incompatible" that Fay may have in mind here, and it is vital to note the differences between the two and to consider the respective implications. For the sake of convenience, let us name these two senses Formal Incompatibility and Substantive Incompatibility.

*Formal Incompatibility.* It is possible to construe Fay's sense of incompatible to mean that whatever thought derives from its reflection on Being cannot be stated in accordance with traditional logical principles. On this hypothesis the purely formal requirement entailed by logic would distort the innovative ontological character possessed by these linguistic evocations of the process of thinking.

But if this formal compatibility is what Fay intends, then we must question whether he has understood Heidegger correctly. For it would follow that Heidegger could assert, for example, both that "Being is presence" and that "Being is not presence" without fear that this conjunction could be rejected purely on grounds of logical impossibility. Thus, if language about Being is "incompatible" with the principle of contradiction, and if this incompatibility gives Heidegger license to state contradictions (whether explicitly, in the blunt manner just illustrated, or indirectly where contradictions are entailed by utterances which by themselves may appear to be consistent), then surely Heidegger has placed a considerable burden on his audience. If Heidegger's "*Denkweg*" leads him so far from the beaten track as to ask us to make contradictions comprehensible, then this is a form of thinking we must ponder seriously before following it ourselves. (The fact that such an obviously self-destructive consequence must be brought explicitly to view may be taken as an indication of the frequently cavalier treatment accorded to logic by many Heideggerians if not by Heidegger himself.)

*Substantive Incompatibility.* It may be assumed, therefore, that the incompatibility in question should be understood in some other sense. We know from Heidegger's own hand that the scope of his inquiry will not encroach upon the "rightness" of logic (EM, 92). The incompatibility may then lie in the fact that the embedded metaphysics hidden in the formulation of logical principles cannot serve as a locus for revealing the true structure of Being, the stated goal of all Heidegger's thinking. But it is precisely at this point that the interpreter of Heidegger cannot simply *say* that Heidegger's way is incompatible with logic. Thus, when Professor Fay claims that Heidegger felt compelled to show the "limitation" of logic and to "assert the lawful rights of another way," the burden is on Professor Fay (and, of course, ultimately on Heidegger) to state clearly *how* Heidegger shows the limitations of logic and *how* the lawful rights of another way are commensurately lawful with the laws of logic. Although his book provides a useful reproduction of the history of Heidegger's reflections on *logos*, Professor Fay's overall interpretation has, in effect, never moved outside the demarcations of Heidegger's own universe of discourse.[11]

A more incisive approach to Heidegger's position in this regard must take into account the fact that logic has traditionally been understood to be without content by virtue of its pure formality. Therefore, the interpretation of Heidegger on logic must (a) attempt to show the sense in which the relevant metaphysical elements in logical principles can be isolated and identified, and (b) then contrast these elements with the substantive portions of Heidegger's own Denken in order to demonstrate how Heidegger's results are incompatible with the results of (a). Both phases in such an inquiry must be executed—without (a), there is no reason to think that logical principles are anything other than purely formal; without (b), there is no reason to think that Heidegger's own position with respect to Being will differ from whatever the structure elicited through (a) may turn out to be.

My own conviction is that any significant contribution to our understanding of Heidegger must advance into these forbidding regions, and the criticisms raised here against Professor Fay's otherwise worthy account are intended to suggest that at least the attempt should be made. In fact, the text cited above from the "Letter on Humanism" may be read as having even more radical repercussions than those suggested so far. Heidegger has claimed that the rules of logic "become rules only on the basis of the law of Being." It seems clear that priority (in some sense) has been given to Being at the expense of logic. But does this priority mean that the rules of logic could have been formulated somehow other than they have been formulated? If this hypothesis is not what Heidegger means, then logical principles would remain in one sense more primordial, or at least on a different level, than whatever laws pertain to Being. But if Heidegger does intend this radical revisionist thesis, then the resultant dependency of logical principles on the law of Being makes it all the more imperative for the student of Heidegger to render as clearly as possible how the "law of Being" has generated these principles as if they were a sufficient but, perhaps, not necessary standard for meaningful discourse. Here again, what must be shown is the internal connections between the content of logical principles and whatever may be the nature of Being. In fact, it would not be entirely inappropriate to ask for the equivalent of a transcendental deduction showing how logical principles have been deemed, from the traditional standpoint, "formally" necessary while at the same time they depend, from Heidegger's standpoint, on more ontological considerations for this necessity. However, for now we stress only the point that Heidegger's claim must be interpreted to mean something more than a mere paraphrase of that claim.

The arena of discussion must therefore be extended from logic in its purely regulatory function—which Heidegger wants to question because of an embedded and distortional metaphysical dimension—to metaphysics proper. Heidegger's approach to logic in this regard can then be confronted with pertinent questions drawn from various moments in the history of metaphysics. As we shall see, these moments appear in a number of "essential thinkers," and the result of our inquiry will be a series of interrelated problems of considerable generality and also of some difficulty.

This interpretive approach depends for its legitimacy on relating the metaphysical dimension implicit in logic to the structure of Denken. Here again, however, this kind of approach has been disclaimed as antithetical to Heidegger, since it is in league with the argumentative style of representational thinking, the overcoming of which is the point of Heidegger's work. The result is that any difficulties raised on the basis of this approach will arise more from applying this methodology than from anything proper to Heidegger's own texts.

Let us, again, consider the implications of this position. It has been claimed that the "methodology" of applying metaphysical concerns to Denken raises difficulties not applicable to Denken, since Denken has overcome metaphysics. Now one of the difficulties one might raise, e.g., when reading the essays on thinghood in *Vorträge und Aufsätze*, is the apparent inability of Heidegger's formulation and development of the notion of the Geviert to establish conditions for individuating one thing (*Ding*) from another thing.[12] But Denken, we are assured, has overcome this difficulty in principle precisely because of the fact that Denken has overcome metaphysics, that realm of philosophy within which the difficulty first arose. If, however, Denken has overcome the problem of individuating beings, does it follow that Denken need not concern itself with individuation at all, in any sense?

It is one thing to maintain that the problem of individuation, a central concern for many forms of metaphysical inquiry, has been consistently misunderstood by any and every metaphysical attempt to solve it. On this interpretation Denken could still assert that the problem of individuation is a perfectly appropriate matter to be thoughtfully addressed, but that its solution is *in toto* distinct from any solution advanced by metaphysics. But it is quite something else to claim in the name of Denken that in overcoming metaphysics, Denken has overcome the problem of individuation to such an extent that this problem ceases to be of any concern whatsoever. This consequence is surely impossible, and it is difficult to conceive of anyone, Heideggerian or otherwise, who would deny the need for introducing and discussing individuation. For if it does not matter to Denken whether things are individuated from one another, then the routine concerns of living—a medley of considered and unconsidered choices focusing on this rather than on that—is set apart from whatever Denken deigns to consider as its proper province.

In fact, to deny the need to reflect on any sense of individuation renders one subject to the kind of criticism Aristotle levels at anyone who refuses to allow the individuation peculiar to the principle of contradiction. If such an individual were walking to Megara, Aristotle asks, "Why does he not walk early some morning into a well or over a precipice, if one happens to be in his way" (*Metaphysics*,

1008b 15-16). The hypothetical walker does not trod over a precipice because he can distinguish between the individuated entity that is a precipice and the individuated entity that is the path to Megara. And this walker achieves this distinction regardless whether he is an Aristotelian realist, a Platonic idealist, or an advocate of any other metaphysical position. Does the walker who reacts to experience through Denken cease to be concerned with such matters? If so, then the walker guiding his life by Denken will fail to fall into a well or plunge over a precipice only if fate somehow guarantees him a straight path. And fate has been known to be fickle.

This line of argument may appear somewhat flippant, and my apologies are tendered to anyone who is offended by its tone. But I do not apologize for what this brief Aristotelian episode shows— i.e., that fundamental need to recognize and to preserve differences, both grandly speculative and humbly mundane. In my opinion too many students of Heidegger believe that Denken can ignore one or all of the classic problems of metaphysics simply because Heidegger has claimed in a variety of contexts that Denken has overcome metaphysics, or at least is on the verge of doing so. Although drastic measures seem to be required to reorient such sensibilities, these measures need not be without a dash of brusque humor drawn from a classic and normally humorless metaphysician.

In any event this argument is important because it demonstrates that Denken must preserve at least some aspects of metaphysics regardless of whether or not it has in fact overcome metaphysics. Furthermore, the ramifications of this argument may be extended to reinforce the point established earlier concerning the appropriateness of second-order terminology when dealing with Denken. In this case the issue revolves around the seemingly vexed use of the word "ontology" to describe Heidegger's reflection.

Heidegger once described his own thoughtful way as a road leading through the restoration of metaphysics (*WM*, 251). In his earlier works, that way was named *ontology,* or *fundamental ontology.*[13] However, Heidegger discovered that naming his thinking in this manner invited comparisons with other types of ontology, especially since the word itself and the prior thinking denoted by that word possessed a rather checkered history of its own (*EM,* 33-34). Heidegger then saw that such comparisons resulted in concealing the radical quality of his own thinking from the contemporary philosophical public (*WM,* 188). Consequently, in the later works, Heidegger refers to his own reflections as Denken, or, as he does in *Unterwegs zur Sprache,* "without a name" altogether (*US,* 42). Now given this gradual shift in titular nomenclature, the Heideggerian might object that "ontology" is yet another of those words that should not be applied to Heidegger's own work on pain of distorting the uniqueness and intent of that work. *Logic and Ontology in Heidegger* is thus a premier example of a book that is doomed to irrelevancy by its very title—regardless what may follow that title.

I suggest, however, that the juxtaposition "logic and ontology in Heidegger" remains valid in this regard for the following reasons:

A. Speaking of his own technical term *Sorge* (concern) as it had been employed in *Sein und Zeit,* Heidegger remarked that the word *Sorge* itself is of little consequence (*KP,* 213). But if the word *Sorge* is itself of little consequence in conveying this important phase of the teaching of *Sein und Zeit,* then the word *ontology* (employed to designate the totality of Heidegger's reflections) can, by itself and apart from the content of those reflections, hardly be of any more importance. What, we may ask, is in a name?

B. In the "Letter on Humanism" (*WM,* 173-74), Heidegger says that his own thinking has not advanced beyond that of *Sein und Zeit* (1927). If this stern self-assessment would hold for all of Heidegger's work after the *Humanismusbrief,* then whatever name Heidegger himself applied to *Sein und Zeit* would be no less inappropriate for everything he wrote after *Sein und Zeit,* since it would be hubris to christen later works with a different name simply because they were later and not because they represented further development.

Both reasons A and B above are, of course, *ad hominem* and therefore should be something less than conclusive. More persuasive reasons for retaining the word *ontology* in relation to Heidegger's thinking may be detailed as follows:

C. Heidegger's expression of his own thinking is necessarily conditioned by the distinctive modes of representational thinking common to the history of metaphysics. Consider, for example, this crucial passage from *"Zeit und Sein,"* where Heidegger announces his intention "to say something about the attempt to think Being without regard to its being grounded in terms of beings" (*SD,* 2), an attempt that Heidegger felt "necessary" to pursue himself. Notice that the structure of this formulation implicitly includes a number of typical metaphysical distinctions—identity (e.g., of Being to itself), difference (between Being and beings), unity (of Being, and presumably of beings as well), relation (between Being and beings), priority (of Being to beings), and process (within Being as such). This list is, of course, not exhaustive.

The implicit presence of these metaphysical concepts in Heidegger's utterance has consequences impossible to overlook. For if this kind of analysis of Being requires the introduction of such metaphysical concepts, then understanding Heidegger's position is necessarily conditioned by an analogous comprehension of these concepts as developed within Heidegger's own utterances. In other words we must know how the metaphysical elements function in Heidegger's thinking in order to be able to discern how that thinking moves beyond the restrictive (and, if Heidegger is correct, distortional) effect of the metaphysical factor. Indeed, Heidegger himself has admitted the necessary presence of metaphysics in both the process and the product of Denken.

To overcome metaphysics is not to abolish metaphysics, and there is good ontological reason for making this qualification explicit. The history of metaphysics is, after all, an essential dimension of Being as long as Being is itself historical. Thus, Heidegger freely admits that questioning the truth of Being requires both thinking metaphysically and yet not thinking metaphysically (*WM*, 100), the former because our ontological presence includes our historical past, the latter because our ontological presence also includes an historical future that in an essential sense transfigures this past. This transfiguration will be of considerable magnitude, so much so that Heidegger even speaks of a "change in human nature" (*Wandel des Wesens des Menschen*—*WM*, 197) that will have to be effected before the appropriate products of Denken can assume their final form. This revisionist strain is never far from the surface of much of Heidegger's thinking, and it is perhaps worth noting as an aside that his optimism seems to approach utopian dimension. After all, if Marxism has had dubious success in revamping the ways all mortals look at the world, then it would be premature, to say the least, to expect Heideggerian Denken to succeed where other and far more practicable philosophical creeds are still struggling. In any event we shall watch his own efforts to make some headway in effecting this change, especially in chapters 5 and 6 below. For now, however, it must be admitted that even the most percipient thinker cannot jump over his own metaphysical shadow.

D. Furthermore, even if the structure of Being turns out to be entirely different from the configurations imposed on it by virtue of some or all of the metaphysical concepts implicit in Heidegger's own formulations, the undeniable fact remains that most, if not all, students of Heidegger continue to dwell to some considerable extent within the sweep of the history of metaphysics. Even if Heidegger's own thinking does succeed in overcoming metaphysics to some degree, his audience nonetheless is rooted in a metaphysical frame of reference. Now if the real possibility of a uniquely Heideggerian ontology is granted, then it seems plausible to assume the equally real possibility of interpreting that ontology, however unique it may be. In order to prepare for this interpretation, some attempt must be made to situate the distinctively Heideggerian pronouncements about Being by constructing illustrative parallels between the purely metaphysical aspects that remain in Heidegger's statements about Being and some of the classical problems commonly cohering with these aspects. Thus, if only from heuristic considerations, it becomes essential to work through a metaphysical approach to Heidegger's thinking just to be in a position to appreciate how the results of Denken differ from the tradition from which Denken originated.

As we shall see, these parallels will in turn engender a series of difficulties. Heidegger's thought may or may not be sufficiently along its own way to produce anything like definitive answers to these and related problems. But the actual wealth or poverty of Heidegger's texts is irrelevant to the point argued here in this Introduction. The point is that the interpreter must pursue Heidegger's teaching as if it yielded answers of this sort. For without such pursuit, the interpreter does not know the extent to which Heidegger's thought is truly innovative or, in the end, reducible to a set of variations on long-standing metaphysical matters. This burden must, I suggest, be assumed by the interpreter before it can be shifted to where it ultimately must rest—on Heidegger himself.[14]

The problems raised in this study do not therefore constitute a "refutation" of Heidegger. Such refutation does not seem to be possible. The nature of the disagreement between those Heideggerians who believe that Denken has overcome metaphysics without remainder and those philosophers who believe that metaphysics still remains viable is so fundamental that little if any common ground would command mutual consent. However, one of the primary purposes of this study is to show how the Heideggerian cannot simply assert that Denken has overcome metaphysics without also explaining how certain key problems essential to metaphysics—and apparently just as essential in their own way to everyday concerns—are also overcome. The analyses of these problems offered in this study detail the apparent consequences of Heidegger's own Denken and then point to the paradoxical character of these consequences. I would suggest that this method compels that Heideggerian to address the issues raised below. For if the Heideggerian remains silent in the face of this challenge, then this silence is tantamount to an admission not only that the demonstrable multiplicity of paradox is inherent in Heidegger's Denken, but also that for some reason this multiplicity can simply and safely be ignored.

Yet it cannot be ignored. And once the Heideggerian sees the need to speak, what is said in defense of Denken will concern either how the metaphysical interpretation of Heideggerian Denken offered here has failed to appreciate the direction and subtlety of that Denken—and must therefore be replaced by another interpretation, or how the various paradoxes emerging in this interpretation can in fact be resolved. Thus, the presentation of these paradoxes and problems has been organized, in part, to invite further inquiry into the rich textures of Heidegger's thinking for anyone who cares to attempt such a task. The Heideggerian's consent to address the issues raised in this study then becomes an implicit admission that Denken does not exist in a historical vacuum, i.e., that it is to some essential degree beholden to the metaphysical tradition from which it originated. Therefore, at least some of the classical problems of metaphysics would remain just as classic for Denken even as Denken itself reorders the distortions prevalent in the metaphysical formulations and solutions of these problems. The bare assertion that Denken overcomes metaphysics would then be recognized as essentially incomplete.

Some students of Heidegger may nonetheless persist in refusing to accept these troublesome implications and the challenge they present to anyone who has fully understood them. The realization of the need to take up this challenge may occasion a variety of reactions, some perhaps unpleasant, but more is at stake than realizing that one has fallen prey to hasty trust. For to continue to believe this Heideggerian assertion at face value, without exploring additional and supplementary argumentation, is to risk embracing a virulent form of philosophical idolatry, an adherence to a style of reflection that lacks any recognizable rules by which to assess its significance and its affect on the way we live.

Metaphysics obeys rules. These rules are the principles of logic. Thus, a metaphysical argument concerning, say, the structure of being must, as a minimal condition for intelligibility, be consistent. If the argument is inconsistent, then that argument is self-contradictory. Now elementary logic tells us that a contradiction implies every proposition. If, in questioning the metaphysical presuppositions of logic in general and the principle of contradiction in particular, Heideggerian Denken ceases to be bound by the principle of contradiction, then Denken, whatever it may say on the surface, ultimately permits every conceivable proposition to follow. But if every proposition follows, then *pari passu* every form of life can follow, its existence justifiably inferred by the lack of logical constraints inherent in Denken. Everyone knows that in Heidegger's own lifetime a particularly barbaric form of life arose and threatened to become world-dominant. Whether or not Heidegger the man reacted justly when confronted with Nazism is not an issue to be discussed below—a variety of opinions are already available in print.[15] However, whether or not Heideggerian Denken is compatible with—or in principle unable to deny—a form of human existence that helped to define the limits of evil is a philosophical question, and one of paramount importance. The traditional conception of logic, in particular the extent to which Denken becomes distant from the constraints imposed by logic, offers one essential backdrop for determining the limits of Denken when confronted with at least a residue of metaphysical intelligibility.

Heidegger himself said that "all refutation in essential thinking is foolish" (*WM*, 167). If Heidegger's own thinking is essential, then attempting to refute Heidegger is also foolish. Apparently for Heidegger all instances of essential thinking in the history of metaphysics simply remain standing as they were originally propounded, despite those critical students of metaphysics who believe that any or all such instances can, with appropriate care, be refuted or seriously thrown into doubt. The implication is that essential thinking, whether as a whole or instance by instance, hovers above at least some forms of critical assessment. But is Heidegger then asking us to accept an extensive body of metaphysical reflection that is, at times, internally inconsistent? Is it "foolish" to be sensitive to the presence of such contradictions, and to attempt to eliminate these contradictions once they have been recognized as such? Surely not. Again, while speaking of the attempt to interpret Hegel, Heidegger said that properly reading a philosophical work requires the effort to unfold its presuppositions (*HP,* 52-53). If an essential thinker of Hegel's stature can be read with this purpose in mind, then it is not completely unreasonable to attempt to do the same for Heidegger himself. This study offers an introduction to this kind of critical appreciation from one and only one perspective. It does not purport to be the last word.

To juxtapose Heideggerian thinking with various metaphysical problems by way of logical principles is, I suggest, one legitimate "way" to read Heidegger, just as Heidegger's own thought is, by his own admission, just one "way" to think. Such juxtaposition may or may not be illuminating, but only after the process of interpretation is completed can the product be evaluated. Simply rejecting the possibility of this kind of interpretation implicitly elevates Heidegger's thought beyond a level on which that thought can be confronted, questioned, and if required by honest inquiry, made subject to criticism. We do thinking in particular and philosophy in general a grave disservice if we spare Heidegger this assessment. It is worth repeating that the purpose of this confrontation is not to refute Heidegger, but simply to describe in some detail the kinds of problems that protagonists of Heideggerian *Denken* would have to face if they intend to take metaphysics seriously. Whether or not such protagonists then resolve to address these problems is a matter for them to decide.

# CHAPTER 1

# The Challenge of the Principle of Contradiction

LOGICIANS HAVE GENERALLY SAID LITTLE ABOUT HEIdegger's thought. However, the converse is not the case. The following passage summarizes Heidegger's position on the status of the Greek *logos* as developed by contemporary symbolic logic:

> Symbolic logic is itself only one kind of mathematics applied to propositions and propositional forms. All mathematical logic and symbolic logic necessarily place themselves outside every sphere of logic, because, for their own purposes, they must fasten on *logos*, the assertion, as a mere combination of representations, i.e., basically inadequately. The presumptuousness of symbolic logic in posing as the scientific logic of all sciences collapses as soon as it becomes apparent how limited and thoughtless are its beginnings (*FD,* 122).

These are strong claims expressed in language that, perhaps with intent, is provocative in the extreme. Logicians will be immediately vexed by Heidegger's highhanded tone and by his summary dismissal of the premises that form the foundation of their work. In fact, even those sympathetic to Heidegger's speculative ontological investigations must pause at this juncture. Can his ringing denunciation of symbolic logic be translated into an articulated argument? If not, then there may be no good reason to pay much attention to what Heidegger has just said about symbolic logic. But if an argument does substantiate this denunciation of the principles of symbolic logic, then this argument may produce insight into both the hidden structure of formal logic and substantive issues of fundamental ontological concern. In any case, however, Heidegger's position on the "presumptuousness" of symbolic logic must be clarified and developed before judgment can be rendered on the vision or arbitrariness of that position.

An appropriate point of departure is Heidegger's careful distinction between two very different types of logic. Heidegger frequently writes logic as "logic." The quotation marks indicate that "logic" refers to logistics (*Logistik*) or symbolic logic—i.e., the axioms and procedures of logical calculi (*WD*, 10).[1] But for Heidegger, not all that is properly logic need be, perhaps even can be, rendered symbolically. There are possibilities in logic, logic understood in the original Greek sense of *logos*, that have been gradually obscured in the advance of Western metaphysics. Logic, then, may encompass more than "logic." In fact, one of the problems in resurrecting these possibilities is precisely the emergence of symbolic logic as the paradigm for rigorous thinking, especially in American academic circles. Rigorous philosophy has become more and more equated with philosophy expressed in symbolic languages. And this growth has not occurred within an isolated academic vacuum. Heidegger detects an intimate connection between the advance of symbolic logic and its actual and potential application for the ends of technology. As technology increases its hold on all aspects of contemporary life, the belief that symbolic logic and philosophy are equivalent will become more and more prevalent (*WD*, 10). Therefore, to appreciate the full force of Heidegger's challenge to the principles of symbolic logic, we must be as open as possible to experiences and types of utterance that may perhaps run counter to what, in an age defined by technological devices and technical languages, is considered appropriate to philosophical discourse.

The distinction between logic as *logos* (in a sense to be discussed later in this chapter) and logic in its present calculative format— "logic"—allows Heidegger to infer that symbolic logic is "only *one* interpretation (*Auslegung*) of the nature of thinking."[2] Furthermore, this interpretation had a specifiable historical origin. For "logic" was the result of the "fall" (*Verfall*) occurring in the thinking of Plato and Aristotle (*EM*, 130).[3] Once thinking became rigidified in this formal manner, the pressure of "logic" led to hiding the nature of Being (*WM*, 237).[4] For Heidegger, the historical character of "logic" testifies to the fact that it is in principle substantive rather than, as many contemporary observers believe, purely formal or operational.[5] However, he also attempts to fashion a more rigorous account of the substantive nature of "logic" by pointing to the fact that the usage of the term "logic" is ambivalent. Thus, in one sense "logic" includes the claims that "sentences follow closely as a consequence of a given state of affairs" and that such consequences are controlled by formal rules (*HE*, 186). At the same time, "logic" can be taken to refer to things that, as we say, have "in themselves" a "logic," a material logic (*Logik der Sachen*—*HE*, 187). Heidegger then infers that this confluence of logic as formal rules and as material content results in a "peculiar state of affairs" (*seltsame Bewandnis*—*HE*, 187). And he concludes that this ambivalence is a hint that neither logic as rules nor logic as material content nor as both combined constitutes "the authentic logic" (*die eigentliche Logik*—*HE*, 196).

One perhaps hesitates to call this account an argument, although the tone of the discussion suggests that Heidegger intends it to approximate one. For, after all, the account merely points out that the same word is used differently in different contexts. We do speak of a matter's "logic" (cf. the later Wittgenstein), but it is not at all clear that the production of such "logics" would justify concluding that logic in general cannot be merely formal but must necessarily become substantive in order to accommodate two divergent senses of one word. It is nonetheless relevant to conclude a discussion of this phase of Heidegger's thinking by noting that Heidegger felt, at least at this point in his development, that claiming logic to be necessarily substantive must require some kind of justifying account. Whether or not the particular discussion just outlined succeeds in this regard must, it seems, remain moot.[6]

If the principles of logic are in fact "limited and thoughtless," does it follow that thought can do without them? The answer, with certain crucial qualifications, is no. Heidegger is well aware that questioning these principles in the manner he intends will be taken by many observers as "dark rumblings," as "lawless arbitrariness," as "pure nihilism."[7] But Heidegger insists on pursuing the question "Why are laws of thought laws" (*L*, 37)? For him, it is ontologically naive to take logic as something "given by God" (*HE*, 258). Yet even Heidegger's questioning will observe certain limits. Heidegger explicitly asserts that he does not wish to deny "the logical" in the sense of "what is thought correctly" (*recht Gedachten*—*EM*, 92).[8] He does maintain, however—and here he specifically employs the technical vocabulary of another philosophical tradition—that truth as correctness is a necessary but not a sufficient condition for truth as such (*PI*, 189). Furthermore, even this purely formal understanding of logic as rules necessary for correct thinking rests on a metaphysical ground (*MA*, 129). In fact, Heidegger holds out the possibility that the use of rules for purposes of mere formal regulation may itself be without any ground whatsoever (*MA*, 130). But if such rules are not merely dispensed by a divinely benevolent logician, if there is a ground for such rules, then the statement of this ground must assume a certain metaphysical shape. In either case, therefore, whether it is substantive or purely formal, logic must be thoughtfully scrutinized in order to yield its hidden preconceptions.[9]

Subsuming the supposed formality of logical notions and principles under substantive conditions is not an invitation to arbitrariness in thinking. Heidegger dismisses the possibility that skepticism and relativism will inevitably result once the formality of "logic" has been recognized as ontologically derivative (*L*, 24). On the contrary, he insists that the type of thinking appropriate to Being will be "stricter" (*Strengeres*) than thinking according to the formal structures inherent in "logic" (*EM*, 94). It must nonetheless be noted that Heidegger never developed or even hinted at how this strictness may be recognized, or how it would differ from the rigorousness guaranteed by "logic." Although Heidegger does assure us that the strictness of such thinking will indeed be governed by a "rule" (*Regel*), the structure of this rule is "hidden" (*Verborgenen*—*WM*, 251) at this moment in the history of thought.

The precise sense in which logical correctness will not be questioned by Heidegger is not elaborated, but presumably correctness includes (but may not be restricted to) the formal validity of an argument. Therefore, if, e.g., the principle of contradiction is essential for correct thinking, then Heidegger does not deny that contradiction plays a fundamental role in determining the conditions for the formal validity of reasoning. What then does Heidegger find deficient in contradiction, especially if it is held to be the exemplar of logical principles? The answer is straightforward: although the principle of contradiction and other principles of "logic" have served to coordinate correct thinking, these principles have never become the "theme of ontological interpretation" (*SZ*, 159). Heidegger proposes to pursue such an investigation: "A reflection which presses in this direction is not turned against logic, but rather is applied to a sufficient determination of *logos*, i.e., that saying (*Sagen*) in which Being (*Sein*) brings itself to language as *the* most notable matter of thought" (*WM*, 306—italics in text). Heidegger will thus attempt to locate appropriately "concrete" questions (*L*,

79) about the meaning of Being by reflecting on whatever presuppositions underlie the principles of "logic."[10]

Since contradiction may be construed as the most fundamental principle of logic in this form, primary consideration must be devoted to those ontological dimensions hidden behind its presently unquestioned apodictic status. I have selected the principle of contradiction for examination here rather than, say, the principle of identity because the structure of contradiction is more immediately complex than that of identity. Nevertheless, both logical principles must eventually be examined at the requisite ontological level (see chapter 3 below):

> The principle of contradiction and the principle of identity are presupposed as self-evident without questioning whether something ultimate is present along with these principles; not that these principles are reducible to simpler principles—but rather that the "principle" of contra*diction* must be questioned as to whether it is only a determinate "expression" for a fundamental grounding relation which does not lie primarily in the dimension of language and these principles. . . . (*L*, 23—italics in text)[11]

As we shall see, this question will be answered by Heidegger in such a way that the grounding relation is indeed located outside the dimension of language.

The word Heidegger uses for "contradiction" is *Widerspruch*, and it is relevant to keep in mind that what Heidegger refers to as contradictory includes considerably more than the purely formal sense expressed in "not (P and not-P)." Here are several representative examples of contradictions in Heidegger's sense:

a. "The rose—without why and yet not without why" (*SG*, 70).
b. "To say that something is near and yet at the same time that it remains at a distance . . . is tantamount either to violating the fundamental law of ordinary thought, the principle of contradiction, or of playing with empty words" (*EH*, 24).
c. "To our customary way of thinking, the converse nature of pain—that its sweep carries us truly onward only as it sweeps us back—may easily seem contradictory" (*US*, 64).
d. "The sentence 'the triangle is laughing' cannot be said." In such cases, "the terms do make a declaration, but contradict each other" (*WD*, 100).
e. . . . the "becoming of God as eternal is a contradiction for ordinary thinking" (*S*, 136).[12]

Two points should be made: first, Heidegger does not observe the distinction between object language and metalanguage; thus, entities or states of affairs are no less "contradictory" than are statements about those entities or states of affairs. Second, some examples of contradictions refer to what many logicians would call contraries (i.e., they cannot both be true, but can both be false—e.g., passages b, c, e), and others are perhaps more accurately designated as category mistakes (e.g., d). However, Heidegger's rather expansive usage of "contradiction" does not affect the fact that he intends the wider sense of the term to include the narrower and purely formal sense. Thus, Heidegger explicitly mentions that whenever something is possible, this possibility means that "it entails no contradiction" (S, 183). This remark is a clear indication that he has not lost sight of the purely formal character of contradiction within an axiomatic context. For our purposes we will therefore assume that Heidegger's challenge to the notion of *Widerspruch* can be directed at contradiction in the technical sense employed by most systems of formal logic.

Heidegger initiated his reflections on the underlying ontological structure of logical principles already in *Sein und Zeit*. At that time his remarks on the principle of contradiction were more introductory than definitive, but they were nonetheless important in indicating the direction of subsequent analyses. Heidegger had contended that the principle of contradiction (as well as Newton's laws and all other "truths") is true "only as long as Dasein exists" (*SZ*, 226). He proclaims that there are "eternal truths" only when it can be satisfactorily demonstrated that "Dasein was and will be through all eternity" (*SZ*, 227).[13] Heidegger leaves the obvious premise unstated, namely that for him such a demonstration is unavailable, if not theoretically impossible, and that consequently there is no good reason to hold contradiction as an "eternal" truth. He adds, in partial justification of this claim, that the very notion of an eternal truth is the residue of an "idealized absolute subject" of theological origin (*SZ*, 229). Presumably no such absolute subject exists, at least in the theologico-metaphysical sense in which its nature has been traditionally defined. And without such a subject, no ontological ground exists on which to base the derivative eternality of a logical principle.

Two related aspects of this discussion must be noted. First, the status of contradiction as a truth of special significance is made dependent upon the mode of existence of an extra-logical entity. Heidegger insists that to construe this truth as eternal requires a prior demonstration connecting contradiction and Dasein, that mode of Being (*Sein*) that determines mortal man as the speaker of language. Although the principle of contradiction may be logically necessary because of considerations based on properties of language as such, it is ontologically necessary that contradiction is an *eternal* truth only if Dasein itself as the speaker of language eternally exists. Two different characteristics of this extralogical entity—its capacity to communicate in language and its mode of temporality—have emerged and intersect in a context where they would not appear to be related. Given this intersection one wonders whether Heidegger would also contend that the necessity of contradiction is grounded on Being insofar as it is temporal rather than on Being insofar as it can be rendered linguistically. This possibility will be considered later in this chapter.

The second noteworthy point is that the unique status of contradiction is not only dependent on the existence of an extralogical entity, but also on one particular mode of that existence—the sense in which it is related to temporality understood as eternity. Heidegger denies special status to contradiction solely on the basis of conditions pertaining to temporality rather than on considerations derived from purely linguistic or conceptual sources. If eternality is a distorted apprehension of the true nature of time, then if contradiction *is* somehow privileged, it must be for reasons other than its putative participation in a realm of timelessly valid truths.

The essential relation between temporality and the ontology presupposed by logical principles has emerged in the *Sein und Zeit* discussion of contradiction. Thus, if contradiction is a formally necessary principle of correct thought, then for Heidegger that formality is itself not independent of temporal determination. In fact, the essential function of time within the ontological structure of logic becomes more and more manifest as Heidegger's reflections on that structure deepen. The denial that contradiction is an "eternal" truth is complemented by the affirmation that contradiction is substantiated differently at various moments in the history of Western metaphysics. The emphasis shifts from what contradiction cannot be (eternally true) to what it must be understood as (historically conditioned). Heidegger insists that whoever holds contradiction to be a timelessly valid principle not only misapprehends time but also "does not consider that this principle has an essentially different content for the metaphysics of Aristotle, and plays another role for Leibniz and again is of a different truth in the metaphysics of a Hegel or a Nietzsche" (*NII,* 159). In fact, since the appearance of Hegel's *Logik,* the "towering peak of Western metaphysics" (*WD,* 146), it is not immediately certain that "that which is self-contradictory could not also be actual (*wirklich*)" (*SG,* 38).[14] For Heidegger, the history of modern metaphysics is, by itself, sufficient evidence to prove that contradiction cannot be considered abstractly, as a purely "formal" logical axiom.

The post-*Sein und Zeit* reflections presuppose that an essential factor in the hidden ontology of logical principles is the progressive history of metaphysical speculation in relation to the bare statement of the principle of contradiction. Thus, the full complexity of those ontological patterns discernible in speculative metaphysical interpretations of the "inner" structure of contradiction depends on the truth of the premise that history is a necessary part of the ultimate ontological nature of symbolic logic. This merger of ontology and history is axiomatic for Heidegger. But clearly it is one feature of his thought that is particularly susceptible to attack. A contemporary logician could maintain, with apparent propriety, that the principle of contradiction remains fundamentally the same throughout the checkered history of Western metaphysics, and that the various metaphysical speculations grafted onto that principle are completely irrelevant to the principle construed in its intrinsic formality.

To justify the full Heideggerian program in light of this anticipated criticism would require a lengthy and difficult analysis of history and its relation to the ontological content of logical principles. But for now, this issue in its full complexity need not be addressed. It will suffice here to examine only one formulation of contradiction insofar as it constitutes a single moment in the history of metaphysics, since on Heidegger's understanding of history what is true of the process as a whole must be true of any one moment in that process. We cannot attempt at this point to show all the ontological dimensions presently concealed by the principle of contradiction when taken as a formally neutral axiom. But what can and indeed must be demonstrated is that hidden ontological presuppositions are present in one historically significant formulation of that principle. For if presuppositions of this sort can be located and specified in one instance, then there is support for Heidegger's claim that such ontological hiddenness permeates the entire metaphysical tradition.

Aristotle will serve as the locus of this demonstration, with particular emphasis on several of his formulations of the principle of contradiction. It is true that Aristotle was not the first metaphysician to appreciate the importance of contradiction—both Parmenides and Plato, with varying degrees of explicitness, articulated the fundamental character of the principle. In fact, Heidegger at least once referred to Plato as the originator of "logic" (*HE*, 233), but he has not addressed this occurrence of contradiction, at least in his works published to date. However, even if Aristotle's formulations are not historically the first, they certainly contain hidden ontological presuppositions, at least to the same extent as and perhaps even greater than the later developments of contradiction in e.g., Leibniz, Hegel, and Nietzsche.

Heidegger asserts straightforwardly that "Aristotle's principle of contradiction is also an ontological relation and a law of Being (*ein Seinsverhältnis und Seinsgesetz*)," and he immediately adds that the precise nature of this relation and law is "unclear even today" (*L,* 23 n). The fact that contradiction is a law of Being justifies the need to "question what this principle presupposes" in order to determine the sense in which contradiction can become instituted as "a regulative principle of thinking" (*NI,* 601). The lack of clarity Heidegger speaks of may well remain after all his other related comments have been analyzed, but I believe that the apparently unbounded scope of the context surrounding this lack will be considerably narrowed. We may hope that once it is evident how Heidegger approaches the Aristotelian presuppositions, it will become less difficult to detect what has been hidden in other subsequent metaphysical developments of the principle.

It should perhaps be stressed that my purpose is not to interpret Aristotle on contradiction, but rather to interpret Heidegger's understanding of Aristotle on contradiction. Whether or not Heidegger has understood Aristotle correctly is, of course, important to determine. But the end pursued in this study is the presentation of a coherent account of the implications hidden in the Aristotelian formulations of contradiction as elicited by Heidegger's commentary. For even if Heidegger has misread Aristotle, it is—ironically, under the circumstances—still logically possible for true conclusions to follow from false premises. In short, my account is guided by the hope of disclosing potentially important philosophical considerations rather than by the intent to evaluate the letter of Heidegger's interpretations according to established, but perhaps philosophically questionable, standards of historical or philological accuracy.

For Heidegger, Aristotle is "the father of logic" (*SZ*, 214).[15] It is Aristotle who, in the *De Interpretatione*, interprets *logos* as propositional forms of affirmation or negation. These forms are composed of nouns that carry no reference to time and of verbs that do carry a reference to time (*De Int*, 2-3). A proposition (*Aussage*) is defined in terms of the grammatical unity of a noun and a verb. This view of the essence of *logos* becomes "representative and decisive for the subsequent development of logic and grammar" (*EM*, 44). And it is this view of *logos* that provides the components for the principle of contradiction as defined in the *De Interpretatione*, and, later, in the *Metaphysics*.

Aristotle's formulation of contradiction depends on the notion of propositional form, and the notion of propositional form depends on his understanding of *logos*. Heidegger initiates his ontological reflections at the point of origin. He contends that Aristotle failed to investigate the "phenomenon within which the structure of *logos* permits and obliges us" to characterize propositional forms as combinatory and divisional (*SZ*, 159). The primordial meaning of *logos* is based on what "*logos* whose essence logic and dialectic, which stem from metaphysics, are never able to experience" (*WM*, 237). At this fundamental ontological level, *logos* is the "foreword" (*Vorwort*) to language—it describes, as it were, the conditions for the possibility of spoken language becoming ontologically revelatory (*HE*, 383).[16] Heidegger intends to pursue this sense of *logos* and, perhaps, bring it partially to light. Therefore, he will analyze the Greek word *logos* according to what he believes is its original meaning. Then he will compare the original meaning of *logos* with its Aristotelian interpretation as propositional form. The difference between the two senses of *logos* will provide the substance for determining what is hidden in Aristotle's understanding of *logos* and, derivatively, in Aristotle's subsequent formulation of the principle of contradiction.

For Heidegger, it is unquestionably true that "the audibilized Greek word" brings us "immediately into the matter at hand" (*WP*,

12). The matter at hand is the original meaning of *logos*. Heidegger contends that "in the decisive beginning of Western ontology, *logos* functioned as the single clue for entrance into the proper nature of beings and for the determination of the Being of these beings" (*SZ*, 154). Thus, the more we know about the original meaning of *logos*, the more we know about the meaning of Being as disclosed by language spoken in relation to determinate beings. Heidegger then asserts that *legein*, the infinitive form of *logos*, originally meant to lay before (*Vorlegen*), to lay down (*Darlegen*), to lay upon (*Überlegen*), and that the meaning of *legein* as to say or to speak was derived from these more primordial meanings (*WD*, 121).

When *logos* is translated as word or proposition, these translations must therefore be understood in the context of the ontological meaning of the infinitive *legein* and not according to the derivative meaning as the process or product of making statements. If this original meaning is restored, then *logos*, when it does become distinctively linguistic in meaning, would be understood as that which allows beings to appear "as they are" in their Being (*US*, 237). When named through the proper sense of *logos*, Being is "that which gathers all that comes to presence in presence" (*VA*, 227). In a word, "Being is gathering—*logos*" (*WP*, 13). And a determinate being is an entity gathered in such a way that its determination in relation to Being as presence is allowed to appear in and through language spoken and understood as *logos*.

The transition from *logos* as the gathering of Being to *logos* as propositional form in abstraction from Being was brought to completion by Aristotle. Heidegger concisely summarizes the transition:

> Initially *logos* as gathering *is* the happening of unconcealment, grounded in concealment and in service to it. Now *logos* as statement becomes the locus of truth in the sense of correctness. And this process culminates in *Aristotle*'s principle that *logos* as statement is that which can be true or false. Truth that was originally unconcealment, a happening of the dominant being itself and governed by gathering, now becomes a property of the *logos*. (*EM*, 142—italics in text.)[17]

Heidegger's contention is that an utterance functions differently when *logos* means the unconcealment of the gathering of Being than when *logos* stands for the utterance construed as a statement judged true or false according to a standard of correctness. If the utterance is understood as a statement subsumed under the representational abstraction of correctness between the speaking of the statement and the object spoken about, then Heidegger insists that Being can no longer become unconcealed through the utterance as it once could when the utterance was governed by the original meaning of logos.

We are now in a position to offer a Heideggerian critique of the Aristotelian approach to contradiction by describing two presuppositions that may be derived from a given formulation of that principle. The following passage appears in the *De Interpretatione* (17a, 25-31). "Now it is possible both to affirm and to deny the presence of something which is present or of something which is not, and since these same affirmations and denials are possible with reference to those times which lie outside the present, it would be possible to contradict any affirmation or denial." It is clear that if truth and falsity are defined exclusively in terms of the correctness or incorrectness of a relation between statement and being, then the establishment of a principle that preserves a formal distinction between true and false propositions is inevitable. But the necessity granted to this principle depends on the meaning given to the components of the principle: truth as a function of propositions that affirm or deny, the proposition as a grammatical conjunction of the verb and the noun. But what if the correct is not equivalent in all respects to the true (*HE,* 94)? Although Aristotle's treatment unifies a diverse set of elements into a principle apparently bearing the force of necessity, the result of that unity omits reference to the appropriate ontological dimension. The first presupposition in the original formulation of the principle of contradiction may now be stated within the context of this omission.

*First Presupposition.* As defined by Aristotle, contradiction is possible only on condition that the propositional forms of language are taken in isolation from the ontological totality within which language occurs. Thus, the necessity of contradiction depends, at least in part, on abstracting the proposition as such from its grounding relation to Being. The modern device of representing a propositional form by symbols—"p", "q", etc.—merely accentuates the abstractive process initially present in Aristotle's decision to separate the propositional form of language from the Being of the referents of that language.

In the vocabulary of *Sein und Zeit,* the historical origin of logic was marked by the "crude ontology of that which is at hand" (*SZ,*

129). In this case, that which is at hand (*Vorhandenen*) is the fact of spoken language as such. This fact generates a "crude" ontology when language is taken as an activity so complete and whole in itself that it can be subsumed under principles of generality (e.g., contradiction) without taking into account the essential relation between that activity and Being. For Heidegger, it is axiomatic that "every proposition is a mode of Being (*ein Sein*) toward the being of the thing itself" insofar as the thing referred to becomes unconcealed through that proposition (*SZ*, 218). Thus, there is a unique intimacy between the referent as such and the referring language, so much so that this language becomes part of the very Being of a particular referent. In fact, this intimacy is so complete that Heidegger feels free to assert that the principle of contradiction becomes operative as a regulatory device if and only if *logos* is construed as a "proposition" (*Aussage*—*L*, 22-3).[18] Presumably if language were not defined in the ontologically crude way that divorces it so stringently from Being, then investigation into the nature of language and its relation to Being would attain results significantly different from those derived from the principles implicit in Aristotle and echoed throughout the subsequent history of metaphysics. Once such an original perspective on language has been secured, however, it will then be possible to resurrect some, perhaps all, of the ontological characteristics that were manifest when *logos* meant the gathering of Being.

For Heidegger, language as it appears in Aristotle's formulations of the principle of contradiction has been subjected to an abstraction—the transformation from spoken utterances as such to "formal" representations of spoken utterances—which presupposes that the process of abstraction has no ontological effect on the product of abstraction. Now, in general, an exposed presupposition need not critically affect all or even some of the elements to which that presupposition is related. And, at this point, no reason has been given by Heidegger to show that the reductive process during which the meaning of *logos* shifted from the gathering of Being to propositional form *necessarily* distorted the relation between language and Being. But the tone if not the content of Heidegger's account of that transition certainly suggests that Aristotle, building upon a certain unexamined notion of *logos*, formulated the elements of language in such a way that contradiction became essential as a regulative principle of correct thinking—and yet contributed by that very essentiality to a distortion of Being. The explicit connection drawn between logic and ontological crudeness supports the forceful immediacy of this suggestion.

But at this point we must pause. It is not sufficient for Heidegger merely to claim that the principle of contradiction is based on an abstractive presupposition derived from the original meaning of *logos*. Heidegger must also demonstrate that contradiction is an abstraction that, whether actively or passively, interferes with the unconcealment of Being. For if it is the case that the principle of contradiction *is compatible with* both Heidegger's account of Being and with accounts of Being that differ from Heidegger's, then there is no reason to reflect further on this principle, at least from the standpoint of the dictates of ontology. The true nature of Being will be accessible in any case. Thus, our discussion of the first presupposition as such must close on an indeterminate note. Although the awareness of presuppositions is always important in a philosophical inquiry, the presupposition just outlined may prove in this instance to be ontologically indifferent, even if the formality it has engendered has become rigidified throughout the history of metaphysics as the most fundamental principle legislating the correctness of thought.

*Second Presupposition.* The first presupposition can therefore become significant only if it is substantiated by a second presupposition that is more definite and more conclusive. The first presupposition, simply put, is that the Aristotelian principle of contradiction is based on a one-sided abstraction from the original ontological meaning of the Greek word *logos*. The second presupposition may be stated provisionally as follows: The principle of contradiction can be restructured only in such a way that that structure hinders the unconcealment of Being as determined through the original meaning of *logos*. This tentative formulation of the second presupposition is itself based on a presupposition of a different order, i.e., that Heidegger can put forth an account of Being sufficiently detailed to show, by implication if not directly, the detrimental character of the implicit process of abstraction described by the first presupposition. For now, it is essential only to connect the function of contradiction with the demands of Being so that this function will be approached from the proper perspective of Denken.

This perspective becomes evident when one compares P. F. Strawson, a philosopher discussing the matter from a very different angle, and Heidegger on the principal effect consequent upon the utterance of contradictory propositions. First, Strawson: "The *standard* purpose of speech, the intention to communicate something, is frustrated by self-contradiction. Contradicting oneself is like writing something down and then erasing it, or putting a line through it. A contradiction cancels itself and leaves nothing."[19] Now Heidegger: "Through contradictory assertions, which man can, unhindered, bring forth concerning the same thing, he displaces himself from his nature into the absence of that nature, he annuls the connection to beings as such" (*NI*, 603).

On the surface Heidegger's description of the effect of contradictory assertions appears to be similar to Strawson's. But there is an absolutely crucial difference. For Strawson, a contradiction is completely self-destructive; nothing linguistic remains once a contradiction has been uttered. It is as if the speaker of the contradiction had never really spoken in the first place. But for Heidegger, the nothingness of a contradiction is informative. The very possibility that language is so structured that it can be expressed in a self-contradictory manner tells us something both about language as such and also about the beings to which language refers. Heidegger claims that the nothingness present after the utterance of a contradiction is not the same as the absence of language altogether. In each case there is silence, but Heidegger believes that the silence ensuing after a contradiction is necessarily replete with ontological significance whereas silence as the mere absence of speech need not be determinable in this respect. The significance of that logical principle that can generate such ontologically revealing silence is not exhausted simply by the fact that, as Strawson contends, its presence nullifies meaningful discourse.

In fact, Heidegger insists that contradiction says "something" about Being, that contradiction "contains the essential outline of *on he on*, of beings as this particular being" (*NI*, 601). Heidegger then stipulates (and the entire claim is italicized) that "the essence of beings exists in the standing absence (*Abwesen*) of contradiction" (*NI*, 603). Note that Heidegger has made this ontological claim in the context of beings, not in the context of propositions about beings. The relevant formulation of the principle of contradiction is now located not on the level of propositions, but on the level of beings (about which contradictory propositions may be uttered). This shift from the formal to the material mode is in keeping with the original meaning of *logos* as the unconcealment of Being with respect to languge spoken about beings. The shift reorients the perspective on contradiction from language as such to beings, a reorientation that is essential before the sense in which language enters into the ontological picture can be accurately depicted.

For Heidegger, the implicit ontological structure of contradiction says that every determinate being is an intersection of what that being *is* and what that being is *not*. The element of negation thus assumes cardinal importance, and we shall consider Heidegger's treatment of it in some detail in chapter 2. For now, we note that this primordial conjunction is an ontological prerequisite that grounds the purely logical impossibility that any single proposition about being cannot be both true and not true at the same time. The contemporary logician will quickly respond that Heidegger's approach obscures the fact—a fact that a philosopher such as Strawson would never deny—that contradiction as such is an essentially formal principle, i.e., that it asserts nothing about the mode of Being of those beings to which it necessarily applies. Heidegger's response is just as prompt—this supposed ontologically neutral formality is precisely the dimension of logical principles that must be subjected to thoughtful scrutiny. The pure "formality" of the principle of contradiction is, in fact, based on a number of fundamental notions, each of which is capable of receiving divergent metaphysical interpretations. Unity, difference, negation, simultaneity, and conjunction are examples of these notions. Is it self-evident that a principle of such intrinsic complexity can simply be labelled "formal" without specifying, or at least investigating, what this formality consists in other than an indifference to propositional content? Heidegger insists that this position is not self-evident.

However, this insistence places Heidegger in a dilemma. He has maintained that he does not question logical principles insofar as they control the correctness of thinking. But correctness of this sort depends on taking logical principles as formal, i.e., as indifferent to the content of the language they regulate. If this formality is subjected to scrutiny, then correctness becomes dependent upon certain metaphysical positions (e.g., on the nature of temporality, as we shall see). And if these positions turn out to be ontologically unsound, then it is possible that the formal validity necessary to correct reasoning distorts the subject matter of thought, especially philosophical thought, simply by virtue of the "formally" self-evident immediacy of logical principles. Thus the dilemma: If Heidegger acknowledges the need for contradiction in some formal sense, then he seems bound to accept an underlying metaphysical stance that may conflict with the stated principles of his ontology; but if he rejects the metaphysics of contradiction in favor of that ontology, then there is no longer a discernible standard for preserving the formal correctness of thought, including the thought necessary to state Heidegger's own ontology.

This dilemma epitomizes the difference between Heidegger and less ontologically-inclined philosophers such as Strawson, and also serves to highlight the full scope of the second presupposition in the Aristotelian formulations of contradiction. To escape the dilemma, and also to illustrate the ontological distortion indicated by the second presupposition, Heidegger must accept contradiction as a regulative principle while at the same time substantiating its abstract character in light of his ontology, with a view toward correcting the original misdirected assumptions of Aristotle's metaphysics. Heidegger must now state precisely how the Aristotelian formulations of contradiction presuppose a metaphysical stance that deflects thinking regulated by the formality of that principle away from the nature of Being as such.

According to one of Aristotle's formulations, "the same attribute cannot at the same time and in the same respect belong and not belong to the same subject" (*Metaphysics* 1005b, 18-20). Although cast in the material mode, this formulation locates the primary metaphysical assumption of contradiction, an assumption which in its own way also permeates the formal mode statement of the principle. The assumption originates in the qualification "at the same time." For what does the notion of simultaneity mean in this supposedly formal context?

One answer, consistent with Aristotle's position as developed in the *Physics* (219-20), is that time can be represented in terms of discrete and denumerable moments. Thus, the implicit metaphysical structure of Aristotle's material mode formulation of contradiction may be illustrated as follows: if an entity possesses a certain property at one moment, then it is logically impossible for that entity not to possess that property at the same moment. But notice that only on the assumption that time can be divided into such moments is it (ontologically) possible to think the (logical) impossibility of the entity possessing and not possessing that property "at the same time." Thus, the Aristotelian formulation of contradiction depends on the possibility that time can be partitioned into distinctly different moments. For if two such moments could, in ontological fact, be the same, then it would also be possible for the entity both to possess and not possess the property "at the same time." Thus, the formal necessity of contradiction is based on the metaphysical position that it is impossible to divide time into such coincident moments.

According to Heidegger, Aristotle did not investigate the fundamental character of the phenomenon that originally grounded the possibility of logic.[20] This phenomenon is time. The assumption that time can be divided into discrete moments sanctions the eventual possibility that beings can be subsumed under a principle defined, in part, by the presence or absence of such moments. And Aristotle has recourse to this possibility when he defines two crucial components in the formal mode definition of contradiction. The first component is discussed in the *De Interpretatione*, where the noun is stipulated as having "no reference to time" (16a20) and the verb is stipulated as carrying with it "the notion of time" (16b6).[21]

But on what grounds does Aristotle decide that a term that names a being lacks reference to time but a term that designates activity or motion possesses reference to time? If Heidegger's ontology of temporality as presence is correct, then there is no cause to exclude temporality from the definition of a noun; this part of language, as all parts of language, should show how the being denoted by the noun is a modality of time. It is true that a noun and a verb may be connected grammatically in such a way that an indirect form of temporality is given to the noun through the verb—e.g., "the tree is growing." But if the noun as such represents a being as something without any essential temporal determination, which Aristotle expressly stipulates, then the only temporal features discernible in the noun (and, derivatively, in the being denoted by the noun) will be imported from those residues of time signified by the verb, or by other grammatical modifiers. The fact that Aristotle has defined the parts of a proposition so that this temporal exclusion becomes unavoidable is, on Heideggerian principles, one of the seminal steps in the generation of a logic that drives language and thought away from the structure of Being.

The ontological arbitrariness in the separation of time from the *logos* as noun is not rectified when the second component of contradiction is formulated, the proposition as a unity of noun and verb. However, Heidegger is careful to note that Aristotle never defended the view that the proposition as such is a simple conjunction of noun and verb, either expressed affirmatively by synthesis or negatively by diaresis. Heidegger contends that, for Aristotle, every proposition, whether it affirms or denies, whether it is true or false, is "equally and primordially both *synthesis and diaresis*" (*SZ*, 159—italics in text). The correct ontological ground for the Aristotelian proposition is therefore not that it is either true or false, but that it can be true or false (*L*, 135).[22] Heidegger's stress on this conjunction of apparent opposites is important because it forces the unity of synthesis and diaresis proper to every proposition to be characterized and defined in a more primordial and nonlinguistic context. If, for example, a proposition that appears to be strictly affirmative (e.g., All S are P) is, as Heidegger contends, both affirmative and negative concurrently, then affirmation and negation cannot refer simply to the immediate logical form of this proposition (since it contains no negative elements). As a result, the proposition's joint affirmative and negative character must be connected somehow to the ontological nature of that to which the proposition refers, i.e., to a being (or beings) in relation to Being.

Aristotle's formulation of the structure of the proposition is sensitive to the fact that Being, the ultimate ground of any proposition, includes both the positive and negative dimensions reflected in the structure of the proposition. It is a formulation theoretically open to an ontological interpretation that would show the specific content of Being with respect to the proposition. Thus, Aristotle's notion of the proposition is, as such, less subject to ontological distortion than is his notion of the noun as part of that proposition. As Heidegger puts it, the Aristotelian formulation of synthesis and diaresis is "half logical, half ontological" (*L*, 168). But, for Heidegger, the fact remains that Aristotle did not carry through an explicit ontological interpretation of the joint unifying-and-divisional property of the proposition in terms of Being as such. The nature of what the proposition both unifies and divides is thus left at a purely formal and unspecified metaphysical level.

The separation of time from the noun and therefore from the ontological character of the being that the noun denotes, and the abstract formulation of the proposition as a whole are the most prominent results of the second presupposition in Aristotle's formal mode formulation of contradiction. But temporal exclusion and formal abstraction are also found in the material mode phase of this presupposition. Thus, the simultaneity that underlies the qualification "at the same time" in this version of contradiction is based on the metaphysical assumption that time can be divided into discrete moments. But, the Heideggerian will ask, what constitutes the difference between such discrete moments? In fact, what does it mean to divide time into moments in the first place? Is such division ontologically feasible?

Now if time for Heidegger is a kind of presence that, as a continuum of sorts, cannot properly be divided into moments distinctively different from one another, then simultaneity understood as the coincidence of discrete moments is ontologically suspect, if not impossible. But if simultaneity cannot be defined in terms of discrete moments, then the very notion of simultaneity may be merely a distortion resulting from an originally deficient metaphysics of time. And if simultaneity in this sense is inappropriate to the structure of time, then contradiction may well lose one of its apparently essential grounding metaphysical notions. If, on the other hand, contradiction as the regulative principle of correct thought cannot be articulated without the notion of simultaneity, then simultaneity must somehow be preserved. In short, if contradiction must be preserved, then so must the notion of simultaneity. But surely in order to maintain the essential rightness of thinking, contradiction must be preserved. Therefore, since time understood in terms of discrete moments cannot support the notion of simultaneity, then simultaneity must be reinterpreted in light of the appropriate ontology of time.

One might attempt to circumvent any such introduction of an ontological reference to temporality by shifting the principle of contradiction from the material mode back to the formal mode. But on Heideggerian grounds this attempt cannot succeed. Although there is no apparent indication or even suggestion of temporality in a symbolic statement of contradiction, this lack of reference is due to a double abstraction—from beings as such to propositions about beings, and from propositions about beings to symbols that represent propositions about beings. This double abstraction generates a symbolic world that, in its immediate appeal to the calculative aspect of thought, appears to be self-subsistent and distinctively nontemporal. But the process of abstraction necessary for the generation of this world strips away the essential temporality of whatever referent such symbolism may eventually designate. The decision to separate time from the principle of contradiction must be evaluated in conjunction with what is, for Heidegger, the ontologically necessary fact that time is the essential determinant of the beings to which this and the other logical principles apply. The material mode formulation of the principle of contradiction merely brings into the open what its formal mode counterpart conceals behind a propositional or symbolic front—time as a necessary element in the metaphysical structure of the principle of contradiction.

We may conclude this initial phase of our study by observing that, for Heidegger, the structure of contradiction must be articulated in accordance with the principles of an appropriate ontology of temporality. Now if Heidegger's critique of the Aristotelian formulations of contradiction is sound, or even simply on the right track, then Heidegger's own ontological approach to temporality must cohere with contradiction more adequately than does Aristotle's uncritical metaphysics. If there are notions that specify both Being in relation to beings as well as the conceptual structure of contradiction, then there must be an isomorphism of sorts between Being in relation to beings and the notional structure of the principle of contradiction. And the temporality that defines these notions in the context of ontoloy must be commensurate with the temporality of these notions in the context of "logic." This commensurability will become ontologically secure only if the formal and material modes of the principle of contradiction are defined at a level of abstraction which ensures that their respective differences are jointly compatible with the structure of Being as such.

The properties necessary to determine the unique presence of an entity will not, of course, be equivalent in all respects to the properties necessary to differentiate a proposition about that entity from the contradictory of that proposition. Nevertheless, all distinctively linguistic features of the formal mode must, at some degree of abstraction, exhibit temporality in the same way that temporality is exhibited by the purely entitative mode. For if this sameness cannot be specified, then the Heideggerian ontology will result in the same serious defect as that present to the Aristotelian metaphysics and to all other metaphysical interpretations of contradiction—an abstract cleavage between word and object, between language and Being.[23]

In the next three chapters, we shall examine the ways in which Heidegger has attempted to analyze the apparent formality of other fundamental logical notions and principles—negation, sameness and difference, identity—in order to indicate how ontological factors have been concealed in them. As we should expect from the investigation of the principle of contradiction just concluded, the direction of Heidegger's reflections becomes increasingly pointed toward elucidating the hidden dimensions of temporality in these logical components. Heidegger's thinking on these matters is always daring—but it is also not without profound difficulties, as we shall soon see.

CHAPTER 2

# The Ontological Structure of Negation

TOWARD THE BEGINNING OF THE ESSAY "*WAS IST META-physik?*," Heidegger proposes to determine the essence of metaphysics by reflecting on the question "Why is there something rather than nothing?" In the course of developing his opening thoughts on this question, he raises a formal consideration that appears to undercut the very possibility of this inquiry. He asserts that any discussion of this question must first concern itself with the word "nothing" (*Nichts*), but adds that to speak about the nothing is apparently a contradiction (*EM*, 19). Thus, either this formulation of the question cannot be pursued or the principle of contradiction must be reoriented to cohere with the demands of thinking on this fundamental ontological level. Heidegger's strategy for resolving this dilemma will be revealed as this chapter progresses. Worthy of note now is the intimacy he detects between the principle of contradiction and the attempt to think substantively about a basic logical notion. Heidegger's recognition of the formal pressure exerted by the principle of contradiction is of considerable interest—but of even greater interest is the fact that according to his interpretation of the regulative function of that principle, all discourse about negation becomes illogical, and therefore irrational. By analyzing the presuppositions of this claim, we will extend our understanding of Heidegger's position on contradiction as well as initiate an appreciation of his position on negation.

In chapter 1 we saw that the metaphysics underlying the Aristotelian formulation of the principle of contradiction is characterized, in part, by the notion of simultaneity. But that formulation also includes the notion of negation—i.e., a contradiction includes the simultaneous affirmation and denial of a specific proposition. Without some application of the notion of negation, the Aristotelian formulation of contradiction becomes impossible. But if the notion of simultaneity contains embedded metaphysical elements, there is then reason to think that the notion of negation may also contain them. Heideggerian Denken cannot rest content, as many logicians are prone to do, with taking negation as a logical "primitive," or as the (uninformative) "opposite of affirmation." Heidegger has already pointed to the substantive role of negation by specifying that an essential ontological characteristic of a referent is what that referent is *not*, a mode of negation already present in the material mode formulation of the principle of contradiction. Although the conceptual structure of negation as such may not be as complex as that animating contradiction, the fundamental status of negation in a sense transcends its function as part of the more diversified logical whole, i.e., the principle of contradiction. To preserve and specify the character of such transcendence is, in fact, part of Heidegger's own approach to negation.

Heidegger's most concentrated treatment of negation appeared in the essay "*Was ist Metaphysik?*," first published in 1929 and later included as the lead essay in the collection entitled *Wegmarken*. A Postscript was added to a 1943 reprint of the essay, and an Introduction, almost as long as the original essay, was included for a 1949 reprint. It seems fair to assume that Heidegger considered "*Was ist Metaphysik?*" to be of no small importance, since instead of simply writing another work to extend the way first explored in the 1929 version of the essay, he preserved that version intact and appended fore- and after-thoughts to it. Consequently, we shall approach these three compositions as a unity of sorts, but not without losing sight of the possibility that subtle differences, of emphasis if not of content, may be present within that unity. The rest of this chapter will review the development of the original essay, concentrating on those elements dealing with negation as such and adding introductory commentary (Section I) and then offer a tentative assessment of Heidegger's position (Section II).

I. Toward the conclusion of "*Was ist Metaphysik?*," Heidegger summarizes the effect his thinking on negation, or the nothing, would have on the primacy of "logic": "When the power of the intellect in the field of inquiry into the nothing and into Being is thus shattered, then the destiny of the reign of "logic" in philosophy is thereby decided. The idea of "logic" itself disintegrates in the turbulence of a more original questioning" (*WM*, 14). Again, a strong claim. Heidegger tells us that inquiry into the ultimate ontological character of negation has touched the very core of "logic" to such an extent that this body of rules "disintegrates" (*löst sich auf*) in the face of this inquiry. Whether or not such an effect pertains to the purely regulative function of logic remains to be seen. In any event the precise nature of this "more original" questioning must be examined with care as a prelude to accepting Heidegger's position concerning the disintegration of logic in this particular ontological context.

Heidegger's own inquiry into the nature of negation is typically broad-based. In fact, the analysis he offers is intended to range as wide as the title of the essay—What is metaphysics?—suggests. And the notion of negation, once properly formulated and understood, will lead directly into that region of thinking in which the answer to the question "What is metaphysics?" can be pursued and enunciated. Thus, establishing the nature of nothingness becomes just as important as thinking the nature of Being and the relation between Being and beings.

The 1929 version of the essay is divided into three sections. In the first section, Heidegger stipulates that any legitimate inquiry into the nature of metaphysics will be guided by two principles: "First, every metaphysical question always encompasses the whole range of metaphysical problems. Each question is itself always the whole. Therefore, second, every metaphysical question can be asked only in such a way that the questioner as such is present together with the question, that is, is placed in question" (*WM*, 1). Heidegger does not argue for the cogency of these principles but merely states them as axiomatic (commentary on these principles follows in Section II).

The one metaphysical question Heidegger analyzes as a pathway into the essence of metaphysics as a whole concerns the nothing, negation as such. His analysis begins by contrasting philosophy and science in the broad sense (i.e., *Wissenschaft*). Heidegger shows how science systematically ignores the nature of nothingness— "Science wants to know nothing of the nothing" (*WM*, 4). But Heidegger himself, as a protagonist of philosophical thinking, persists in questioning the notion of the nothing if for no other reason than to determine with some degree of certitude that this question cannot be meaningfully asked.

In the second section of the essay, the initial step taken is one that Heidegger describes as having an "unusual" (*ungewöhnliches*) consequence. To question the nothing presupposes that the nothing exists in some sense. But how can nonexistence exist? It cannot. Heidegger's thinking runs as follows: "The commonly cited ground rule of all thinking, the proposition that contradiction is to be avoided, universal 'logic' itself, lays low this question. For thinking, which is always essentially thinking about something, must act in a way contrary to its own essence when it thinks of nothing (*WM*, 5)." The unusual consequence is therefore that logic, through the stringency of the principle of contradiction as the ultimate standard for rightness in thinking, forces this problem to silence itself as soon as it has been voiced by thinking.

Heidegger takes this consequence to justify his subsequent claim that the negation so essential to logic cannot be located in the realm of thinking, but rather emanates from a more primordial phenomenon. The argument leading to this conclusion may be outlined as follows: If reason inquires into the nothing, then reason falls prey to the principle of contradiction. Reason cannot so fall prey and remain what it is. Therefore, reason cannot inquire into the nothing. But the nothing is nonetheless still present. Thus, if nothingness can be inquired into at all, then it must be given in advance. Since the givenness of this phenomenon necessarily lies beyond the bounds of rational thinking, and apparently beyond any restrictions placed on thinking by logical principles, Heidegger feels free in the second section of the essay to shift the analysis toward locating the origin of that phenomenon in a certain "mood" (*Stimmung*), that of "anxiety" (*Angst*).[1]

This initial argumentative step is important. It reveals that Heidegger rejects as ontologically inappropriate the seemingly relevant metaphysical distinction between meaning and reference. According to this distinction, "nothing" could be considered to have no referent while having a meaning, just as "gold mountain" can be meaningful without necessarily being referential. This distinction became prominent in our time primarily from Frege's work, but of course the sense of the distinction with respect to negation did not originate with him. In the *Sophist* Plato carefully introduces and describes a sense of nothing which renders the meaning of that notion equivalent to one sense of difference (257 b). And in the *Metaphysics*, Aristotle cites with apparent approval that "in the case of that which is not, some, emphasizing the linguistic form, say that that which is not is—not is simply, but is non-existent" (1030ª 25-26). Heidegger is therefore perhaps precipitous when he asserts that thinking "must act in a way contrary to its own essence when it thinks of the nothing." For the thinkers Plato and Aristotle, the attempt to construe the meaning of nothingness did not prove to be a self-destructive project. Whether or not their thinking represented that meaning properly is, of course, another matter.

It is not difficult to see why the meaning/reference distinction would not be suitable to Heidegger's approach. The reason is that the distinction permits nothingness a mode of existence that Heidegger's formulation of the problem of the nothing cannot allow. For even if "nothing" does not refer to anything, the fact that it can lay claim to be meaningful implies that the meaning ascribed to the nothing, or at least the statement of that meaning, has some kind of existence. And for Heidegger the nothing is properly characterized as "the negation of the totality of beings" (*die Verneinung der Allheit des Seienden*—*WM*, 5). But although this characterization is posited as a "definition" (*Definition*—*WM*, 6), the quotation marks indicate Heidegger's fundamental reservations about this form of representational categorization and all that such "logical" procedure entails as far as metaphysical distortion is concerned. He nonetheless repeats the claim that "the nothing (*das Nichts*) is the complete negation of the totality of beings" (*WM*, 6), and presumably he would contend that even a strictly semantic determination of negation remains within the totality of beings and thus cannot be thought of as nothingness in the requisite sense.

Heidegger pairs his phenomenological approach to determining the nature of nothingness with a similar approach to understanding the kind of nothingness that is falsehood. If falsehood is taken as an example of untruth, then the utterance of a falsehood entails the concealment of beings as a whole (*WM*, 93). A false proposition, insofar as it hides the being of its range of reference, carries with it the ontological consequence of concealing everything about every other being as well. Hence, Heidegger asserts, the resulting need to approach the problem of falsehood from a phenomenological perspective (*L*, 208). Every false utterance is *verstellend*,[2] a word that may mean, according to context, either "otherness" or "wrongness." This ambivalence is, of course, crucial in the context of negation. Is a false proposition one that says something simply other than the truth, or is it one that says something wrong, something opposed to the truth? If the former, then the principle of contradiction need not apply to the conjunction of a true and false proposition, since the false proposition as signifying something other than the true proposition need not necessarily be incompatible with that proposition. If the latter, however, then the principle of contradiction would seem to apply in full force. As far as I know, Heidegger never clarified which sense he had in mind, so we will again assume that he intended at least the stronger sense, i.e., that a false proposition is opposed to a true one not just in the sense of being other than true, but in the sense of being wrong in relation to the true.

How then can negation so defined be experienced and articulated? At this point Heidegger introduces an important distinction. The totality of beings is given at some fundamental ontological level; however, it is one thing to comprehend that totality as such, quite another simply to find ourselves existing within that totality. The first is impossible, the second is happening all the time (*WM*, 7). It is from the latter mode of existence that Heidegger begins his analysis of the foundational phenomenon of nothingness in terms of anxiety, the distinctive mood of Dasein that provides access to the ontological structure of the nothing.

By mood in this sense, Heidegger does not mean "merely a way of being determined in our inner being;" rather, mood is "precisely the basic way in which we are *outside* ourselves," i.e., "the way we are essentially and constantly" (*NI*, 119—italics in test). Furthermore, such a condition manifests itself in feeling directed toward what we are and what we are not (*NI*, 62).

The externality proper to this sense of mood is such that it unites human beings existing in that mood with the distinctive "feel" produced by that mood. Whereas "mood" typically refers to a condition that comes and goes, Heidegger intends to evoke a sense of mood that transcends such evanescence by the continual projection of self toward what is not self. Thus, I feel hatred or love toward something that, as other than myself, is the originator of that feeling. Heidegger then specifies the ontological locus of such intentionality by describing it as, in part, "what we are not," a specification which in turn locates the source of nothingness as such. The question nonetheless arises whether such a mood and its correlative feeling (anxiety in this case)—which in ordinary, i.e., non-ontological, contexts seems essentially transitory—can be made to sustain the ontological weight Heidegger wants it to bear in his analysis of the structure of nothingness. This point will be examined further in Section II below.

Although anxiety as a mood of ontological dimension also played a pivotal role in *Sein und Zeit*, the emphasis of this role was somewhat different in that early work. Anxiety provided "the phenomenal basis for explicitly grasping Dasein's primordial totality of Being" (SZ, 182). This totality is "being-in-the-world," and anxiety makes manifest to Dasein "its *Being-free* for the freedom of choosing itself and taking hold of itself" (SZ, 188).[3] In "*Was ist Metaphysik?*," the relation between anxiety and Dasein remains fundamental, but now there is an equivalent emphasis on the way in which anxiety reveals the structure of nothingness as such, i.e., not simply for Dasein but also as an integral component of Being itself. As Heidegger puts it in another early work, "*Angst* is *Angst* before Being itself" (PG, 405). The ontological thrust of anxiety assumed the widest possible scope as Heidegger advanced from the thinking of *Sein und Zeit* to that of "*Was ist Metaphysik?*."

Once the fundamental character of anxiety is understood, "we have arrived at that happening in human existence in which nothing becomes revealed and from which it must be interrogated" (WM, 10). It is therefore vital to keep in mind that Heidegger has not erected a simple equation linking anxiety with the nothing: anxiety is only the ontological phenomenon within which the structure of nothingness can and must be discerned. Thus, Heidegger in effect distinguishes between anxiety as the essential medium through which the nothing is revealed and the structure of the nothing as such.[4]

In the actual experience of anxiety, there is, as Heidegger tersely states, "nothing to hold on to" (WM, 9). Anxiety is never anxious about some specific object or event—rather, anxiety always concerns the totality of objects, all beings taken as a unity. Anxiety touches everything precisely as everything. It is this factor of unity in totality that provides the key to the structure of nothingness—"in anxiety, nothingness is at one with beings as a whole" (WM, 10). Heidegger expands on this function of the nothing as follows:

> The nothing does not attract; it is essentially repelling. But this repulsion is itself as such a parting gesture toward beings that are submerging as a whole. This wholly repelling gesture towards those retreating beings as a whole,

which is the action of the nothing that oppresses Dasein in anxiety, is the essence of the nothing: nihilation (*WM*, 11).

"Nihilation" (*Nichtung*) is therefore a kind of process. It is the movement generated when the totality of beings recedes from Dasein in such a manner that this movement can be experienced by Dasein only as a mood of a distinctive sort—i.e., anxiety. Stated in the more abstract terminology of classical metaphysics (which at several points in the essay Heidegger is not averse to using), nothingness reveals the totality of beings "as pure other" (*schlechtin Andere*—*WM*, 11), a mode of expression repeated in the Postscript (*WM*, 101). We should also note that this speculative contention, although tendered here in the material mode, is also mirrored in the formal mode. Since the confrontation between Being and not-being happens preeminently in language (*HG*, 66), Heidegger infers that every proposition includes what it does not refer to as well as what it does. Any distinction between the material and formal modes will therefore not affect the description of the nothing on the level at which Heidegger undertakes this description.

But why anxiety and not some other mood? To the objection that anxiety is arbitrarily chosen for this essential ontological function, Heidegger's reply in the Postscript takes the form not of arguing that anxiety and only anxiety is the appropriate mood, but of describing a counterpart mood to anxiety—i.e., "courage" (*Tapferkeit*). The strategy of this response seems to rest on the belief that the primordial ontological character of anxiety is not something open to demonstration. All that the thinker can do is complement the potential negative effect risked in elevating anxiety to this fundamental position by describing a sense of courage serving as a counterpart to this mood. According to Heidegger there is a palpable ontological sense in which beings threaten us as "non-being (*Nichtsein*—*WM*, 274).[5] As a result the "ground of courage" is located in the ontological fact that man, or Dasein, "is *not* who he is" (*HE*, 375). We may attempt to interpret this cryptic claim as follows: Whatever is represented as a threat can be projected into an experiential realm in which the threat, as something other than ourselves, moves beyond our control. But since this realm is, in fact, part of our mode of existence, Heidegger is justified in designating the ground of courage as that ontological level on which humanity is *not* what it is. Thus, in acting courageously while facing a threat, a human being is extended beyond whatever its present limits may be, i.e., into regions where the intentions and actions of a given individual are not yet present. It is precisely this element of nothingness within both our world and our reaction to a certain threatening part of that world which makes the realization of courage the uncertain affair that it often is.

But even if courage and anxiety are allowed to coexist as ontological complements, there are other obvious objections to anxiety in this sense. For one might contend that anxiety as an ontological phenomenon has no experiential grounding in any of the typical instances of negation (e.g., those in ordinary discourse). Heidegger responds to this query by asserting that "anxiety is there. It only sleeps" (*WM*, 14). The reference to sleeping is an effective personification—neatly compatible with the human element of Dasein—for what is, we are assured throughout the essay, a strictly ontological phenomenon. Just as we are not conscious of sleeping while sleeping is our state of being, so also we are not conscious of anxiety even though anxiety remains an unceasing component of our ontological mode of being. However, whether or not this personification can stand critical questioning is a matter that will be considered later in this chapter.

In any event once we recognize the ontological region in which the nothing properly resides, then we will see that "the nothing does not remain the indeterminate opposite of beings but reveals itself as belonging to the Being of beings" (*Sein des Seienden*—*WM*, 17). It follows that the question of the meaning of Being (*Sein*) becomes also the question of the meaning of *non-being* (*Nichtsein*—*HE*, 276). Furthermore, since as we might put it, Being entails the nothing and the nothing entails Being, the nothing permeates the entire realm described by the various approaches taken toward determining Being throughout the history of metaphysics.[6] The task of Dasein, both as thinker and as participant in this history, is to evoke the meaning of Being through considering the nothingness that differentiates Being at the same time that it belongs to Being as such.

But where should such difficult thinking begin? In any case it will not originate in the classic interplay of "positive" and "negative." Heidegger asserts that this well-entrenched metaphysical distinction does not preserve any significant relation to Being (*HE*, 157).

The terms *positive* and *negative* possess a manifest and particularly accessible type of opposition, but for Heidegger this opposition becomes more and more nugatory the more one attempts to specify its ontological ground. How therefore can this derivative distinction be properly thought? The answer must begin with the correct approach toward the negative in relation to its source in negation as such. Heidegger carefully situates the relational priority between nothingness in the fundamental sense intended and the "not" found in logical negation. His claim is that the logical "not," the not of negative propositions such as "S is not P," depends on the nothingness of nihilation—not vice versa.

Heidegger attempts to demonstrate the point in this passage:

> But how could the deniable and what is to be denied be viewed as something susceptible to the not unless all thinking as such has caught sight of the not already? But the not can become manifest only when its origin, the nihilation of the nothing in general, and therewith the nothing itself, is disengaged from concealment. The not does not originate through negation; rather negation is grounded in the not that springs from the nihilation of the nothing. But negation is also only one way of nihilating, that is, only one sort of behavior that has been grounded beforehand in the nihilation of the nothing. (*WM*, 13).[7]

This important discussion stands at the center of Heidegger's thinking on negation, and it will be examined in Section II of this chapter. For now, we note the crucial ontological point that if Being is limited by the active presence of the nothing, then Being itself becomes finite in nature by virtue of this necessary limitation—a conclusion that Heidegger does not shrink from drawing (*WM*, 17). It is also worth noting that the notion of finitude in this context is not at all easy to grasp. For if Being has limits, then whatever will limit Being could not itself have Being on pain of generating a contradiction (i.e., the limits of Being both have Being insofar as they serve as limits of Being, and do not have Being insofar as Being itself is made finite by these limits). The implications of the "finitude" of Being are thus of considerable importance, and they will be developed and discussed in chapter 8 below.

II. Heidegger prefaced the analysis of negation by laying down two axioms as guides for the subsequent course of that analysis. Our critique of Heidegger's position on negation will be drawn from the ramifications of these two axioms (Section IIA). It will also test the strength of Heidegger's thinking by producing two alternate accounts of negation that follow the guidelines established by these axioms (Section IIB).

IIA. The first axiom is that "every metaphysical question encompasses the whole range of metaphysical problems." Since, by implication, Heidegger's response to the question of the meaning of negation will affect every other metaphysical problem in its ontological setting, the attempt to determine the structure of negation as derived from anxiety must be examined with special care.

A suitable point of departure for this attempt is the long passage cited above, in which Heidegger shows the way in which an ontological sense of nothingness has priority over a derivative logical sense of "not" in, e.g., negative propositions. The first sentence of his discussion asks, "How could the deniable and what is to be denied be viewed as something susceptible to the not unless all thinking as such has caught sight of the not already?" This passage seems to inaugurate an argument, in structure if not in intent. But if the passage is read in this way, then surely the nature of the "not," whether it be logical in a formal sense or ontological in some substantive sense, is precisely the point at issue. As a result Heidegger cannot simply affirm that the logical "not" has already been caught sight of in a more fundamental experience of negation without assuming what is to be proved, i.e., that the logical "not" is, in fact, less fundamental than some form of extralogical negation—but this, again, is the point. When Heidegger then goes on to assert that "the not does not originate through negation; rather negation is grounded in the not that springs from the nihilation of the nothing," his claim seems guilty of a straightforward *petitio*. He simply assumes that the "not" of logical negation must be derived from some other source, says that it is so derived, and then concludes that this assertion proves the claim.

The objections that may be raised against this apparently flawed thinking go straight to the core of Heidegger's later ontology. We may preface these objections by noting that in a later essay, *Zur Seinsfrage* (1955), Heidegger discusses the tendency of his audience to ignore the specific sense of negation he had been analyzing in "*Was ist Metaphysik?*." That essay, Heidegger asserts, "asks about *this* nothingness." It does not ask haphazardly and vaguely about "the" nothingness. It asks: how about this totally different other to each being, that which is not a being" (*WM*, 246—italics in text)? Now this clarification is itself susceptible to misunderstanding. When Heidegger refers to "this totally different other to each being," he could be taken to mean "other" in the sense of all those beings that are other than this particular being. According to this interpretation, the totally different other would comprise the universality of beings minus one, i.e., whatever the given being might be. But, upon reflection, this interpretation could not be Heidegger's meaning. Rather, the reference to "each being" in the phrase "this totally different other to each being" is to every individual being but as a member of the set of all beings, and therefore to all beings, both in their particularity and as a totality. Thus, the "totally different other" is totally different precisely because it does not contain any one being or collection of beings; it refers to something that is completely other than the totality of beings as such. For Heidegger, the proper locus of negation is not in the interstices of reality, i.e., in the differentiating relations between and among determinate beings as determinate—it is outside the domain of beings altogether. Thus, if the nothing does display some measure of reality, then the fact that it cannot be reduced to any kind of determinacy means, according to Heidegger, that the nothing can be justifiably situated on an ontological par with Being itself.

The fact that Heidegger emphasizes that nothingness is opposed to the totality of beings is of considerable importance. When Heidegger describes that totality as "retreating" in the face of the nothing, then the totality as such is in retreat. Now as noted, if the totality of beings is involved, then there is no being of any sort outside that domain. Therefore, when the totality of beings retreats in the face of the nothing, the totality must remain the same throughout this retreat. But two problems arise from this sameness, the first in the direction of Being as such, the second in the direction of the totality of beings as such.

1. It is important to note that in both the 1943 Postscript and the 1949 Introduction, Heidegger couches the ontological character of the nothing in terms of "otherness," thus recalling, with or without intent, the Platonic position on negation developed in the *Sophist*. In the Postscript, for example, he writes: "This, the purely other than anything that is, is non-being (*Nicht-Seiende*). Yet this nothing (*Nichts*) is present (*west*) as Being" (*WM*, 101-2). And at

another point in the Postscript, the nothing is described as "pure other than what is" and as "the veil of Being" (*Schleier des Seins*—*WM*, 107).

The problem is simply this. We cannot rest content with the relation between Being and nothing described as a "veil." The matter must be developed further, and in more precise language. The problem is whether such development is possible. For how can nothing be "part" (using this term as loosely as possible for the moment) of Being if negation and the totality of beings are distinct from one another? If beings have being by virtue of Being, then Being and beings are always related to one another. But if nothing is completely other than the totality of beings, then how can nothing maintain this otherness and at the same time be said to be "part" of Being? If nothing is part of Being and if beings exist as beings by virtue of a relation to Being, then either nothing is part of all beings taken individually (which contradicts the claim that nothingness is completely other than beings) or it is only part of some beings (which implies that Heidegger's explanation of the place of nothingness in the metaphysical construal of the Being/beings relation remains incomplete, since some beings would be different from Being by a factor other than negation). One might then attempt to locate the opposition between Being and the nothing on a plane that excludes any relation between Being and beings. But this attempt would not only run counter to what Heidegger has explicitly said about the ontological differences between Being and beings, but it would also be liable to criticism on the grounds that the opposition is purely nugatory because of the extreme abstraction of the notions involved. For if Being had no relation to beings, then how could it have any character such that it would be different from nothing?

2. Let us grant for the moment, and in spite of the problems just raised, that it is possible to understand how nothingness can be part of Being. But even so, how can the nothing maintain this ontological equivalency with Being and also provide the source of the differentiation required to distinguish between that particular being that is X and some other particular being that is not X? Thus, the "otherness" between nothingness and beings as totality cannot be identical to the otherness between a determinate being X and another determinate being Y. The image of the *totality* of beings "retreating" before the nothing does not explain how nothingness can become a factor *within* the totality of beings. Consider, within this totality,

that case in which X is not Y. The negative "not" allows X to be any being other than Y. But in the case of the nothing existing in a manner other than beings as totality, the range of possibilities ascribable to nothingness is necessarily limited—it is, in fact, unique, since nothing can be other than the totality of beings in only one sense for the simple reason that the totality of beings is only *one* totality. It seems therefore that the notion of nothingness resulting from Heidegger's ontological description cannot do justice to a straightforward type of metaphysical differentiation required for that concept, as well as for any thinking that purports to be capable of distinguishing between different beings.

Let us now consider Heidegger's second axiom, that "every metaphysical question can be asked only in such a way that the questioner as such is present together with the question, that is, is placed in question" (*WM*, 1). The sense in which the questioner is present in the detail of Heidegger's own answer to the problem of negation is defined, in part, by anxiety—that distinctive human mood recognized by Denken as an ontological phenomenon of ultimate significance. Insofar as negation originates in anxiety, its structure affects Dasein in every possible way, since it is precisely nothingness that allows Dasein to differentiate itself from all other modes of Being. But it will be sufficient for present purposes to discuss only some of the more abstract ramifications of anxiety once it has assumed ontological proportions within the general notion of negation itself.

In his description of negation as such, Heidegger speaks of the nothing as a "wholly repelling gesture towards beings that are in retreat as a whole." What retreats in the face of the nothing is not this or that determinate being, but the totality of beings taken precisely as totality. This totality provides the ontological underpinning, so to speak, for Heidegger's selection of anxiety rather than, say, love—an alternative condition of Dasein which is in fact mentioned by Heidegger (*WM*, 8) but is not explored in this particular context. Anxiety is that condition which, as Heidegger has eloquently described, cannot pinpoint its object because that object is a disorienting pervasiveness inclusive of all Beings. The totality intended by the mood of anxiety is therefore equivalent to the totality of beings taken in opposition to nothingness. The relevant point is not how many beings in the set of all beings Dasein actively dreads, but rather the fact that Dasein exists dreading all the beings that circumscribe the full range of its experiences.

We have already noted that in the 1943 Postscript, Heidegger attempted to disarm the negative reaction to the use of anxiety by articulating an approach to courage as a counterpart in mood to anxiety. But this defense is no less problematic than the line of thought that occasioned the need for such defense in the first place. For if courage is the counterpart to anxiety *in all relevant ontological respects*, then the need to explain how anxiety is present in all forms of negation now becomes compounded by the further need to explain how courage, the counterpart to anxiety, is also present in all forms of negation. Therefore, to produce its opposite as an essential complement does not establish an adequate defense against the charge that anxiety is arbitrarily chosen. For the opposite of something arbitrarily chosen is itself no less arbitrary than its original counterpart.

Furthermore, in the Introduction of 1949, Heidegger's response to the matter of the ontological primacy of anxiety is even less pronounced than that delivered in 1943. The Introduction contains very few direct references to anxiety. Instead, Heidegger asks, "What more can thinking do but endure in anxiety?" (*WM*, 200). The discussion of the active presence of anxiety is considerably diminished in the Introduction, with the tone of Heidegger's question in the above passage seemingly more rhetorical than substantive. The suspicion is that he did not wish to admit that anxiety ceased to function in his ontological reflections, but that he wanted it to be understood as perhaps more personalized than it was in the earlier exploration of this particular way of approaching negation, more appropriate to the actual process of the thinker thinking negation than to the product of that thinking. For in the Introduction, there is much more emphasis on thinking nothingness as the relation between Being and beings than on attempting to think nothingness as such. Given this gradual shift in emphasis, it would be natural if Heidegger wanted to reduce—but, perhaps, not entirely eliminate —the sense in which nothingness had been previously depicted as an ontological notion grounded in a specific mood possessing an unavoidably human perimeter.

If such conjectures on the diminished importance of anxiety are sound, another question must be raised at this point: Is Heideggerian anxiety replaceable by another mood of ontological dimension? If so, then there is no compelling reason to believe that anxiety ever could provide *the* ontological substantiation to nothingness. And if anxiety can be replaced by another explanatory source, mood or otherwise, then does not this possibility of substitution at least partially justify the belief that logical notions and principles are essentially formal and are not reducible to, or derivable from, anything other than their own privileged domain of reality?

IIB. We have stressed the fact that the Heideggerian approach to nothingness in "*Was ist Metaphysik?*" possesses the apparent analytic virtue of attempting to break down the traditional ascription of formality to logical notions. His account of nothingness is determined, if not defined, by the presence of anxiety, a determinate mood of Dasein. Thus, the structure of nothingness as such could not be derived without some kind of informing relation between nothingness and the experience of anxiety. Therefore, Heidegger's denial of the irreducibly formal character of this particular logical notion depends for its plausibility on showing that the subsequent articulation of the structure of nothingness, as directed by the mood of anxiety, can be correlated with the actual experience of that mood.

This step in Heidegger's thinking is clearly crucial. For if it can be demonstrated that some, if not all, of the requisite functions of "not" can be derived from a source *other than* Heideggerian anxiety, then one could maintain that "logic" need not necessarily suffer the self-destruction that Heidegger has assigned to it in his pursuit of an appropriate ontological ground. In such a situation, it might be possible to generate *competing* accounts of the origin of this logical notion, each as plausible as any of the others. If so, then it would seem that we may be thinking in an essentially speculative domain, one that may not provide sufficient basis for establishing a definitive determination one way or the other. Yet we would then be all the more justified in accusing Heidegger's analysis of nothingness via anxiety to be an instance of the genetic fallacy. For even if the origin of nothingness could be effectively isolated in some sense (and regardless what the precise content of that origin may be), the revelation of this origin would not affect the formal regulatory function of the "not" as a logical notion.

At the beginning of this chapter, we noted that Heidegger prefaced his discussion of negation as a paradigmatic metaphysical problem by positing two axioms: (1) each metaphysical question entails every other metaphysical question; (2) any metaphysical question necessarily includes the being of the one who thinks about this question, an inclusion that itself becomes part of the problem to be questioned. In attempting to produce accounts of the source of negation competing with Heidegger's own, we must therefore begin by accepting these axioms and showing how they are satisfied in these other accounts. Without such acceptance and implementation, the Heideggerian could claim, with a certain justification, that apparently competing accounts are not in fact on an explanatory par precisely because these accounts fail to explain the phenomenon of negation in a manner compatible with Heidegger's own ultimate concerns. After all, the theme of negation is, for Heidegger, merely a pathway into the nature of metaphysics as such (recall the title of the essay—"What is Metaphysics?"). The burden is therefore on the critic of the Heideggerian approach to sketch alternative accounts that satisfy these two fundamental heuristic principles.

We shall consider two accounts here, the first that of Whitehead as laid down in *Process and Reality*, the second Plato's provisional approach to negation as discussed in the *Sophist*.

Whitehead clearly indicates the fundamental character of negation in consciousness: "Consciousness is the feeling of negation: in the perception of 'the stone is grey,' such feeling is in barest germ; in the perception of 'the stone is not grey' such feeling is in full development. Thus the negative perception is the triumph of consciousness."[8] Later, Whitehead states the necessary presence of negation in consciousness even more forthrightly: "There is no consciousness without reference to definiteness, affirmation, and negation." He then adds that "affirmation and negation are alike meaningless apart from reference to the definiteness of particular actualities" (*Process and Reality*, 372). In general, the negative intuitive judgment—"the triumph of consciousness"—includes "a conscious feeling of what might be, and is not." This feeling is "the feeling of absence, and it feels this absence as produced by the definite exclusiveness of what is really present" (*Process and Reality*, 417).

The Whiteheadian analogues to the Heideggerian account of negation may be thus identified: First, Whitehead locates the basic metaphysical context of negation in consciousness; Heidegger locates it in Dasein, that distinctive mode of human being which, although perhaps not reducible to consciousness, must nonetheless include consciousness as an essential component of its structure. Second, Whitehead specifies that negation is something *felt* by consciousness, thus mirroring in a sense Heidegger's insistence that negation derives from that one type of felt mood that is anxiety.

Furthermore, the Whiteheadian account in its own way satisfies Heidegger's two hueristic axioms. First, if, as Whitehead asserts, there is "no consciousness without reference to definiteness, affirmation, and negation," and if every metaphysical problem involves these three factors, then the Whiteheadian feeling present in negation—together with the fact that negation (as well as affirmation) is "meaningless apart from reference to the definiteness of particular actualities"—must be such that this feeling permeates every substantial metaphysical problem. In other words as long as a metaphysical problem concerns either some definite entity or something having to do with human consciousness, the mere posing of that problem will introduce the element of negation. How relevant this factor becomes in the problem at hand will be determined in the actual course of thoughtful analysis—but *that* negation is present is undeniable. Second, the fact that it is the unconsciousness of the questioning metaphysician (and, indeed, of everyone in an unreflective way) that experiences the feeling of negation implies that the questioner, as that type of being who can feel on this privileged ontological level, becomes an integral part of what the questioner has questioned. Of course, whether or not the questioner intends the analysis of that problem to include the metaphysical status of self as questioner is, again, another matter. But the fact of the questioner's presence in this regard must be admitted.

Whitehead's account thus meets both Heideggerian criteria for ontological propriety. Given this shared character, the differences between the two positions become all the more prominent. First, the Whiteheadian feeling of negation is presumably unique to negation and is not based on a feeling of another qualitative sort—e.g., a specific mood—as the Heideggerian standpoint would have it. Second, Whitehead insists on grounding negation on the mode of existence of determinate beings in their particularity—not on the totality of such beings, nor on Being as something distinct from that totality. Thus, Whitehead adopts as ontologically axiomatic precisely what Heidegger would deny, i.e., that consciousness depends on the "definite exclusiveness" of beings for recognizing the negation that exists there and in all other contexts in which negation can become present. For Whitehead, negation originates from the difference between determinate being A and determinate being B, a difference that is felt by consciousness while perceiving these two beings as, in fact, distinct. The "not" of negation, as represented by such rudimentary linguistic claims as "A is not B," thus receives its metaphysical underpinnings from the fact that beings can be described as "given"—at least in the sense that consciousness can feel how differences obtain between and among these beings.

One could argue that the Whiteheadian account has a certain advantage over the Heideggerian position in that for the former, the feeling of negation is immediately and universally present whenever distinct beings are experienced as different while for the latter, negation depends on the unique kind of feeling that is the mood of anxiety. The Heideggerian might object that what Whitehead calls the feeling of negation is so diluted qua feeling that there is little if any justification in describing it as a feeling rather than as some other mode of consciousness. This objection may have some merit, assuming one accepts the premise (shared by both Heidegger and Whitehead) that consciousness of negation must be localized in feeling of some sort rather than, say, apprehended through some type of cognition. This particular point need not be addressed now; but the mention of an alternative, i.e., a cognitive mode of apprehending negation, establishes a thematic link to the other account of negation we shall introduce.

In several relevant aspects, both Heidegger and Whitehead on negation were prefigured by the account in the *Sophist*.[9] At 256e the Stranger asserts that "it must, then, be possible for 'that which is not' to be" (Cornford's translation). Why can the Stranger say this? Because it is the nature of the Form of difference to make a thing "different from existence" and so make that thing "a thing that 'is not'." The Stranger concludes about the objects of such predication: "Hence we shall be right to speak of them all on the same principle as things that in this sense 'are not,' and again, because they partake of existence, to say that they 'are' and call them things that have being." The Stranger continues to develop the sense in which existence both is and is not: Existence likewise 'is not' in as many respects as there are other things, for, not being those others, while it is its single self, it is not all that indefinite number of other things (257a). And finally: "When we speak of 'that which is not,' it seems that we do not mean something contrary to what exists but only something that is different" (257b). Nothingness in this sense becomes sheer otherness, with the specific character of this otherness determined by the nature of whatever is other than the negated referent. The contrast between being (of the referent) and non-being (of what is other than the referent) is therefore closely analogous to the mingling of Being and nothingness at the apex of Heidegger's ontology.

The treatment of negation in the *Sophist* remains a worthy candidate in the quest to think through this particular ontological problem. Notice, again, that the account satisfies both Heideggerian prerequisites for ontological inquiry. For our purposes, it is not necessary to enter into the disputed status of the "greatest kinds" with respect to the other elements of the Platonic metaphysics. The relevant comparison concerns only the sense in which the notion of negation in the *Sophist* has been developed within a suitably complex metaphysical background. Thus, concerning the Stranger's account of nothingness, we may presume that the recognition of difference as implicit in the predication of "is not" may be substituted for Heideggerian anxiety. The Stranger's notion of "is not" can itself be understood as participating in, or existing in relation to, that which "is." Furthermore, the "is not" is, by its very nature, predicable of everything, including the Forms, since one can affirm not only that one Form is not another Form, but also that a given Form is not a particular instantiated by that Form. Thus, "is not" functions metaphysically in a manner analogous to the Heideggerian notion of the "complete negation of the totality of beings," since "is not" can be predicated of any single being or of the totality of beings taken as totality (e.g., that this totality is not equivalent to Being). The parallel would then run: "is not" is to "is" as beings and the totality of beings are to Being. It will follow that every metaphysical problem involving the Forms (as well as the greatest kinds, assuming that they are distinct from the Forms) will also involve negation, since negation can be predicated on all levels of the Platonic metaphysical hierarchy.

Second, the questioner becomes an integral moment in the process of predicating negation in the sense that it is the questioner who speaks the "is not" in propositions of the form "S is not P." Although it is not clear from the Platonic standpoint how the metaphysical status of the speaker of the "is not" would enter into the "is not" as such, one may plausibly assume that perceptual or cognitional activity will become an integral part in such predication, and must therefore be included as essential to the complete description of negation as such.[10]

These similarities are sufficient to establish the Platonic account of negation as a possible candidate on the basis of the axiomatic phase of the Heideggerian approach to negation. But of course the differences are obvious and considerable. Unlike both the Whiteheadian and Heideggerian analyses, the notion of negation defined as pure difference seems to lack any kind of inherent qualitative "feel." Furthermore, this primarily cognitional notion of negation is cut off from any ontological dependency on temporality or history, an aspect that would make this characterization of negation completely unacceptable from the Heideggerian standpoint. At this juncture we confront yet another substantive impasse, one that would require considerable analysis and argumentation for its resolution (discounting for the moment the possibility that neither account is correct). Again, however, this issue need not occupy us any further at this time. The relevant point is only that we recognize the sense in which the position advanced in the *Sophist* exhibits ontological plausibility, not that it will necessarily carry the day.

Let us grant that the two accounts of the origin of negation introduced above are at least equivalent to Heidegger's in explanatory power. Under what conditions could the Heideggerian defend the account based on anxiety as more appropriately elucidating the nature of nothingness as such than these alternate accounts (and of course any others as well)? I suggest that such a defense would be possible if two conditions are met:

1. If each and every instance of negation found in experience incorporated within the experience of that instance some element of, or some relation to, anxiety in the Heideggerian sense. Without specifying such connections, Heidegger's claims for the primacy of anxiety as *the* mood for deriving the structure of nothingness must remain unpersuasive by reason of the abstract character of this mood when placed in appropriate ontological and logical contexts.

2. However, even if (1) could be shown, it would not by itself constitute an adequate defense. The Heideggerian must also demonstrate that such universal applicability of anxiety cannot be claimed for *any other* potential source of negation, whether that source is derived from some aspect of consciousness or from some other sector of reality.

If the first condition is not met, then anxiety is not universally applicable in the context of negation; if the second is not met, then there is always the possibility that anxiety can be replaced with another phenomenon of equivalent explanatory power. Now if, in the final analysis, no one account can be seen as preferable to any other account, then this indeterminacy may be taken as evidence for the belief that logical notions (and, by implication, logical principles as derived from logical notions) are "simply" formal.

But, by itself, this particular bit of evidence is not conclusive. For from the fact of many diverse and competing accounts attempting to substantiate the formality of logical notions, it does not necessarily follow that these notions are, simply as a result of this diversity, neutral in content. It may be the case that there is in fact one correct account, but that it has not been seen to be correct when confronted with other (incorrect) accounts. In short, it is possible that Heidegger on negation is not so much incorrect as incomplete. And if his account of negation is incomplete *but on the right track*, then the results of the critique sketched in this chapter are far more positive than negative. The burden is, however, on the Heideggerian to complete what Heidegger himself has only begun. But the suspicion lingers, despite this proviso, that this way may perhaps be as difficult to follow to the end as it was to discern in the first place.

The problem of determining as precisely as possible the range (or ranges) of opposition inherent in negation is important not only with respect to the general understanding of negation in logic and metaphysics, but also with regard to the particular question of how negation should be understood within the more limited context of Heidegger's own thinking. The studied indeterminacy in the *Sein und Zeit* distinction between authentic and inauthentic has now become almost classical, but there are many other examples of problematic negation as well: Thus, what we are to make of claims such as truth and untruth "belong together" (*zusammengehören—WM,* 86), along with Heidegger's admission that there are all kinds of untruth (*WM,* 82); that what is sayable comes from what is unsayable (*NII,* 484), whereas the unsaid comes from what is said (*WM,* 109); that we can learn only if we unlearn (*WD,* 8); that the condition of nonwilling, so essential to the realization of entities as things (in Heidegger's technical sense of thinghood), is "willingly to renounce willing" (*G,* 30); and finally, that truth is "the unsaid" that exists as "remaining unsaid" (*HE,* 180).[11]

Given this panoply of fundamental distinctions, each of which is defined by the presence of negation, we must ask whether Heidegger's analysis of nothingness in "*Was ist Metaphysik?*" should be incorporated into the fabric of his own thinking on other ontological matters. This problem becomes especially important when we consider that Heidegger characterized, if not defined, "essential thinking" (*wesentliche Denken*— WM, 105) as absolutely determined by what is "other" than what is. Thus, is the "otherness" between any one pair of opposites identical to the "otherness" in every other pair of opposites? The answer must be either affirmative or negative. If affirmative, then how can Heidegger also claim, for example, that there are many kinds of untruth (*WM*, 82)? The burden lies on the Heideggerian in this case to extend the analysis of negation as grounded on anxiety in order to demonstrate how negation can be differentiated in the multifold context of "untruth." And if the answer is negative, then the burden still lies on the Heideggerian to demonstrate the differences which obtain between whatever types of negation are, in fact, distinct from one another. In either case the analysis of negation is incomplete with respect to understanding Heidegger's Denken as an exemplification of that phase of his own thinking which concerns negation.

We have already noted the apparent progression in Heidegger's thinking on nothingness, i.e., that specifying the nature of nothingness in terms of an aspect of Dasein becomes unavoidably anthropocentric (despite his earlier claims that "anxiety" was not to be understood as a mere evanescent mood). In the later works, the emphasis is on the notion of the ontological difference between Being and beings as the appropriate locus for determining the sense in which Being is *not* beings.[12] Thus, the notion of nothingness as such is no longer quite so open to ontological inquiry as an isolated phenomenon—rather, its sense must be derived from whatever modes of determination are required to substantiate the difference between Being and beings. Part of the burden of chapter 7 below will be to examine in some detail the implications for the notion of negation when its characterization is approached from this particular ontological direction—i.e., thinking the ontological difference.

# CHAPTER 3

# Sameness and Difference

IN THE LECTURE SERIES ON LEIBNIZ GIVEN AT MARBURG in 1928, Heidegger notes that the order of the laws of thought has never been satisfactorily established—"In which order, in which inner connection (*Zusammenhang*) do they stand" (*MA*, 24)? Is the principle of contradiction the most fundamental law, since without it the very possibility of meaningful discourse is rendered null? Or, perhaps, is the principle of identity the most fundamental? For if it is possible that a thing may not retain identity with respect to itself, then such a basic and chaotic lack of stability would make even the attempt to formulate any kind of discourse a seemingly self-destructive endeavor. For Heidegger, it is clear that the relation of ontological priority between the principles of identity and contradiction has never been properly decided (*FD*, 136).

Heidegger raises a difficult problem here, one which as far as I know he himself never attempted to resolve. Of course, those who adopt a purely formalist approach to logical principles might respond to this problem by asserting that there is no real need to establish any substantive priority among logical axioms. But from Heidegger's standpoint, to adopt a position of formal neutrality on these matters is naive and, as it were, begs the ontological question. In this chapter we shall examine how Heidegger interrogates the elements of sameness incorporated within the principle of identity, an interrogation that both extends the ontological inquiry into contradiction and illustrates how negation functions as difference when negation becomes integrated with the notion of sameness.

The capacity to recognize how things are the same as and different from one another is essential in order to stabilize the flux of human experience. And the abstract articulation of this correlative notion is equally essential to the structure of an ontology. This requirement holds even for Heidegger's speculative vision. In fact, the notion of sameness is especially crucial to the thinking of Heidegger's middle and late periods. Its importance within a concrete setting may be illustrated by the following claim: "Metalanguage and Sputnik, metalinguistics and rocket technology are the same" (*US*, 160). At first glance such a claim may perhaps be dismissed as just another virulent specimen of the Heideggerian penchant for abusing language. What does Sputnik have to do with metalanguage? And are those who study metalinguistics and those who study rocket technology actually studying the same thing? It would seem that the predication of "the same" could not possibly be meaningful in this context. But to reject so abruptly Heidegger's apparently eccentric usage of sameness presupposes that we can determine what he means by sameness and that we can also show that whatever he means by sameness is threatened with problems that defy solution. These two projects occupy our attention in this chapter.

I. What does Heidegger mean by sameness (*das Selbe*)?[1] Although the answer to this question must be pieced together from a variety of sources, it is an answer defined by consistency and unity of thought. But before we attempt to present a connected version of the answer, it is important to acquire additional first-hand experience in the extensive application of the terms to be analyzed. Here is a series of texts containing references to sameness or to derivatives of sameness:

1. Therefore, in a good conversation, what is said and what is heard are the same (*EH*, 124).
2. That which is said in poetizing and that which is said in thinking are never identical; but at times they are the same (*WD*, 8-9).
3. The subject-object relation and Newtonian physics . . . are and remain metaphysically the same (*VA*, 63).
4. We do not maintain that Nietzsche teaches what is identical to Descartes, but . . . that he thinks the *same* in its historically essential completion (*NII*, 149—italics in text).
5. We must also learn first to read a book like Nietzsche's *Also Sprach Zarathustra* in the same rigorous way as a treatise of Aristotle; in the same way be it noted, not in the identical way (*WD*, 68).
6. Thus, both of them, the dwarf and Zarathustra, say the same thing (*NI*, 307).

7. The will to power and the eternal return of the same say the *same thing* and think the *very same* fundamental character of beings as a whole (*NI,* 481—italics in text).
8. It would be a delicate and genuinely difficult task for contemporary thought as representation to show in what respect the characterization of Being as objectivity and as will say the same (*SG,* 115).
9. Thus, the essential determination of thinking in Plato is not identical to that in Leibniz, but it is the same (*VA,* 220).
10. *Aletheia* . . . and *logos* are the same (*VA,* 220).
11. The *energeia,* which Aristotle thinks as the basic character of presence, of *eon,* the *idea,* which Plato thinks as the basic character of presence, the *logos,* which Heraclitus thinks as the basic character of presence, the *moira,* which Parmenides thinks as the basic character of presence, the *chreon,* which Anaximander thinks in that which is present in presence—all name that which is the same (*HO,* 342).
12. Russia and America are both, seen metaphysically, the same; the same hopeless frenzy of uncontrolled technology and excessive organization of common men (*EM,* 28).
13. Thinking and Being belong in the same . . . (*ID,* 90).

Although far from exhaustive, this series of texts is sufficiently diverse for present purposes. We note how sameness has been predicated of language as spoken and heard, of language as poetry and thought, of epistemology and physics, of metalanguage and rocket technology (the introductory example above), of numerous apparently unrelated moments in the history of metaphysics (from the pre-Socratics to Nietzsche), and even of the metaphysical character of two national superpowers. Is there any pattern to this diversity? If there is a pattern, its ordering principle has probably been expressed in the final utterance, that thinking and Being belong "in the same." Thus, to understand sameness in this most fundamental sense is to understand the relation between thinking and Being, which in turn presupposes thoughtful insight into the nature of Being as such. If understanding sameness on this global scale can be formulated, then it should be possible to discern the less universal but equally essential instances of sameness when that notion is applied to individual beings and to individual linguistic events.

The notion of sameness is normally applied in two distinct philosophical senses. The first sense is ontological, e.g., when two beings are determined to be the same as one another (at least in one respect); the second sense is linguistic, e.g., when two propositions are said to have the same meaning or to intend the same referent. In the texts cited above, sameness is applied to the meanings of individual words (10,11), to the meanings of different parts of the teaching of a single philosopher (6, 7), to the meaning of the teachings of different philosophers (4, 9), to types of language differentiated in various ways (1, 2), to predominant features in the character of two nations (12), and to an entity in conjunction with a linguistic activity (the Sputnik-metalanguage text). Therefore, by applying sheer numerical preponderance as a standard, the texts seem to indicate that sameness should be understood in a linguistic rather than in an ontological context.

But this conclusion is surely premature. The predication of sameness with respect to an entity such as Sputnik shows that Heidegger does not reserve the notion of sameness strictly for the context of language. In fact, the final instance of sameness cited (13) must imply that Heidegger intends the notion of sameness to be understood at a level that transcends what, for Heidegger, is the purely metaphysical distinction between beings as such and language about beings. To affirm that "thinking and Being belong in the same" can only mean that the structure of Being and the structure of thinking about Being—including the linguistic expression of such thought—must share properties that are defined by the nature of sameness (a nature as yet unspecified). As a result the fundamental character of sameness may be distorted if some currently viable theory of meaning is introduced for purposes of eliciting comparisons between this theory and Heidegger's apparently unique version of sameness. A theory of meaning is derived from a more general understanding of language, and a theory of language is ultimately derived from explicit conceptions or implicit presuppositions concerning the relation between language and Being. Therefore, if the nature of Being that grounds this theory of meaning differs from Heidegger's grasp of Being, then it will be inappropriate to evaluate Heidegger's notion of sameness by comparing it to a theory of meaning which, in its ontological foundation, is incompatible with Being insofar as Being belongs to sameness.

My procedure in determining the ontological structure of sameness and difference follows the leads provided by various seminal texts. I then attempt to reproduce this structure in outline form, to the extent that an outline is possible on that fundamental level where Being, thought, and sameness are mutually constituted.

It is not accidental that the majority of the texts cited concern relations of sameness that occur within the history of philosophy. In fact, the connection between sameness and the history of philosophy leads into the structural core of sameness and difference. For Heidegger, "the essential thinkers continually say that which is the same (*das Selbe*). But that which is the same does not mean: identity." (*WM*, 193). We need not discuss the unspecified criterion by which Heidegger separates essential from nonessential thinkers. The relevant point here is the distinction between the sameness that has continually concerned these thinkers, whoever they may be, and the fact that such sameness is other than identity. The elucidation of the distinction between identity and sameness will point the way toward establishing the appropriate ontological structure of Heidegger's notion of sameness and difference.

In many contexts pertaining to ordinary language, sameness and identity are synonymous. "A is the same as B" frequently does not mean anything different from "A is identical to B." But Heidegger sharply distinguishes between identity as predicated of unity and sameness as predicated of unity. The unity of identity "is the indifferent likeness of the empty, endlessly repeatable identity: A as A, B as B" (*SG*, 152).[2] But the unity of sameness is in no way such a "faded emptiness" (*ID*, 87). What then in sameness? Sameness is "the belonging together of what is distinct" as found in "the gathering by means of difference" (*VA*, 193). Since, for Heidegger, sameness can be predicated only "when it is thought with respect to difference" (*VA*, 193), sameness must be defined in relation to difference. Therefore, Heidegger contends that sameness first breaks open "the indifferent likeness of that which belongs together" and at the same time "holds it in the most distant unlikeness" (*SG*, 152). This "holding together in holding apart from one another (*Zusammenhalten im Auseinanderhalten*) is a characteristic which we name sameness" (*SG*, 152).

The historical origin of sameness in this sense of the belonging together of distinct properties is "in the enigmatic word *to auto*, the same" (*VA*, 249), as found in, e.g., Parmenides' dictum that thinking and Being belong in the same. Locating the historical origin of sameness is essential for two reasons: first, because "the distinction concerning beings and Being turns out to be that sameness from which all metaphysics springs" (*NII*, 208)—according to Heidegger, every metaphysician, ancient or modern, necessarily thinks Being and the relation between Being and beings as sameness of some sort. And second, because the distinction between Being and beings "is that sameness, which concerns the Greeks and us in different ways" (*HO*, 310). Here Heidegger assures us that the way in which the Greeks construed Being and beings is different from the way in which modernity has represented Being and beings; thus, the expression of sameness is somehow historically conditioned. Furthermore, regardless of the greatness of an individual thinker, and of the time in history during which that thinker happened to exist, the sameness of Being and beings "is so essential and rich that a single great thinker never exhausts it" (*NI*, 46). If finished answers to problems derived from this particular fundamental notion are available, these answers do not reside in the works of any one of philosophy's greatest minds.

The previous two paragraphs develop a textual basis for determining the ontological scope of Heidegger's notion of sameness and difference. We may initiate a description of this notion by continuing to trace some of the characteristics distinguishing identity and sameness. For Heidegger, the most important difference between the two concepts is that identity remains formally abstract while sameness becomes ontologically concrete. Heidegger does not deny the logical correctness of the identity statement "A is A," but he does claim that the unity of A with itelf is "empty" and "faded" when the being that A represents is construed as identical to itself in such a way that nothing in that being becomes differentiated in any manner whatsoever. Heidegger intends to correct this abstraction by introducing a notion of sameness which is so structured that it can manifest more concretely the ontological composition of those beings to which it is applicable. Whereas identity can be understood as a purely logical concept indifferently predicable of any and every being and type of being, sameness is an ontological notion that applies only to certain types of being and in ways that elucidate the hidden structure of those beings. This chapter is primarily devoted to elucidating the intricate ontological structure animating Heidegger's notion of sameness. The description of relevant similarities and differences between sameness and Heidegger's notion of identity, in particular the distinctive Heideggerian inclusion of history within identity, will be resumed in chapter 4.

The following outline isolates and describes the principal properties of sameness and difference as derived from the set of texts cited above. An outline of this sort should facilitate understanding the complexity of the notion stipulated by Heidegger's various references to that notion. Once this set of properties is tested against the passages just cited, the results should vindicate the overall soundness of these properties, both in number and in content. However, I might note that these properties may not correlate with every single predication of sameness found in the entire Heideggerian corpus.

A. Sameness always refers to beings as wholes (unlike identity, which can be predicated of part of a whole—e.g., an identical hue of greyness in two grey jugs).
B. Sameness cannot be predicated of a whole which is simple, but only of a whole which is complex, i.e., having distinct parts or properties.
C. If the various parts or properties of a whole "belong together," then presumably sameness applies only to those beings that have either a natural or an imposed order (e.g., a flower and a flower garden).
D. Although identity can be predicated of a being with respect to itself, sameness always refers to two distinct beings.
E. These two beings must be both equal to and different from one another. The sense in which they are equal to is not yet clear, and more will be said on this aspect of sameness in Section II of this chapter. The sense in which they are different depends on the difference in properties between the two beings. In general, two beings that are the same are both like and unlike one another.

Sameness defined in this sense runs counter to the term's typical meaning in most occurrences of ordinary language, for we do not normally think about differences when we say that two beings are the same. In instances of this sort, however, ordinary language is naive, for if two beings are in fact the same in all respects, then they are not two beings but one being, misleadingly reduplicated in language as two distinct beings. When we want to say that two beings are the same without worrying about the sense in which they are different from one another, then according to Heidegger's terminological recommendations we may more properly call them identical, i.e., predicate of them the "empty" relation that binds two beings together without further specification.

F. Once the properties that determine the difference factor necessary for sameness are gathered together and specified, these properties must be "held apart" from one another in "the most distant unlikeness." The use of the superlative degree in this stipulation imples that, for Heidegger, there are gradations or levels of unlikeness; thus, if two beings can be more or less unlike one another with respect to a given property or properties, then sameness is correctly applied only when this unlikeness is maximally displayed.

G. In addition to its predication with respect to particular beings, sameness can also be predicated of Being in relation to beings. We may ask here whether it is possible for sameness to function in the relation between Being and beings in a manner equivalent to sameness when predicated of particular beings. The point will be discussed in Section II.

H. Unlike identity, which is typically understood as a purely formal concept without any temporal definition, sameness is historically conditioned, at least when it is applied to the relation between Being and beings. The Greek notion of sameness and our notion of sameness are different because the nature of history—for Heidegger, an essential aspect of the relation between Being and beings—somehow necessitates this kind of differentiation.

I. If the sameness in the relation between Being and beings has never been exhausted by a single great thinker, then we may wonder whether that sameness has not been exhausted even by the sum total of great thinkers, however many that may be and whoever they may be. If this hypothesis is in fact the case, then it may follow that sameness in this fundamental ontological context is in principle impossible to state completely. The profundity of the relation between Being and beings would then always outstrip any attempt to express the full scope of that relation.

It is evident, both from the number and the stipulative content of these properties, that sameness and difference is one of the most important structural notions in Heidegger's ontology. However that ontology will eventually be substantiated, the coordination of its respective elements will depend in large measure on the capacity of this correlative notion to provide stability and coherence to those elements. Therefore, the notion as defined in this complex sense must be evaluated with special rigor. For if sameness and difference as such become problematic, then the ontological substance that Heidegger will mold by means of sameness and difference cannot avoid becoming disfigured, perhaps beyond recognition, by the imposition of this apparently neutral bit of "formal" terminology.

II. In the second half of this chapter, I propose to initiate an assessment of Heidegger's notion of sameness and difference by sketching a series of problems. These problems, five in number, have been derived from the properties enumerated and described in Section I, and may be taken as one pathway toward critically evaluating the ontological structure of sameness and difference. Unlike the account of negation offered in "*Was ist Metaphysik?*" and discussed in chapter 2, Heidegger's use of sameness is more abstract, more developed, and more prevalent throughout the body of his work. As a result, there is less need to test the complex structure of sameness by comparing it with other existing positions outside the Heideggerian realm of thought. We may remain within the spacious confines of Heidegger's own development of the notion in order to discover its distinctive problems.

Properties A through D listed above are fundamental for all the following properties. The specific nature of each problem enunciated below arises from one, or several, of the subsequent properties; the relevant property or properties will therefore be indicated at the beginning of each discussion.

1. (Property E) If two beings are the same, then at least one property is different with respect to the conjunction of these two beings, a difference that is maximized if sameness has been accurately predicated. But is this difference one of degree or of kind? If A and B are the same, is A different from B because A has a property B lacks altogether or because A and B share an identical property but manifest that property in different degrees? As far as I have been able to determine, Heidegger never directly speaks to this question. And his silence in this regard is especially significant in view of the fact that potentially serious repercussions will ensue regardless of which alternative should prove most applicable.

If the difference Heidegger intends is one of kind, then any two distinct beings, regardless of their respective constitution, will satisfy this condition. For example, Sputnik is made of various kinds of metal, i.e., a type of being completely distinct from everything proper to the definition of a metalanguage. Surely this instance of sameness must be construed as a difference in kind. But if, in general, no restrictions are placed on the types of properties that will constitute a difference of this sort, then designating the relation (e.g., between Sputnik and metalanguage) as difference in the technical sense required by sameness dilutes the force of the relation to the point where it can mean little more than sheer and simple otherness. This notion of difference can be predicated of *any* two beings, regardless of the extent to which they are like or unlike one another.

But such an ontologically bland notion of difference can make no difference, so to speak, as far as the substance of an ontology is concerned. Thus far, the treatment of Heidegger's notion of beings seems to render them metaphysically similar to "bare particulars." But of course this mode of reference is only an abstraction, and a more concrete rendering would become feasible once Heidegger's substantiation of the nature of beings was in full view. Presumably the difference factor of sameness is intended to gather together differences between two beings in such a way that their mutual unlikeness does not remain sheer otherness, sheer nothingness, but somehow helps to illuminate both their likeness to one another as beings and their mutual relation to Being as such. However, if the difference essential to sameness means simply a nonrestricted difference in kind, then this ontologically heuristic function cannot be fulfilled.

If, again, the difference is one of kind, then there is a second and perhaps even more serious problem: How can a given example of difference be held apart in the "most distant unlikeness" (*SG,* 152)? If properties are different in *kind,* is it even possible to speak of a *degree* (e.g., "most distant") of unlikeness between them? Is the difference between metal and the sound of spoken language more or less unlike the difference between metal and a grammatical explanation of the sound of spoken language? One is strongly tempted to answer that this question cannot even be asked, because the nature of the difference in this case precludes the common ground that is essential before degrees of likeness or unlikeness can be specified. Therefore, if Heidegger intends to preserve the degree-aspect of difference—as his reference to "most distant unlikeness" seems to indicate—then it is not clear how difference can be defined as one of kind: if in fact the difference *is* one of kind, then it is not clear how Heidegger can preserve the degree-aspect of difference.

But perhaps the difference Heidegger intends is one of degree and not of kind. The presence of the above-noted reference to unlikeness in the superlative degree supports this alternative, which, should it prove applicable, would obviate the second problem, since properties can admit of degrees of difference if these properties are of the same kind. But if we return to the Sputnik-metalanguage example, then yet another serious problem arises. As noted above, the comparison of two properties different in degree presupposes that these properties are the same in kind. But what then would be the "kind" that grounds, e.g., Sputnik and metalanguage? One could perhaps appeal to the fact that both are products of human activity. But this ground is surely too inclusive. Although both activities are of human origin, producing Sputnik and producing a metalanguage are so heterogeneous—both in their respective processes and in the products of those processes—that it is not sufficient simply to note their common origin.

To circumvent this objection, we might attempt to narrow the scope of the ground from human activity as such to human activity as derived from a technological attitude toward nature. This shift is adequate up to a point, for it results in showing how different aspects of Sputnik and metalanguage can be related in sameness to one another. The sense in which Sputnik is technological is obvious; and a metalanguage is also technological as a purely formal construct based on a natural phenomenon and designed to illustrate at least part of the "real" underlying structure of that phenomenon. But is this shift in ground sufficient to justify the predication of sameness based on kinds? Many differences between Sputnik and metalanguage remain, even after both are located on a common ground situated within technological boundaries. And if any one of these differences is sufficiently diverse to disrupt this common ground, then it would follow that the difference in properties could not be established as one of degree.

Heidegger insists that difference is essential to the structure of sameness. Furthermore, he stipulates that difference must be understood according to certain specifications. But it is not entirely unfair to conclude, at least provisionally, that the Heideggerian must clarify whether the properties in question are different by degree, by kind, or according to some as yet unstated principle of determination. We may also note that if the complexities in the notion of difference must be traced to a form of ontological nothingness, then the account of negation in terms of anxiety discussed in chapter 2 offers little if any assistance in resolving these complexities.

2. (Property E) If sameness is to be employed as a technical term without complete loss of its ordinary language meaning and if the sense of identity that the term possesses in this context must nonetheless manifest an ontological connotation, then the nature of whatever is "in" two beings that justifies the predication of sameness must be stated as clearly as possible. Now if Heidegger's ontology is substantiated in such a way that beings are subject to generic or type distinctions, then sameness could refer to that which is common to beings that share a given genus or type. But two reasons militate against adopting this interpretive gambit. First (as far as I know), the notion of sameness has never been discussed by Heidegger in a context centered on genus or type; second, and more importantly, Heidegger was never disposed to describe the ontological character of beings in terms of explicitly generic distinctions, which he would have to do if he intended to ground different ontological senses of sameness. Therefore, it seems that this potentially attractive gambit cannot be introduced, given Heidegger's fundamental approach to the relation between Being and beings. The ontological status of types in relation to particular beings as instances of types is an important phase in Heidegger's approach to "thinghood," and the point will be discussed in greater detail in chapter 5 below.

On the assumption that Heidegger would deny the relevance of such generic distinctions, the only apparent alternative is to base the element of identity in sameness on the simple fact that particular beings determined as the same are "in" being. However, it would then appear to follow that in this respect every being is necessarily the same as any other being. But if all beings are the same as one another simply by virtue of possessing being, then the ascription of sameness carries no real significance. Sameness of such a universally undifferentiated scope is equivalent to the nonrestricted difference of kind discussed above—neither can serve the ontologically heuristic function that both are seemingly intended to perform. If the identity aspect of sameness cannot be specified, then the predication of sameness becomes a simple conjunction of entities for purposes of drawing comparisons between some or all of the properties of those entities.

3. (Properties F and G) Heidegger maintains that thinking and Being "belong in the same" and that the distinction between Being

and beings is "that sameness from which all metaphysics springs." We have already seen sameness predicated of particular beings and of individual linguistic expressions. But if "belonging" can be taken as establishing a relation between Being and sameness, and if sameness in this relation can be properly predicated of Being as such, then it appears to be the case that there is no significant difference between sameness as predicated of the relation between Being and beings and sameness as predicated of two particular beings. If this inference does not result from a radical misrepresentation of Heidegger's thought in this regard, then two questions should be asked: (a) In what sense can sameness be predicated of the relation between Being and beings? (b) Can the meaning of sameness in this relation be equivalent to the meaning of sameness when predicated of particular beings?

(a) For Heidegger, a qualitative difference exists between Being and the totality of beings. Therefore, regardless how this difference is ultimately defined, it is at least certain that the difference factor essential to sameness has been fulfilled. The problem will be to identify that which is common to both Being and beings insofar as sameness can be predicated of this identity. Now as traditionally defined, sameness is a symmetrical relation: If A is the same as B, then B is the same as A. And this symmetry pertains to the predication of sameness to particular beings. Notice, however, the implications that attach to the nature of Being if sameness is symmetrical in the Being/beings relation just as it is symmetrical in the relation between particular beings. Before we detail these implications, however, it should be noted that the number and type of beings are never stipulated in the relation between Being and beings. Presumably the absence of this stipulation is not significant—Being and beings will belong in sameness regardless whether some or all beings are involved in this relation. But if we assume that sameness is symmetrical in all respects, then paradoxes result from predicating sameness of Being and beings. And these paradoxes arise independently of the number or type of beings stipulated.

Consider: If beings are different from one another, then according to the definition of sameness all such differences must be gathered into Being and held apart from one another *within* Being in such a way that Being can be discerned as distinct from beings. The structure of sameness requires that Being be viewed from that perspective which allows Being to become differentiated according to whatever properties are found in those beings that comprise the other terminus of the sameness relation. But there must be something present to Being over and above the set of differences held apart within Being. For if this something is not present, then Being becomes identical to beings. And the "most distant unlikeness" between Being and beings cannot be recognized as such if Being is simply identical to the various differences proper to beings. But in light of the symmetry of the sameness relation, this something must be present to beings as well as to Being, regardless of the precise specification of that something. For if Being possesses something that is not possessed by beings, then this essential asymmetry means that sameness cannot be predicated of both Being and beings. But how can sameness be predicated of Being as such if the difference aspect of sameness requires that one *part* of Being constitute this predication, i.e., that part which allows the maximization of the difference between Being and whatever beings have been included in the predication of sameness?

Thus, if Heidegger intends to maintain that Being is in some difficult and undefined sense "greater than" beings, then it becomes virtually impossible to see how he can also maintain that both Being and beings belong in sameness. The only identity aspect of sameness possible in this case is that derived from whatever is common to *part* of Being and to *all* beings. But sameness must be predicable of Being *as such* and as a whole in order to justify the claim that Being and beings belong together in the symmetry of sameness. Therefore, it does not seem possible to ground sameness according to this hypothesis. If, however, he continues to maintain that sameness can be predicated of Being and beings, then it is difficult to see how Being can be anything other than a mere synonym for the sum total of beings. In this case the requisite sameness is generated from the fact that everything in existence possesses Being insofar as each thing is a being. However, it also follows that Being as such loses all significance as a unique and distinctive ontological factor, since the meaning of Being will be reduced to the meaning of whatever beings are at hand. And this conclusion, if sound, undermines Heidegger's life-long labor to establish the question of the meaning of Being— not the meaning of this or that individual being or even of beings taken collectively—as the primary locus of authentic philosophical thought. This question could not assume this exalted status because it could not even be asked. And it could not be asked because Being would be nothing more than a name for beings—whether one, some, or all.

The predication of sameness to Being engenders yet another related problem. This problem concerns the function of difference within Being as such. If the differences that distinguish beings from one another become an essential part of the structure of Being, then Being as such is differentiated according to those distinguishing properties. Now if it is possible to isolate Being from its relation to beings and to analyze Being from the perspective of this differentiation, then one must ask about the nature of the ontological difference between a property (as specified in the above manner) and a particular being. What distinguishes the relation between that property and Being from the relation between a particular being and Being? A property of Being cannot be the same as a particular being—how then can one account for the ontological difference between the two?

(b). If the predication of sameness is univocal with respect to the relation between particular beings as such and to the relation between Being and beings, then whatever is "in" two particular beings that are the same is identical to whatever is "in" Being and beings when they belong to sameness. But surely whatever is predicated as the same in two particular beings cannot be identical to whatever is in Being that justifies the predication of sameness between Being and beings (assuming that such predication is somehow possible). For this identity would imply that particular beings are no longer recognizably particular but become in fact indistinguishable from Being as such, at least with respect to the predication of sameness. It would follow either that Being as such is reduced to the level of particular beings or that particular beings are elevated to the level of Being as such. But in either case, the difference between Being and beings cannot be preserved. This problem is obviated if sameness could be predicated of Being and beings in such a way that the common element in this relation is different from the common element in the predication of sameness with respect to particular beings. But, of course, this obviation would then imply that the notion of sameness cannot be univocally predicated of all ontological regions. Therefore, if it is the case that the notion of sameness must be analogically predicated of different ontological regions, then Heidegger is either incorrect or, at best, misleading when he attributes sameness to Being and beings as well as to particular beings without stating that the notion cannot be understood univocally in these two distinct ontological settings.

4. (Property H) If sameness is historically conditioned, then it is possible that the structure of sameness for the Greeks will be different in some essential respect from the structure of sameness for modernity. And Heidegger has asserted that there is such a difference present in modernity in relation to the Greeks. In general then, at any moment in the history of philosophical thought, the specification of sameness and difference is subject to alteration, both in the relation between beings and in the relation between Being and beings. But if, in this most fundamental ontological context, the content of what is predicated as the same can shift with history, does the notion of sameness retain its elementary and foundational significance? For if the content of sameness is somehow dependent upon its occurrence within an historical epoch, then whatever is "in" two beings that are determined as the same in one epoch may be incompatible with, perhaps even contradictory to, whatever is "in" two beings that are determined as the same in another epoch. And the same transepochal consequences would also apply to predicating sameness of Being and beings.

Heidegger's notion of sameness is marked by a form of historicism. We must therefore assume that this historicism is intrinsic to the structure of sameness. Two alternatives then appear open as a response to this historicism. The first alternative is to reject this view of sameness as such because the historicist factor of its structure renders the notion virtually self-destructive. But of course, this rejection is based on the truth of the premise that the historicism in question is, in fact and as such, self-destructive. And one would accept this premise only if one were disposed to believe that sameness as an ontological notion must be essentially nonhistorical, in a manner similar to the logical formality of the concept of identity. But if Being as such is necessarily defined by the appropriate form of historicism, then it follows that a nonhistorical formulation of sameness would distort the authentic character of Being. Therefore, the problem of whether or not an historicist definition of sameness is intrinsically self-destructive can be decided only if the nature of

Being is known with some degree of certainty. As such, the problem is resolvable only on the most basic ontological level and will be discussed in more detail in chapter 8.

The second alternative allows for the possibility that such historicism is not intrinsically self-destructive. In this case the content of sameness will vary with historical epochs, but the potential incompatibility between the determination of sameness in one epoch in comparison with its determination in another epoch will never arise. For if the meaning of Being as such cannot be said to straddle all historical epochs, then sameness as predicable of Being must be similarly structured. All such transhistorical comparisons of sameness would then be based on a fundamental misconception of Being as historical.

As a result sameness cannot yield the certainty generated by the application of the logical notion of identity. The only certainty available on this ontological level is that found *within* any historical epoch during which a specific content of sameness has been articulated. To expect a degree of certainty that transcends the limits of an historical epoch is to expect what is possible only on the basis of a metaphysical dimension which, for Heidegger, must remain inappropriate to Being as such.

If this second alternative is adopted, then there is the additional problem of restructuring sameness so that all its stipulated properties are defined in the proper historicist content. Heidegger does not introduce the factor of history as essential to sameness in the majority of references to its structure; for example, the careful delineations of the relation between like and unlike properties with respect to difference would not, by itself, lead one to expect that these properties were historically conditioned. But this element and all other elements of sameness *are* so conditioned. Although presumably that aspect of the abstract structure of sameness by virtue of which different properties are held apart from one another will not vary from epoch to epoch, that which is held apart will become subject to epochal variation. And it is the epochal content of sameness that will manifest the nature of Being and beings insofar as they belong to sameness.

These two alternatives, here only sketched, have been derived from those aspects of the structure of sameness that are more readily accessible in their historical determination. In chapter 7 below, both of these alternatives will be reexamined in conjunction with the complex sense of history that Heidegger envisions as essential to their full ontological structure.

5. (Property I) Heidegger has maintained that the sameness of Being and thought is "inexhaustible." Perhaps the most potentially damaging repercussion of this claim is the threat of skepticism, with the possible cessation of the philosophical enterprise. For if we know *a priori*, so to speak, that the ontological ground of sameness is inexhaustible, we can hardly avoid wondering how to react to this fact. Should the thinker simply stop short because the project of thinking sameness can never be completed in principle or should the thinker carry on in the face of this fact because of the intrinsic grandeur traditionally associated with this project? Adopting the first alternative is perhaps a subtle form of indolence, but in the long run it may be the most prudent course; pursuing the second alternative indicates intellectual diligence, but in the end it may also be simply quixotic.

Now there are grounds to substantiate an attitude of skepticism only if sameness is inexhaustible for certain reasons. Is the relation between Being and beings inexhaustible because of the historicism proper to sameness, i.e., because the articulation of the nature of Being in relation to beings depends on its position within an historical epoch, or is it inexhaustible by virtue of a complexity that is present in sameness over and above the historical transformation to which the relation between Being and beings is subject?

As far as I am aware, Heidegger never addressed this problem. The problem is important, however, and must eventually be discussed. If the reason for the inexhaustibility of sameness is that sameness necessarily remains historicist in its forms, then skepticism is unwarranted. Since the efforts of any thinker are bound by the limits of his or her historical epoch, it would be ontologically impossible for that thinker to attempt to say anything more about sameness with respect to Being and beings than what can be said from within that epoch. The thinker knows that Being is inexhaustible because the manifestations of Being are epochally plural and the existence of the individual thinker is epochally singular. But that knowledge need not hinder the attempt to say whatever it is possible to say about the sameness of Being and beings from within the epoch in which the thinker exists. In fact, such knowledge may well excite the thinker's efforts all the more, given that sameness is epochal and that in each epoch a thinker has glimmerings of what can be said about Being and beings. For if what can be said in this regard is in fact not said, then the consequences of this silence may be something less than beneficial, both for the thinker as an individual and for the world as a whole.

If, on the other hand, the reason for the inexhaustibility of sameness is nonhistoricist in origin, i.e., it has to do with an element in the structure of sameness other than its historicity, then skepticism is perhaps a more fitting reaction. In this case it would not matter how perceptive or energetic the individual thinker may be, or how many historical epochs will transpire—Being remains inexhaustible for a reason that is, perhaps necessarily, impossible to determine and equally impossible to alter. And because this inexhaustibility is of nonhistoricist origin, it would be present to each and every historical epoch, thus affecting the efforts of every thinker within that epoch to express the nature of sameness appropriate for that epoch. But even in this eventuality, skepticism is not the thinker's only recourse. For if the sameness of Being and beings is complex, then it would be premature to assume that all aspects of this complexity were equally inexhaustible. And if some aspects of sameness *are* open to expression, then all thinkers shirk their duty if the attempt is not made to articulate these aspects. This possibility must at least be entertained, if not actively explored, before any thinker slips into the safe but sterile haven of skepticism.

*Concluding Remark.* The analysis of sameness and difference presented in Section I of this chapter culminated in a list of nine properties. These properties illustrated the breadth and also the complexity of the notion. The commentary in Section II set these properties in relief by suggesting some problems that emerge if the notion of sameness and differences is taken as an integrated whole. However, in their present format, these problems can perhaps be appreciated only as a source of abstract exercise, for they are drawn from an ontological world inhabited solely by the terminology and concepts introduced by Heidegger to define the structure of sameness and difference.

But this relatively abstract world of sameness and difference is, in fact, coterminous with the concrete world of Being as temporality that is described in, e.g., Heidegger's late work "*Zeit und Sein.*" We find this passage on the second to the last page of that austere and highly condensed essay: "What remains to be said? Only this: Appropriation appropriates. By this, we say the same of the same toward the same (*vom Selben her auf das Selbe zu das Selbe*—SD, 24). In the course of this work, Heidegger discusses the nature of appropriation (*Ereignis*) in some detail, and chapter 8 below will be devoted in part to the apparent meaning of the word at this crucial point along Heidegger's ontological way. However, nowhere in this essay is there any explicit indication either of the importance or of the complexity proper to the notion of sameness as such. Unaware of Heidegger's important and perhaps unconventional handling of this notion, even the most sympathetic reader might experience philosophical vertigo when confronted with this peculiar trio of seemingly synonymous terms. One may hope that a study of the complex structure of sameness and difference would allow Heidegger's audience to withstand the onset of this not entirely unexpected reaction, and to integrate that complex structure with the equally complicated structure of appropriation.

Two related points should be made in conclusion. First, the notion of sameness and difference is intimately connected to the substance of Heidegger's ontological ventures, especially his attempts to think Being as the temporality of presence (*Anwesen*) and as appropriation. Any effort to understand and to reconstruct the Heideggerian doctrine of Being as time will necessarily be fragmented unless an interpretation of sameness becomes an essential component of that doctrine. The second point is a corollary of the first. Even if the purely temporal aspects of the doctrine of Being as presence assume an integral and coherent ontological whole, that whole must also be evaluated in conjunction with the notion of sameness and difference as a constituent part of the structure of that whole. The problems raised in Section II of this chapter should be taken into account in any such evaluation. However, in terms of Heidegger's overall philosophical project, these problems must be resolved not in the narrow domain of sameness and difference as an isolated and abstract phenomenon, but in the far richer world of Being as the temporality of presence.

This analysis of sameness and difference in the abstract, as it were, isolated from the relevant forms of ontological substantiation, will have served its purpose if students of Heidegger's more immediately appealing doctrines will also recognize the need to concern themselves with a notion that is as ontologically pervasive as it is metaphysically pedestrian. The notion of sameness and difference has been generally overlooked in secondary work on Heidegger, but it was never overlooked by Heidegger himself. The extent to which Heidegger's later ontology is coherent and incisive will depend in no small measure on the extent to which the formal structure of sameness and difference can be understood in conjunction with the substance of that ontology. This chapter might then be considered as an introduction to a critical discussion of sameness and difference in the context of Being defined as the temporality of presence. In chapter 8 the doctrine of Being as presence will be assessed using the results of this inquiry into sameness and difference as one guiding parameter.

# CHAPTER 4

# Identity and the History of Metaphysics

IN THIS CHAPTER WE WILL EXAMINE HEIDEGGER'S analysis of the principle of identity by discussing two cardinal premises of that analysis. The first premise concerns the relation between identity taken as a purely formal principle and identity viewed in terms of its underlying ontological structure; the second premise deals with the function of the history of metaphysics on the supposed formality of that principle. The texts are taken from "*Der Satz der Identität*," the first of the two essays that comprise Heidegger's important opusculum *Identität und Differenz*. The premises to be discussed are stated almost immediately in the order of the essay's exposition; they are also first in the order of the argument's logic. Agreement or disagreement with the direction of Heidegger's thinking, particularly with regard to the place of history in the temporality of presence, will depend therefore in large measure on accepting or rejecting these initial premises. Both premises are speculative, but the second is more speculative than the first; the commentary on this premise, which appears in Section II of this chapter, reflects this difference by its proportionately greater length. In general, the discussion offered here is intended to explore interpretive possibilities and several important problems arising from them.[1]

As a preamble to the critical discussion of the two premises, let us briefly review Heidegger's thinking in "*Der Satz der Identität*" up to the point at which the first premise is introduced. Heidegger opens his analysis by stating what he considers to be the customary formulation of the principle of identity: A = A. This formula represents the equality of A with A. But, Heidegger affirms, equality requires two distinct elements and the expression A = A contains only one element. Therefore, a more appropriate formulation of the principle will indicate not simply that every A is *equal* to itself, but rather that every A is itself the *same* with itself (*mit ihm selbst ist jedes A selber dasselbe*).[2] However, Heidegger now asserts that the sameness of A with itself is not equivalent to the equality of A with itself. For A could be equal to something distinct from A by virtue of a common characteristic or a shared perspective. Equality could then be predicated of part of A rather than of A as a whole. For Heidegger, once the appropriate ontological level has been reached, we can see that the predication of identity depends on the predication of sameness and not vice versa. Thus, two things, can be identical to one another without also being the same as one another, since sameness, as we saw in chapter 3, always refers to the thing as a whole while identity can abstract from this holism whenever parts of wholes are isolated for purposes of representing equality (e.g., in the totally abstract formula A = A).

This understanding of identity forces further analysis of the ontological mode of existence of the thing (represented symbolically by A) with respect to the predication of identity. Thus, to say that A is the same "with" (*mit*) itself presupposes, first, an underlying notion of unity, for without a notion of unity, one thing cannot be distinguished from any other thing. And, second, it presupposes an underlying mediation represented by the relational phrase "is the *same* with (*mit*)." At this stage of the analysis, Heidegger concludes that the principle of identity is a logical principle that incorporates a complex ontological stance. The notions of unity and mediation comprise this stance and must therefore be analyzed before the ultimate ontological character of the principle of identity can be fully comprehended.[3]

## THE UNITY AND MEDIATION OF IDENTITY

The first crucial premise may now be formulated. Heidegger has argued that the principle of identity contains two notions of equivalent or even greater generality than that possessed by the principle itself. If therefore the mediation that prevails within unity were disregarded, then identity as a purely formal principle would be represented only by a certain "faded emptiness" (*fade Leere—ID*, 87). For Heidegger, such an abstract representation of identity would become an "abode" (*Unterkunft*) within which are concealed some, perhaps all, of the essential characteristics of Being. It follows that insight into Being will be hindered unless the principle of identity is made as concrete as possible. Therefore, Heidegger's first premise is that an ontological debate must be carried on with the principle of identity, which now can no longer be considered merely a logically self-sufficient "principle of thought." However, Heidegger's questioning of the principle of identity presupposes that identity remains the same throughout all its possible metaphysical applications. Thus, he does not take into account the contemporary studies of the term when it has been predicated of events, meanings, persons, etc.[4] Heidegger nonetheless contends that some form of mediation is present even when we say, in the context of formal logic, that every thing is itself the same as itself.

One might respond to this important ontological claim by asserting that the sameness of identity is logically necessary simply by reason of its formal character, quite apart from the presence of some putative mediation. But Heidegger would press an appeal for necessity of this sort as follows: "A = A" is an abstraction based on the possibility that the denotative device "A" can symbolically represent any entity. But a given entity *as thing* being the same with itself is not equivalent to a given thing *as abstracted* (i.e., in "A = A") being the same with itself. The assumption here is that the relation "is the same with" functions in the formal mode in precisely the same way that it does in the material mode. Heidegger questions this assumption. He questions it because the identity of a thing must include the mediation of the parts of that thing, even while identity denoted symbolically excludes mediation by reason of such representational simplicity and indifference. For Heidegger, the formal character of the principle of identity cannot assume the status of a given or a primitive, but must be explicitly connected to the most fundamental and substantive ontological principles.

But surely identity is so necessary to the correctness of rational thought that it must be assumed, regardless of its metaphysical interior. If the supposed metaphysical notion of unity that underlies identity is subjected to Denken, then the tacit meaning of unity will doubtless become differentiated. And if the notion of unity is differentiated, then unity will have parts. But even as parts within a concrete and more inclusive metaphysical whole, these parts must themselves be identical to themselves. For if they are not identical to themselves, then there is nothing to prevent each part from becoming self-contradictory. Therefore, if an inquiry of the sort Heidegger intends is such that it cannot preclude the imminence of self-contradiction in its results, one could object that it is impossible to analyze the ontological structure of the principle of identity. For the principle must be assumed in the very attempt to articulate its structure.

Two replies, distinct but closely related, may be brought to bear in defense of the Heideggerian inquiry into identity. The first reply appeals to the fact that the objection is based on the apparently undeniable preeminence of the principle of contradiction. But if the ontological significance of the principle of identity can in fact be thrown into question, then the principle of contradiction cannot legitimately be applied to undermine the possibility of determining this significance, since, as we have seen in chapter 1, the principle of contradiction is no less ontological than the principle of identity. The ontologically derivative character of any one "formal" logical principle throws into question the ontological character of all logical principles. Therefore, one cannot assert the impossibility of analyzing the principle of identity by appealing to the principle of contradiction because this appeal in effect begs the question that is being directed toward the principle of identity. The second reply is that the objection, quite apart from the (ontologically illicit) appeal to contradiction, implicitly assumes that the very purpose of the inquiry is fruitless. But even if the principle of identity is accepted as logically inviolate, it is still possible and essential to speculate on the metaphysical nature of that principle. All one must assume is that the principle contains notions that are intrinsically of such a sort as to allow diverse metaphysical developments at the same time that the principle they collectively define retains, coincident with all such possible developments, the same logically necessary status. If, by appropriate reflection, this diversity is forced into the open—and such is precisely Heidegger's hope—then questioning the principle of identity evolves into the discussion of the notional structure of these metaphysical stances. As an exemplar of the regulative function of logical principles in relation to rational thought, the structure of identity may yield insight into Being that is impossible to secure from any other source.

## IDENTITY AND THE HISTORY OF METAPHYSICS

The first key premise in Heidegger's analysis of identity has shifted that principle from a privileged logical to a problematic ontological level. As such, thinking has introduced substantive content into the notion of identity similar to that found in the notion of sameness. The principal distinction between the developments of the two notions is that in thinking about identity in *Identität und Differenz*, Heidegger stipulates that identity must possess unity and mediation, without suggesting, as he does in many places where he discusses sameness, how this unity and mediation is to be understood. Here we shall restrict our attention to that aspect of mediation explicitly introduced and developed by Heidegger in this context. It is the mediation of that temporality defined by history, in particular by the history of metaphysics. As we shall see, this phase of identity is, by itself, considerably complex. But even so, the full measure of the Heideggerian approach to identity as an element in the thinking of Being will emerge only later, in chapter 8, when the doctrine of Being as the temporality of presence comes under sustained scrutiny.[5]

Heidegger's second premise suggests a reason why the ontological structure of identity must be determined according to certain guidelines. The reason is tendered in a general way toward the end of the essay, although it has already been applied more specifically at the beginning of the essay. For Heidegger, it is axiomatic that "whatever and however we may try to think, we think within the sphere of tradition," the tradition of Western metaphysics (*ID*, 106). And, with respect to thinking about the principle of identity, Heidegger had also contended that "since the era of speculative idealism, it is no longer possible for thinking to represent the unity of identity as mere monotonous oneness (*Einerlei*), and to disregard the mediation that prevails in unity" (*ID*, 88). Therefore, to understand the metaphysics hidden in the principle of identity, we must understand the entire tradition of Western metaphysics, from Parmenides to Hegel. And particular attention must be paid to that era of speculative German Idealism—Fichte, Schelling, Hegel—during which identity became the subject of especially intense metaphysical investigation.

The second key premise in Heidegger's analysis of identity asserts the essential connection between the history of metaphysics and the substantive content of the principle of identity. Heidegger's reason for concluding that the principle of identity is metaphysically-bound depends on the historical fact that this principle was first metaphysically articulated in different ways by Parmenides and Plato and was then brought to its metaphysical completeness during the era of German Idealism. The second premise is especially important and therefore must be carefully evaluated. It is important because the substance of the first essay in *Identität und Differenz*—Heidegger's development of identity as sameness and of the appropriation (*Ereignis*) of thinking and Being—concerns the historical utterances of Parmenides, the originator of Western metaphysics. The legitimacy of Heidegger's attempt to reconstruct identity according to the demands of Being depends on the assumption that the thought of Parmenides is ontologically privileged. And the substance of the second essay in *Identität und Differenz*—the rapprochment between Heidegger and Hegel on the role of thinking and the relation between thought and history—rests on the assumption that the tradition of Western metaphysics begun by Parmenides builds upon itself and is necessarily consummated in this respect in the thought of Hegel. Therefore, Heidegger's final position on the principle of identity is based on a premise that contains a certain vision of the process of history, in particular the history of metaphysical thought.[6]

In this chapter we shall isolate one aspect in the intrinsic interrelation between history and identity, an aspect that is vital and yet is one that can be manageably discussed in the space at hand. A provisional critique may bring to light the desired aspect of Heidegger's second premise. We note, therefore, that it does not seem to follow that the principle of identity must be metaphysically conditioned by history simply because there has been a lengthy history of speculative attention paid to that principle. That which pertains to the subject thinking must be distinguished from that which pertains to the object of such thinking. From the fact that thinkers exist in definite historical epochs, each thinker potentially and sometimes actually influencing succeeding thinkers, it does not follow that the object thought about must itself be historical simply by reason of its common occurrence in different historical epochs. What a modern botanist thinks about the nature of trees is not the same as what Aristotle thought about the nature of trees, but does it follow that trees as a type of natural entity must be metaphysically conditioned by history simply because of the historical difference in reflective attempts to analyze their nature? Surely not. The historical attempts to construe the principle of identity must be distinguished from the principle of identity in itself. Heidegger must show that the principle of identity is historical by examining the structure of that principle, not by appealing to the undeniable but apparently accidental fact that there is a history of speculation on that principle.

To answer this objection, we must venture into the core of Heideggerian ontology, to the extent that this ontology is presented in *Identität und Differenz*. Heidegger asserts that "the claim of identity speaks from the Being of beings" (*ID*, 89). Thus, identity is a principle that has become necessary to logic because identity is essential to the structure of Being in relation to beings. This condition is crucial, for if Being possesses properties that, upon discovery and examination, run counter to identity understood as a purely formal logical principle, then this abstract formality must be reinterpreted according to ontological specifications. The formality of identity as a logical principle must be expressable in the vocabulary of the ontological nature of Being in relation to beings.

What then does Heidegger understand by Being? Heidegger announces that "we think Being according to its original sense as presence" (*Anwesen—ID*, 95). Now Heidegger does not explicate the structure of presence in *Identität und Differenz*. Perhaps the most complete articulation of that structure is found in "*Zeit und Sein*," a lecture first given in 1962 and published in *Zur Sache des Denkens* in 1969, twelve years after the publication of *Identität und Differenz*. We shall assume that the notion of presence mentioned in the earlier work is essentially the same as the presence discussed more extensively in the later work. There, Being as presence is defined solely in terms of time. The details of Heidegger's analyses are extremely dense, and it will be the purpose of chapter 8 to attempt a coherent reading of Heidegger's thinking on this topic. For now, the fact that presence entails temporality is sufficient for our purposes. It follows that the extent to which the logical formality of identity obscures the underlying temporality of identity is the extent to which identity necessarily detracts from the expression of Being as such. The formal character of identity must eventually yield, or at least be isomorphic with, the ontologically substantive temporality of presence.

The principle of identity is, in fact, characterized by two different modes of temporality. The first mode is the past-present-future interplay that determines the nature of presence (an interplay developed in *"Zeit und Sein"*). The second mode of temporality is the temporality proper to the history of metaphysical speculation on the principle of identity. The final sentence of *"Der Satz der Identität"* asserts that "only when we thoughtfully turn toward (*zuwenden*) what has already been thought will we be turned in readiness (*verwendet*) for what must still be thought" (*ID*, 106). Thus, a necessary condition for determining the nature of identity is the thoughtful turning toward what has already been thought about identity in the past. But this turning is not, by itself, a sufficient condition. It would be a mistake to assume that Heidegger intends the pastness of the past history of metaphysical reflection on identity to be equated with the pastness that the ontology of presence must incorporate into identity.

Nevertheless, it is not inappropriate at this point to assume that the temporality of the history of metaphysics is analogous to the temporality of Being as presence. The analogy is based on the notion of sequential order. Let us assume that the history of metaphysics and Being as presence both exhibit some kind of sequential order. The sequence of historical metaphysics certainly possesses order, not only in the obvious sense that Parmenides chronologically precedes Hegel, but also in terms of the fact that the content of what each thinker has said about identity depends on what prior thinkers have already said about that principle. If, therefore, the ontology of presence is ordered analogically with the history of metaphysics, then it follows that the structure of order in the history of metaphysics reflects to a certain degree the structure of order in the ontology of presence. It would then become important to understand and to evaluate the notion of sequential order that underlies Heidegger's belief that the history of metaphysics is itself an integral component in the nature of identity. The sequential analogy will not be pressed in this chapter with respect to Being as presence, but will be taken up again in chapter 7.

We have now located an aspect of the relation between identity and the history of metaphysics that can be fruitfully discussed in light of one crucial set of alternatives. From this point on, the commentary in this chapter will be restricted to the exploration of the sense in which the sequence of metaphysical thinking from Parmenides to Hegel may be characterized either as contingent or as necessary. Important implications ensue in either case.

If, for example, the sequence is contingent, then the extent to which each moment in that sequence is accidentally related to every other moment is analogous to the extent to which the structure of Being is itself contingent, at least with respect to the status of identity within that structure. But if, on the other hand, the sequence is necessary, then it should be possible to discern some form of overarching structure that determines why each moment follows necessarily upon its predecessor. The more we know about this superstructure, the more we would know about the nature of Being insofar as it is ordered in an analogous fashion. However, we should keep in mind throughout the following discussion that the contingent/necessary distinction is itself of metaphysical origin and therefore is part of that very tradition that we are now attempting to situate from the standpoint of an ontological position which is, in some essential respects, different from that tradition. Therefore, the distinction may not be entirely appropriate for such a project. But the advantages gained by interpreting Heidegger's second premise in light of this distinction outweigh the risk of perhaps distorting that position to a certain extent.

There are several readily available reasons for arguing that this sequence is contingent. After all, none of the individual philosophers who comprise the sequence need have existed or, if they had existed, need have been philosophers or, if they had been philosophers, need have thought what they had thought. But, in fact, none of these alternate possibilities were realized. As a result the sequence has a kind of necessity in the sense that it is as necessary as any other demonstrable historical fact. But surely if the sequential order of the history of metaphysics is necessary, its necessity cannot lie in what amounts to merely a restatement of a historical fact. The necessity must somehow derive from the structure of Being in relation to the content of metaphysical thought.

For reasons that perhaps lie deep in the nature of Being—and thus must remain unstated for now—let us posit that the sequence is necessary. If the sequence is necessary, then within the full sweep of the history of metaphysics that necessity may move in either a generally progressive or generally regressive direction. There are, of course, other possibilities—e.g., a zigzag course with no discernible omega point at all. But if the necessity is neutral or indeterminate, neither progressive nor regressive, there would be no reason to single out any one moment in the sequence as privileged in any way. Since Heidegger does select one such moment (i.e., Parmenides), we may infer that the sequence is not neutral, and thus must be either necessarily progressive or necessarily regressive.

Now if the sequence is progressive, then there is no need to consider any moment in the sequence other than the last, for it is not unreasonable to assume that the fact of progression implies that the possibilities in the sequence will be realized most completely only at the point when the sequence has reached its final moment. But if the sequence is regressive, then for purposes of determining the appropriate ontological structure of identity, it is not necessary to consider that part of the sequence that follows whatever moment marked the most adequate metaphysical interpretation of identity. If we assume that the regressive movement does not oscillate, then this moment was presumably at the very point of origin of the sequence. The initial spokesman of identity was immediately receptive to the relation between identity and Being, so much so that all succeeding treatments distorted the metaphysical purity of that utterance.

Once the entire sequence of the history of metaphysics is viewed from the standpoint of Heideggerian ontology, it becomes evident that the sequence is definitely regressive. We know this from Heidegger's explicit preference for Parmenides, that thinker who uttered the "first truth for all Western philosophy" (*AM,* 23), that thinker who spoke about identity "most early and authentically in Western thought" (*im abendländischen Denken am frühesten und eigens—ID,* 90). The notion of sequential order may now be subjected to more precise scrutiny, especially in view of the fact that the description of the Parmenidean statement on identity conjoins a straightforward reference to chronology with what appears to be an ontological value-judgment. For example, what does "authentically" (*eigens*) mean in this context? Does Heidegger want to say that all relevant utterances of Parmenides are most authentic *because* they are the earliest? If so, then the metaphysics of identity is determined by temporal accident, since the first observer of identity just happened to be its most percipient student and determined the nature of identity in such a profound but mysterious way that all succeeding students of the principle necessarily and regressively misconstrued it. But if the connection between "authentically" and "most early" is not causal, then the true nature of identity depends not on the fact that Parmenides was the first observer of identity but rather on what Parmenides said in observing it. This explanation implies that the principle of identity need not necessarily be conditioned by the history of thinkers who have examined it—in fact, Parmenides' vision may become ours as well if we could only see identity the way he did. But this hypothesis, if sound, implies that there is no real need to study German Idealism for its teachings on identity, an implication that contradicts the axiomatic historical character of the principle of identity explicitly affirmed by Heidegger.

To summarize: If Heidegger stresses the fact that Parmenides' thought was "most early," then this historical event is not sufficient by itself to warrant accepting what Parmenides has said about identity as "most authentic." If Heidegger stresses that Parmenides' utterances are authentic, then the fact that these utterances were also "most early" appears irrelevant, especially by virtue of the fact that in order for this claim to be true, Parmenides' notion of Being must already have been identical with Heidegger's notion of Being. And if Heidegger intends to stress both qualifications equally, then since no explanation of their relation to one another is given, the meaning of the conjunction must be sought elsewhere than in the apparent meanings of its respective parts.

For Heidegger, the Parmenidean formulation of identity as the sameness of Being and thought straddles the entire sequence of Western metaphysics. But even Parmenides did not speak the nature of identity in the manner required by the ontology of presence. For if these two approaches to identity are themselves the same in all essential respects, then it would be sufficient for Heidegger merely to illuminate the Parmenidean position and to ignore all subsequent positions, including that of Hegel. The fact that identity requires further thought within in the context of Heidegger's ontology demonstrates that something must be added to the original insight of Parmenides. And ultimately the reason for this supplementation is simply that the figure of Parmenides is no less part of that Western tradition than succeeding philosophers, even though his thought helped define its origin and determine its subsequent development. Since the metaphysical tradition is, for Heidegger, a unified whole, we may deduce that Hegel on identity rounds off what was already implicit in Parmenides on identity. For that reason alone, Parmenides' thought is insufficient to serve as the ground for an adequate statement of identity, and despite the possible regressiveness of the metaphysical tradition, that entire tradition must be thought in order to substantiate the ontological structure of identity.

Therefore, will the sought-for Heideggerian understanding of the unity and mediation proper to identity incorporate the history of metaphysics or transcend it? Is Heidegger's notion of identity the next moment in the sequential order of metaphysical thinking or does it, as ontological, stand completely outside that order? Since Heidegger's position on identity is only adumbrated rather than systematically presented, the question cannot be answered at this point. If the ordered sequence of metaphysical thought is in fact regressive, as suggested above, then it would seem to require a qualitative transition, i.e., from Hegel, as the pinnacle of metaphysical speculation on identity (and all other logical principles), to Heidegger as the spokesman for the new and most appropriate ontological treatment of identity. Without such a transition, Heidegger's position risks being reduced to yet another regressive step from the original (but still ontologically incomplete) Parmenidean position. But if such a transition is required, then Heidegger's position becomes in a real sense transhistorical, i.e., sufficiently perceptive of the structure of Being to step apart from and beyond all that has historically preceded that position. On this hypothesis Heidegger would define the metaphysics of Being as essentially historical but then at the same time ground his own ontology in a transhistorical vision of Being.

The suggestions outlined in the previous paragraph will be examined again in greater detail, and from a more comprehensive ontological setting, in chapter 7 below. But regardless how this particular matter is resolved, an evaluation of Heidegger's position on identity which confronts that position on all its explicitly stated levels must take into account:

a. An understanding of Parmenidean thought as the origin of Western metaphysics, especially with respect to the function of the principle of identity in that metaphysics;
b. mastery of the tradition of metaphysics from Parmenides to Hegel as a continuum of necessarily interrelated moments; (this prerequisite ensures that the appropriate differences will be estab-

lished between the Heideggerian formulation of identity—whatever its final specifications may be—and all pertinent metaphysical formulations of identity).
c. recognition that the principle of identity will eventually require some form of ontological substantiation.[7]

Heidegger has already resolved (c) in favor of the ontology of temporality as presence. But once the decision has been made to replace the formality of identity with substantive ontology, the content of that ontology must be selected with extreme caution. For it is surely possible that an appropriate ontology grounds identity through something other than temporal considerations. Heidegger would deny this possibility by appealing to the history of metaphysics as the source of legitimacy for his selection of presence, but this reason is precisely the pivotal aspect of the second premise, and it is precisely this reason that we have suggested is not entirely persuasive. The possibility of a nontemporally oriented ontology must be kept open, at least until a demonstration, not a naked appeal to history, is offered to show that Heidegger's ontological choice of the temporality of presence necessarily grounds all other apparently divergent ontologies. Again, one special problem that must be constantly kept in view is the threat of producing multiple substantive accounts of identity in such a way that no one of them could be judged more ontologically appropriate than any other—the same problem that arose with regard to Heidegger's approach to negation as discussed in chapter 2.

These considerations pertaining to the grounding of identity set in relief the relative degree of persuasiveness engendered by the discussion of Heidegger's two premises offered above. It seems to me that Heidegger has given reasons worth considering to justify his claim that the principle of identity must be transformed from a purely formal logical axiom into an expression of ontological substance. The burden would then be on the protagonist of Heideggerian Denken to articulate the notions of unity and mediation so that they cohered with the demands of both the principle of identity as a regulative axiom of thought and also the distinctive structure of Being as the temporality of presence. This project would be difficult, but presumably (i.e., if Heidegger is proceeding along the right path) not insuperable. However, it is not at all clear why this expression must be directed by the history of metaphysics. And, finally, it is even less clear why Parmenides, the principal originator of that tradition, has spoken about identity in such a way as to guarantee that the ontology of presence must be considered as *the* nature of Being. The latter two reservations are doubtless expressions of a potential disagreement with Heidegger's first principles, particularly the function of history within the structure of Being. But we shall not pursue this disagreement now.

If the discussion of these two premises in this chapter has been at all successful, then it should be evident that Heidegger's approach to thinking the principle of identity is far-reaching in speculative vision. Thus, whoever wishes to assess Heidegger on his own ground in this regard must expend considerable energy—but no less energy than Heidegger himself spent in studying identity as a principle of logic and formulating problems arising from that study according to appropriately rigorous ontological standards.

According to the recommendations introduced in this chapter, the gap between substantive ontology and the traditionally ascribed formality of identity as an exemplar of all logical principles must be spanned by attempting to think that formality in light of the temporality of history. If this project of thinking can be accomplished, the result will be a unique ontological identity between thinking as the proper endeavor of one type of being and Being as temporality, the proper object of thinking. One question that might be raised now, but considered later, concerns how the classical differentiation assigned to time within the metaphysical tradition—e.g., past, present, future—can be accommodated within the ontological direction that Heidegger's analysis of temporality seems to portend. In any event it has become clear that Heidegger's extensive examinations of the presuppositions grounding logical notions and principles are all directed at showing the various senses in which history in particular and temporality in general must be thoughtfully integrated as part of the formal structure of these notions and principles.

The principal conclusion of Part I of this study may be briefly stated—if the classical problems of metaphysics are understood to bear directly on the demands of Denken, then the attempt to think the supposed formality of logical notions and principles according to the Heideggerian ontology produces a wide variety of problems and paradoxes. Presumably such problems and paradoxes can be resolved. If not, then we must question whether the way indicated by Heidegger's own thinking is a way that can be followed by others.

In Part II we shall continue the investigation into the ontological content of logical principles, but with the emphasis on the way in which the analytic direction of Heidegger's questioning of "logic" affected his thinking on four problems—the nature and individuation of things, the existence and nature of deity, the status of history, and the structure of Being as the temporality of presence. The central interpretive parameter for this part of the work has a double focus; we will study Heidegger's answers to these problems in order to determine how these answers are open to more primordial ontological specification while at the same time testing these answers to see how they cohere with the formal restraints required by logical "correctness." It will then become evident that the difficulties arising from Heidegger's substantive responses to the topics discussed in Part II (most of which have been classical metaphysical issues) are equivalent to, and in many cases merely extensions of, the same difficulties that arose in our study of Heidegger's prior attempts to subject the principles of logic to ontological scrutiny. It will be argued that the Heideggerian solutions to these four problems appear to be in need of further thought. If so, then the strength of this conclusion will depend in no small measure on the extent to which the principles of logic are allowed to preserve their correctness despite the concerted effort of Denken to relocate the ontological limits of this correctness.

# PART II
Ontology and Logic

# CHAPTER 5
# The Individuation of Things

THE HEIDEGGERIAN THINKER MUST THINK ABOUT THE meaning of Being. This injunction is pronounced frequently throughout Heidegger's works. But the question of the meaning of Being itself is also the question of the meaning of Being as related to but ontologically different from beings. In this chapter we shall discuss and tentatively evaluate one especially important way Heidegger explored for determining the proper ontological character of beings. In the course of this inquiry, we shall also be introduced to the nature of temporality insofar as it substantiates beings and leads to uncovering the nature of Being as such.

Heidegger's concern for elucidating the ontology of beings is evident from the outset of his thinking. In *Sein und Zeit*, distinctions are introduced—e.g., that between what is present at hand (*vorhanden*) and what is ready to hand (*zuhanden*)—with the express purpose of showing more adequately the phenomenological reality of beings. Furthermore, one of the important early essays after *Sein und Zeit*, "Der Ursprung des Kunstwerkes" ("The Origin of the Work of Art"), contains an extended critique of three well-established metaphysical accounts of beings as things—substance/accident, unity of a manifold in sensation, matter/form. And an entire volume, *Die Frage nach dem Ding*, continues to question the nature of things by way of a typically vigorous Heideggerian illumination of certain passages in Kant's *Critique of Pure Reason*. The predominant tendency of these works is critical rather than substantive; Heidegger's purpose is to show the relevant assumptions underlying the various reigning metaphysical attempts to discern the structure of things. But Heidegger has done more in this regard than merely criticize, and I have interpreted the culmination of Heidegger's own thinking on things, understood in at least one phase of their true ontological nature, to be contained in the remarkable doctrine of *das Geviert* (variously translated as fourfold, quadrate, the square, etc.)[1]

The fourfold (as it shall be called here) is a mysterious yet in many ways intriguing notion. The essays developing this notion contain some of Heidegger's most visionary thinking, at times developed in language lyrical if not rhapsodic in tone. Furthermore, since Heidegger insists that thinking on thinghood depends on our ability to think the Being of beings (*HO*, 28), the fourfold will contain specific references to beings insofar as they are determined by presence (*Anwesen*), thus providing at least a hint of the sense in which the Being of beings is to be thought. In this respect concentrating on the notion of the fourfold as Heidegger's most concentrated and complete attempt to think thinghood has the additional advantage of placing us in intimate contact with at least one sense in which temporality enters into the ontological constitution of things. Thus, the more we know about the fourfold, the more we know about beings in their relation to Being.

The fourfold receives its most extensive development in two of the essays in *Vorträge und Aufsätze* and in several chapters of *Unterwegs zur Sprache*; it is also mentioned in a number of other works written during and after 1950. The most systematic account of the fourfold is offered in the two essays *"Bauen Wohnen Denken"* ("Building Dwelling Thinking") and *"Das Ding"* ("The Thing"). These two essays, appearing in sequence, form one-half of the second third of *Vorträge und Aufsätze*. This expositional proximity is important because it allows us to excerpt relevant passages from both essays and to present the result as a narrative unity of sorts. These two essays will therefore serve as the textual basis for an exposition of the fourfold; additional references to other works dealing with this notion and with related material will be introduced whenever such references might prove useful. It should be noted at the outset that the following outline is necessarily selective, although not at the cost of excluding any substantive element in Heidegger's position. Also, the almost hypnotic quality of Heidegger's prose will be virtually absent in this discussion, a quality of Denken that should perhaps be considered as part of the product of thinking just as it is clearly a part of its process.

Thinking about things for purposes of articulating their most fundamental nature is a complex matter, and to do so adequately a number of factors must be considered. One such factor, the correlative notion of sameness and difference, is a crucial structural element of any ontology, particularly when the inherent abstractness of such a notion is applied to concrete individual beings. The proponent of an ontology, or even a "way" toward Being, must be prepared to examine and to define the sense in which any two beings are the same as and different from one another. However, this logical perspective on beings cannot be developed until the ontological nature of beings has been formulated. The problem of individuating beings with respect to sameness and difference can be introduced only after beings have been determined as things within the context of the fourfold.

I. We begin by noting Heidegger's promulgation of the principle that what determines (*bedingt*) a thing (*Ding*) cannot itself be a thing (*FD*, 7),[2] a principle laid down in Heidegger's commentary on the Kantian analysis of thinghood. The sense of this dictum seems to be that the ontological character of a thing depends on certain conditions that allow the very possibility of that character to be realized. In short, what makes a thing to be a thing is not itself that thing. We will have more to say about the implications of this principle in Section II of this chapter, but it is important to emphasize at the outset that Heidegger's approach to thinghood is based on conditions dealing with something other than a being as such, i.e., it is contextual in nature.

Before the discussion of these conditions is introduced, it is necessary to clear away some metaphysical misconceptions about thinghood. Language is, of course, necessary for describing and articulating beings. But Heidegger maintains that, at the dawn of metaphysics, the discernment of the relation between *logos* as a language and whatever characteristics of beings were seen to be at hand (*Vorhandenen*) was an especially fateful moment (*L*, 161). It is fateful because *logos*, in conjunction with the notion that a being could be categorized, stands in a relation that was never properly grounded, neither for Plato or Aristotle nor in any subsequent metaphysical attempt to elucidate the structure of these categories (*HE*, 256). For Heidegger, the traditional categories of thinghood—quality, quantity, relation, etc.—all depend on a prior understanding of the notion of meaning as that understanding is derived from the structure inherent to any proposition (*PG*, 301). And as we have seen in chapter 1, the structure of a proposition contains presently hidden ontological features. On the basis of this position, Heidegger then infers that the ontological priority between the structure of the proposition is as yet unknown (*HO,* 13). Thus, do we say "the jug is grey" because, as a matter of ontological fact, the property greyness belongs to the jug, or do we think that this property and this being are so related because language has evolved in such a way that it frequently bears a subject-copula-predicate structure? Since the correct priority has not yet been established, Heidegger concludes that the entire propositional stance governing this approach to things must be thrown into question, and another approach developed that will not be subject to such unthought presuppositions.[3]

What then, Heidegger asks, is a thing (*Ding*)? Consider the being that is a jug. What is the "thingly" quality of the jug? As noted, no assistance is available on this matter from any of the great minds in the metaphysical tradition. Heidegger asserts that the thinghood of the jug does not consist in the jug's being a represented object (*VA,* 165), as it has been understood, in one way or another, throughout the history of metaphysics. This criticism appears frequently in Heidegger's thought—the point of the criticism is that once a being has become construed as an object of knowledge, the being so represented is stripped of a decisive portion of its underlying ontological character, in particular the appropriate dimension of temporality. For Heidegger, all such objects necessarily lack Being (*EM,* 48). Heidegger's own thinking must therefore attempt to articulate a mode of apprehension of the jug that will be qualitatively distinct from the representational and conceptual status imposed on the being of the jug by all relevant forms of metaphysical reflection.

The jug as a represented object nonetheless does provide a point of access to the demands of Denken (*HE,* 310), and that is the fact that the jug has a specifiable purpose. The path to the jug's thing-character opens up when the thinker reflects on the function of the jug—"the jug's thingness resides in the fact that the jug exists as a vessel" (*VA,* 167). In fact, the jug *is* insofar as it is used to pour liquid—when not in use, the jug becomes, in an ontological sense, virtually indistinguishable from the shelf on which it sits.[4]

The pouring of the jug is a gushing, and Heidegger traces the original meaning of the word "gush" (*Guss*) back to Greek and Indo-European roots as "offer in sacrifice" (*VA,* 171). Although a jug may be used to pour liquid in many apparently nonsacrificial ways (e.g.,—Heidegger's own example—"to dispense liquor at a bar"), the authentic meaning of "gush" is, for Heidegger, always a function of a giving which is basically sacrificial in nature. The history of language thus provides Heidegger with the source of an ontological hint for determining the proper perspective on the nature of a being as thing, in this case a plebian jug that by virtue of its original sacrificial function, is on the way toward assuming an aura of ontological nobility.

The jug pours liquid. But where does the liquid come from, who pours that liquid, and for what purpose is it poured? The jug pours liquid that honors that which is divine, which quenches the thirst of mortals, and which originates in the heavens as water and is drawn from sources in the earth. Heidegger then generalizes: there are four sectors—earth and heavens, the divine and the motal—and they "belong together" (*VA*, 172). Insofar as they precede all that is present, "they are unfolded into a single fourfold" (*Geviert*—*VA*, 172)." Heidegger affirms that the jug is a thing because every thing is a "gathering" (*Versammlung*—*VA*, 172), a gathering of the four sectors that constitute the fourfold.

Heidegger characterizes rather than defines the ontological composition of each of the sectors of the fourfold, and these descriptions are relatively sparse in detail. The following passages (interspersed with brief development) appear on pages 176-77 of "*Das Ding.*"

Earth: "the building bearer, nourishing with its fruits, tending water and rock, plant and animal."[5]

Heavens: "the sun's path, the course of the moon, the glitter of the stars, the year's seasons, the light and dusk of day, the gloom and glow of night, the clemency and inclemency of the weather, the drifting clouds and blue depth of the ether." Note, for both earth and heavens, the careful and concerted emphasis on the process aspect of the beings described.

Divine: "the beckoning messengers of the godhead (*Gottheit*). Out of the hidden sway of the divine the god (*Gott*) emerges as what he is, which removes him from any comparison with beings that are present." It is essential to keep in mind that Heidegger distinguishes between the divine and the deity, or God, and that it is the divine—not God—that constitutes this sector of the fourfold.

Mortals: "The mortals are human beings. They are called mortals because they can die. To die means to be capable of death as death. Only man dies."

Heidegger does not discuss, here or elsewhere, how these four sectors were determined, why there are four and not some other number, and why the four are these four and not some other group of four.[6]

A being becomes a thing in Heidegger's technical sense if and only if it is constituted as a unified gathering of these four sectors. In each ontological thing, the four sectors "belong together from a *primordial* unity" (*ursprunglichen Einheit—VA*, 149—italics in text). Within this unity each of the four sectors "mirrors in its own way the nature (*Wesen*) of the remaining sectors" (*VA*, 178), and when any one sector is named, "we already think of the other three even if we do not consider the unity (*Einfalt*) of the four" (*VA*, 150). As a result all components of the fourfold are "already smothered in their essence if we represent them as simple realities (*Wirkliches*) which are to be grounded and explained from one another" (*VA*, 178). We note now, but reserve commentary until later in Section II, Heidegger's appeal to the notion of unity as a fundamental element in this phase of the fourfold's structure.

A being becomes a thing through the "mirror-play" (*Spiegel-Spiels*) of the four sectors of the fourfold (*VA*, 180). And at this point, the distinctive temporality of Being as presence (*Anwesen*) is introduced, for it is only in virtue of this mirror-play that the jug "comes into presence" (*west*) as a thing. Each sector is allowed to "linger" (*Verweilen*) in the ensuing ontological unity resulting from the interplay of the four sectors as they determine this and all other things (*US*, 22). The unity of this mirror-play is called "world" (*Welt*), and the interplay itself Heidegger refers to as the "round-dance" (*Reigen*) of "appropriation" (*Ereignis*—*VA*, 179). The image of the round-dance is apparently intended to convey a sense of continuous and orderly motion among the designated elements proper to a thing. (The mirroring aspect of a thing's determination will be discussed in Section II below, and the extremely difficult notion of appropriation will be one of the topics of analysis in chapter 8.)

The following passage epitomizes this remarkable phase of Heidegger's doctrine: "The thing things (*Das Ding dingt*). Thinging gathers. Appropriating the fourfold, it gathers the fourfold's stay, its while (*Weile*), into something that stays for a while: into this thing, that thing" (*in dieses, in jenes Ding*—*VA*, 172). Each utterance in this extremely condensed passage is important, but for our purposes, we note only the following: (a) the emphasis on the distinctive internal motion of the thing; (b) the fact that this motion is defined, apparently almost exclusively, in terms of temporality, and (c) the fact that the temporality bestowed by the fourfold to thinghood, its "while," generates "this" thing and "that" thing—i.e., individuated things.

Although some things, i.e., "natural" things, do not depend for their existence on mortals, Heidegger states unequivocally that all things are "meaningless without men" (*AM,* 202). In fact, the ontological effect of mortals on things is so pervasive that Heidegger dramatically makes the point as follows: "The question 'What is a thing?' is the question 'Who is man?' " (*FD,* 189). Since only men are interested in beings to the point of studying and describing them, we must know as much as possible about the mortal source of these activities before the descriptions of beings as things can be assessed as adequate or inadequate. It should come as no surprise then that although theoretically no one sector of the fourfold is any more or less important than any other sector, the one sector that is comprised of mortals receives special consideration.

Mortals are those who "dwell" (*Wohnen*), i.e., who preserve beings as things, and who let a being into its proper essence (*VA,* 149). Thus, mortals are those who "nurse and nurture" the things that grow and who build "properly" (*eigens*—*VA,* 152) things that do not grow. The distinction between these two very different kinds of things (which Heidegger does not elaborate) is important, both metaphysically and, as we shall see in Section II, ontologically as well. For now, however, the relevant point is the intimacy binding mortals to both these kinds of thing. In fact, mortals define *themselves* ontologically by the sense in which they dwell—"dwelling is a *fundamental characteristic* of Being" (*Grundzug des Seins*—*VA,* 161—italics in text). Once this level of dwelling has been achieved, we recognize that the lecture title "Building Dwelling Thinking," a title made idiosyncratic by its lack of punctuation, indicates that to build is to dwell is to think. All three are mutually dependent on one another to such an extent that no one of these activities can be separated from any of the others without destroying the three, for they are constituted as an ontological unity originating in Being itself.

For mortals, "dwelling, as preserving, keeps the fourfold in that with which mortals stay: in things" (*VA,* 151). The precise meaning of "in" found in this passage is not readily translatable into non-

Heideggerian terminology, but since each thing (whether natural or man-made) is determined by the fourfold as ontological totality, mortals will dwell "in" things as diverse as a house, a forest, and a jug. How will such dwelling transpire? Mortals dwell in the sense that the ontological ambit of each thing includes—but is not restricted to—the use to which mortals will put each thing. Hence, mortals can dwell "in" a jug because the jug, in its own way, incorporates the fourfold as a totality which is ontologically more inclusive than the given use put to it by mortals.

Such dwelling is therefore not specifiable in purely spatial terms. In fact, according to the ontology of the fourfold, there is no "space" in any recognizably metaphysical sense. It is the thing as experienced by mortals which produces "place" (*Ort—VA*, 154) and from which the tradition of metaphysics has derived the representational and abstract notion of space (*Raum*). For Heidegger, space comes from place and not vice versa. As a result Heidegger's rethinking of space as place includes notions designating distance in terms of what he calls "the near" and "the far." At this juncture Heidegger's terse prose must again be cited in full: "The thing things. In thinging, it stays (*verweilt*) earth and heavens, the divine and the mortal. Staying, the thing brings the four, in their farness (*Fernen*), near (*nähe*) to one another. This bringing-near is nearing" (*VA*, 176). Thus, nearness and farness originate with the thing (which, we recall, includes the mortal as one of its constituent elements), and not from any relative or "objective" spatial distance between or among things. "Near" and "far" are as precise as thinking can become with respect to indicating the limits of a thing's "place" as that thing is ontologically determined by the fourfold.[7]

The effective spatial limits of a thing will depend to a considerable degree on the ways in which mortals become involved with beings. In the case of artifacts, it is from the primal unity of the fourfold that mortals receive the directive for that building from which places come into existence (*VA*, 159). Presumably mortals receive this directive to build things by thinking in a certain way. However, elsewhere Heidegger has contended that thinking as Denken is "neither theoretical nor practical" because it is appropriated prior to any and all such distinctions (*WM*, 188). And in the very first paragraph of "*Bauen Wohnen Denken*" he says that he does not intend to provide "rules" (*Regeln—VA*, 145) for what should be thought in order to build so that mortals can dwell. Given this fundamental character of thinking, it then becomes difficult to decide how the directive delivered by the fourfold for building should be understood. For it seems that building, even in this ontological sense, must result in the production of a being. And that being either will or will not satisfy the spatio-temporal conditions for thinghood as specified by the fourfold. Thus, there seems to be a certain tension between what Heidegger says about thinking in some of his works and what he then expects thinking to do as far as incorporating the ontological demands of the fourfold. This problem could in fact be pursued solely in the context of thinking, but the scope of the problem is such that a commensurate version of it will arise in the context of the thing understood as an ontological unity. And since building, dwelling, and thinking are all aimed at the realization of things, we will not sidestep the problem, but only relocate it, by discussing it in that context in Section II.[8]

This brief sketch of the fourfold must suffice as far as textual exegesis is concerned. But in order to assist in assimilating its idiosyncratic character, let us attempt to paraphrase its basic structure in somewhat more traditional metaphysical language.[9] The fourfold may then be characterized as, in general, the appearances of certain stipulated regions or groups of (apparently similar) beings that are in motion, presumably in continual motion, and that as a unity depict totality. It should be emphasized, however, that appearances in this sense should not be understood in a manner that reduces them to "perceptions" and all that may be associated with this metaphysically-engendered phase of experience. For Heidegger, how a being appears, how it looks to mortals, is due to the Being of that being (*Sein des Seienden*—HE, 253-54). Therefore, since the Being of each being is still to a certain essential degree in question, the proper reality of perception as such is what Heidegger has designated as a completion of the experience of the being as thing, but a completion that is "no longer and not yet" (*AM*, 206). Heidegger considers perception to be a process still in process, and as such it requires an ontological ground before it can be properly thought. This ground is thinghood—"only thinghood allows a thing to have properties with respect to perception" (*HP*, 124). Therefore, whatever conceptual complexities may result from perception understood as a distinct phase of epistemological activity would be dismissed as derivative until it can be shown that these complexities would also result once perception is integrated with the appropriate ontological foundation.[10]

Each of the fourfold's components may be described as a sector or zone of indeterminate spatio-temporal limits in which beings interact contextually with other beings (e.g., the sector earth as composed of water, stones, grass, etc.). The generation of these sectors is produced by an emphasis on the appearances of beings as a unified set rather than on some opaque form of substantiality proper to these beings taken singly. The appearances of something located in one sector then somehow merge with the appearances of each of the other three sectors to determine that something as a thing. Presumably Heidegger's use of the mirror-play image is intended to suggest how this merger is accomplished. The reflection in a mirror is not real in the way that the appearances of an object are real because the object can be grasped, etc., while the reflected object can only be seen. And yet of course the reflected object *is* the object, and we are doubtless intended to recall that fact. As the distance between mirror and object increases, the image reflected decreases in size while the object itself remains the same. Despite this diminution, however, the reflected object continues to exist, although in ever-decreasing dimension. Thus, if each of the four sectors were to be understood as an ontological mirror of sorts, then the being qua thing would bounce off, as it were, all four mirrors simultaneously, casting a different image as the play of object-as-thing took place through the thing's unique temporality.[11]

These four sectors must preserve the uniqueness of appearances emerging from a given sector and at the same time unify this uniqueness with the uniqueness of each of the other three sectors. Only if this condition is fulfilled can a being attain status as a thing. Heidegger's appeal is therefore to the appearances of beings— appearances completely removed from ratiocination of any sort—in conjunction with a distinctive definition of totality, this whole then thought as a continually moving intersection of totality's four different sectors. It is clear that these sectors must not be reified or reduced to any representational concept of any sort, for such a reduction would effectively nullify both the quest for totality and the contextual medium for attaining that totality demanded by the demarcation and description of the fourfold.

II. We must let the above sketch serve as a summation of the fourfold in terms of a more traditional and, at least by intent, more accessible position. In any event the distinctiveness of this position does not elevate it above the attempt to scrutinize it critically, and to this task we now turn.

If, for the moment, we withdraw from the alluring rhythms of Heidegger's prose account of the fourfold, then we may wonder whether our non-Heideggerian experience of beings correlates with the descriptions just presented. The suspicion is that the answer will typically be in the negative. We then begin to ask questions: Do all beings exist as things in Heidegger's technical sense? And how much time does the process for realizing thinghood require? To the latter question, Heidegger says that a being becomes a thing "apparently all of a sudden;" and to the former, he says that things are "modest" in number (*VA*, 181). It follows that all things are beings, but not all beings are things. And it is perhaps because of the fragility and scarcity of things in our experience that Heidegger spoke of the difficulty of defining thinghood in an ontologically acceptable way and the need for such a definition to be in accord with "destiny" (*Schicksal*—*HO*, 21) before it could be uttered. Apparently we are not to take even the fourfold as a solution to the question of thinghood that is destined to be definitive; writing in the 1930s, Heidegger said that this question was decidable only "in a century" (*FD*, 39), a remark that if taken at face value, implies that nothing Heidegger himself would subsequently put forth could ever sufficiently reveal the nature of things.

What Heidegger has expressed in his thinking on the fourfold should therefore be understood as perhaps more exploratory than definitive. But this exploratory status does not imply that it cannot be critically examined as it stands. Here again, Heidegger's thinking has cleared a path in a certain direction, and it is not inappropriate to determine, if possible, whether it is wise to pursue that path any further.

Although as noted above, the number of things may be "modest," the variety of things is considerable. On the final page of "*Das Ding*," Heidegger claims that "the jug and the bench, the footbridge and the plow" are all things. Furthermore, "tree and pond, brook and hill" are things, "each in its own way" (*nach seiner Weise*). The "heron and roe, deer, horse and bull" are also things, each "in its own way" (*in ihrer Weise*). Finally, "mirror and clasp, book and picture" are things *in ihrer Weise* (*VA*, 181). The qualification "in its own way" remains the same throughout this ontological catalogue. But what does this qualification mean in light of the structure of the fourfold as the locus for one thing becoming individuated "in its own way" from every other thing?

For our purposes we shall consider three examples of individuation as they relate to thinghood and the fourfold: (A) the individuation of things of (apparently) the same type; (B) the individuation of things of similar types; (C) the individuation of things of clearly different types.[12]

A. Consider the individuation of things of the same type—e.g., two jugs standing next to one another on a shelf in a Schwarzwald hut. I have qualified the above mention of "the same type" with "apparently" because there are, it would seem, strong reasons to deny the ontological existence of types. The status of types in this regard will be discussed in (C) below. But even if there are no types in the ontology of the fourfold, the problem of individuating two particular jugs remains nonetheless. An attempt must be made therefore to elicit a principle for individuating two jugs as things by employing the means Heidegger's thinking on thinghood has provided.

And on that basis, the requisite principle seems difficult to secure. Heidegger has told us that each sector of the fourfold has a nature (*Wesen*) that defines that sector to be what it is "in its own way." But if each sector remains the same as a constitutive element in the process of determining thinghood, then how can each sector also remain the same as a part of the unity that is each individuated thing? The fact that the nature of each sector is uniquely the same among all four sectors of the fourfold (itself a unity) seems to preclude the possibility that individual things can be determined as different from one another. For to establish a difference between things, it seems necessary to require the possibility of determining difference in one or several of the four sectors which determine that thing to be one thing and not another thing. But if any one sector must, by implication, become different with respect to the differentiation of individual things, then how can that sector remain the same with respect to its own nature as a distinct sector of the fourfold? If, for example, the earth is the ontological source of the clay for the two jugs, then how can earth-as-clay remain the same as one sector of the fourfold (without becoming an abstraction of some sort and thus representational) while also being different as the source of individuation between the two jugs?

Somehow the sameness that defines each component of the fourfold's interplay must be distinguished into a differentiating principle. One candidate for this principle might be the apparently distinct spatio-temporal locations of the two jugs.[13] Now Heidegger has insisted that the spatio-temporal location of the thing qua thing (not the thing qua represented object) depends on the fourfold. But the spatio-temporal limits of the fourfold describe totality. And the near-far oscillation of this space-time does not seem to be helpful in this regard, given the relative character of "near" and "far" and the fact that no one being or sector can be established as a standard for judging what is near (or far) in relation to what. Therefore, no limits to the spatio-temporal character of each thing can be secured, since each thing possesses the same spatio-temporal character as every other thing—i.e., the totality of space-time delimited by the totality of the fourfold. But how then can the spatio-temporal considerations of the fourfold individuate any one thing from every other thing? In the same vein, how far can the mirror metaphor be pressed, at least as far as experiencing the appearance of this particular thing is concerned? To take a mundane but quite real example, the jug before me must be handled to perform its distinctive "thingly" function. But how can the mirror image of a jug be so handled? The point may be generalized as follows: The mirror metaphor has the virtue of spreading the effective range of a given being throughout the limits of space-time. But it also has the decided weakness of failing to account for the manifest differences in types of experience of beings other than that type which is purely visual. The being-as-thing thus does not display the totality effect that its determination by the fourfold seems to require. And without this effect, the ontology of the thing becomes merely regional rather than holistic.

Heidegger's late essay *"Zeit und Sein"* asserts that the relation between Being and beings must be thought in terms of temporality. Furthermore, we have seen that temporality plays an essential although relatively undeveloped role in the structure of the fourfold. Perhaps temporality provides the principle of individuation for those beings that are things. If so, then it becomes crucial to understand the Heideggerian doctrine of Being as presence (*Anwesen*), especially with respect to the possibility that things will be individuated from one another only when they are properly thought in relation to Being. The final chapter of this study will be devoted to an analysis of Being as presence, so it would be premature at this point to venture much speculation in this regard. However, we may note that, according to the doctrine of the fourfold, the temporality of each thing in its "lingering" (*Verweilen*) requires a certain "preserving" (*Wahren*). But are we to understand this preserving as strictly temporal in character or does it also include what, viewed metaphysically, would be designated as nontemporal factors? How, for example, is the temporal lingering proper to the jug preserved in a way other than simply *using* the jug in the appropriate manner? These are the types of questions that can only be addressed after the examination of Being as presence we shall attempt in chapter 8 below.

B. Consider now the individuation of two things of similar type—e.g., a jug and a bridge, both of which fall under the notion of artifact as a type.

Heidegger emphasizes the fact that both the jug and the bridge are determined as things by virtue of gathering the same four ontological sectors. But the bridge as a being is different from the jug as a being. And surely an analogous difference will obtain for the bridge as thing and the jug as thing. Therefore, the way that the bridge gathers the four sectors of the fourfold must be different from the way that the jug gathers these same four sectors. Without this difference a bridge becomes indistinguishable from a jug, at least on that ontological level where their thinghood has been discerned.

One may wonder at this point whether we impose a purely metaphysical problem in seeking to determine the principle of individuation whereby a jug and a bridge are differentiated as things. The answer must be no. For if this problem were strictly metaphysical, and thus in principle transcended by the demands of Denken, then Heidegger himself would have to be considered blatantly metaphysical in describing the structure of each thing in such a way as to preserve the need for such individuation. The problem may then be posed thus: If each distinct thing is a gathering of the four sectors of the fourfold, then what constitutes the principle of individuation between two things, especially two apparently dissimilar things?

To think of any one sector of the fourfold is necessarily to think of all four as a unity. Therefore, as we argued earlier, it is illicit on ontological grounds to appeal to any single aspect of any one of the four sectors as the potential source of individuation. Now if the sectors of the fourfold each remain the same with respect to the determination of the thing, then perhaps it is the thing *as being* that somehow individuates the mirroring of the four sectors so that different things can be realized. But an appeal to any aspect of the thing-as-being is also illicit, for this appeal would reintroduce precisely the vestiges of the metaphysical approach to beings that the doctrine of the fourfold intends to circumvent. For example, Heidegger explicitly rejects the means/ends conceptual schema as an appropriate path toward apprehending the thinghood of beings (*VA*, 146). Means and ends are designated or specifically built into beings by mortals. But the notions of means and ends are metaphysical. Therefore, they cannot in principle account for the thing's true ontological character. And if this rejection can be generalized, then nothing human beings as mortals do can be made to account for why a jug differs from a bridge. If one may resort to images, the round-dance of the fourfold would go out of step if the mortal sector called the tune.

Perhaps the process of gathering the four sectors rather than the product of such gathering will provide the source of individuation. Heidegger tells us that mortals and *logos* gather in different ways (*HE*, 280). There are then at least these two different gathering processes. But the gathering proper to *logos* cannot be the source of individuation. For if *logos* is synonymous with Being, then one thing cannot be individuated from another thing by the process element in Being because each thing is the same as every other thing *qua* Being—things are distinguished from one another insofar as they *are* beings, not insofar as each thing *has* Being.

The way mortals gather is important even if it is not equivalent to the gathering of *logos* as such. Heidegger emphasizes that mortal gathering has everything to do with preserving (*Bewahren*) which defines in part the ontological nature of mortals as part of the fourfold (*HE*, 289-90). Nevertheless, mortals cannot be the source of individuation while they are in the process of gathering, for the simple reason that mortals cannot be the source of individuation at all, i.e., because the fourfold would be thrown out of balance as a result. It is worth noting here that Heidegger sees the process element of mortal gathering as the ontological counterpart to a type of knowing (*Wissen—HE*, 364) which, to a certain degree, approximates the classic idea of wisdom. If Heidegger is criticized for his lack of concern for the ethical dimension, then this aspect of the fourfold must be considered with great care. However, the gathering of mortals as a kind of wisdom is never developed to any degree, at least in the works published to date, and it is yet another area that must be explored with additional thought. Therefore, for present purposes, the process element of gathering, whether the process originates with Being as *logos* or with mortals as beings, does not produce the requisite source of individuation.

C. Finally, consider the individuation of a jug and a deer, two things that certainly seem to be more different than they are the same. The reasoning that was brought to bear against the possible avenues of individuation introduced earlier also holds in this context, and therefore we need not repeat these arguments. In this case, however, and unlike the two prior examples discussed, there are readily available metaphysical differences. The jug is an artifact and the deer is a living being. Thus, if artifact and living being represent distinct types, then one could begin to individuate a jug and a deer by pointing to the fact that each is an instance of a different type. However, the Heideggerian can make such an appeal only if the ontology of the fourfold can (a) admit types and (b) admit those types that bear the designation "natural" and "artifact." But can the fourfold admit the possibility of a type at all, much less types thoroughly encrusted with what are in fact metaphysical modes of representation?

For Heidegger, a universal is a premier example of representational thinking. A universal arises when cognition derives what is typical of a tree, a pitcher, etc. (*G,* 36), and places that typical property, now transformed into a static mental entity, before the mind. But such a "generic and universal concept" is what Heidegger designates as an "unessential essence" (*HO,* 39). Although Heidegger is willing to permit the word "essence" (*Wesen*) to describe this mental phenomenon, it is precisely because this phenomenon dissolves the experience of particularity that he then qualifies this kind of essence as "unessential."

A universal of this sort is revealed through a comparison of a number of particulars, and Heidegger contends that although the universal does apply equally to every particular subsumed under it, this application occurs in a completely indifferent sense (*EH,* 34). In fact, Heidegger goes so far as to assert that a concept (*Begriff*) of a particular and a concept of a universal type (*Artbegriff*) instantiated in that particular are the same (*AM*, 141). Here, at an especially crucial juncture, we find another instance of Heidegger's notion of sameness, and it is important to keep this technical sense in view when trying to understand what Heidegger has just said about concepts and concepts of types. After all, one could plausibly argue that if a jug is a type of artifact, then the concept of a jug and the concept of an artifact can scarcely be the same concept. If such sameness held, then it would seem to follow that only jugs could be artifacts and that all artifacts would be jugs, both obviously false consequences. Presumably what Heidegger has in mind in predicating sameness of the concept as such and the concept of a type is that the differences between such class divisions are ontologically insignificant when we take into account the fact that lived experience never concerns "jugness" or "the artifact," but rather *this* jug or something that can be designated as an artifact only because it is this jug or this bridge.

It appears that Heidegger's position on the sterility of representational thinking implies an especially stringent nominalism.[14] Universals are little more than names, and the extent to which thinking locates the reality of things in the names for things is the extent to which thinking remains far distant from the true ontological character of those things. In *Die Frage nach dem Ding*, Heidegger emphasizes that "there is no thing in general, only particular things; and the particulars, moreover, are just these. Each thing is one such this one and no other" (*FD*, 11).

According to this interpretation, Heidegger's thinking is nominalistic. If there are types, then these types belong exclusively to language rather than to the beings named by language. However, the final page of "*Das Ding*" may be read in a way that indicates that the doctrine of thinghood in the context of the fourfold perhaps includes something like types. Consider again Heidegger's examples of things:

a. jug, bench, footbridge, plow
b. tree, pond, brook, hill
c. heron, roe, deer, horse, bull
d. mirror and clasp, book and picture, crown and cross

Now notice the careful—and unstated—arrangement of things in these lists: (a) and (d) are all artifacts, (b) and (c) are all natural beings, some living, some not. In (a), all the artifacts are related to what might be called (and without intending to patronize) mundane pursuits, but in (d) all are higher or more "cultural" artifacts. Now I do not want to argue that Heidegger is introducing type-distinctions for things just because he arranges things in a certain order. If this were his intention, it would be an example of expositional subtlety to a fault. For surely if such types are present in the ontology of the fourfold, they should be placed in full view so that thinking can attempt to coordinate them with the explicit structure of the fourfold. We may conclude, at least provisionally, that although it would be premature to infer from the arrangement of Heidegger's examples of things that any type-distinction, much less such types as "nature" and "artifact" as mentioned above, is part of the structure of the fourfold, there nonetheless are textual grounds admitting the possibility that such types might be present within the fourfold.

Moreover, additional textual evidence may be cited for justifying the existence of such types. In this case, however, the relevant conclusions involve a bit more in the way of deduction. Heidegger has explicitly applied the notion of nature (*Wesen*) to the fourfold as such, each of the four sectors of the fourfold, and each thing as determined by the fourfold. Now it is evident on Heidegger's own terms that a thing is different from a sector of the fourfold, and that both the determinate thing and any one sector of the fourfold are different from the fourfold as such. Yet Heidegger uses the same term to refer to the nature of each component. Therefore, either the term is ambiguous or equivocal, or the sense of nature intended is predicated analogously. If ambiguous or equivocal, then the significance of the term will doubtless be difficult to untangle and to apply to these three distinct contexts; if analogous, then the differences among the three usages must be clarified as strictly as possible— clarification that Heidegger himself does not provide—in order to maintain harmony within the fourfold.

Notice, however, that even if these differences can be thought out and articulated, the question arises whether substantive sameness remains in the notion of *Wesen*, sameness despite the differences that allow *Wesen* to be applied to such ontologically disparate components as the fourfold as a whole, each sector of the fourfold as part of a whole, and any one thing determined as such by the fourfold. If such sameness does remain, then *Wesen* seems to exhibit properties that qualify it as an ontological type. The question then is whether the sameness that underlies all the differences found in Heidegger's various uses of this word becomes, at some point, an instance of what he has referred to earlier as an "unessential essence." For if this leveling process does in fact exist, then Heidegger's own use of *Wesen* becomes effectively indistinguishable from precisely the kind of indifferent representational tendencies found in metaphysics.

The same considerations hold for Heidegger's use of "unity." Thus, is the unity of the fourfold as such the same as the unity of any single sector of the fourfold or the unity of any one thing determined as such by the fourfold? If neither, then Heidegger's appeal to unity is incomplete and must be rethought; if unity *is* the same throughout, then unity, like nature, seems to be a type, albeit one of ontological dimension. The rich tradition of metaphysical speculation on the multifold senses of unity—its peak, perhaps, in Plato's *Parmenides*—forces the Heideggerian to subject the notion of unity to considerably more scrutiny than we find in Heidegger's own thinking.

And, in fact, it is difficult to see how unity could be synonymous in all these contexts. The unity of the fourfold encompasses four parts, whereas the unity of each part, each sector of the fourfold, presumably includes many parts (e.g., everything "earthly" in the earth sector). Furthermore, the unity of each thing determined by the fourfold cannot be the same as the unity of the fourfold as such, for then there would be no difference qua unity between the fourfold and a thing. Similarly, the unity of each thing cannot be the same as the unity of each sector of the fourfold, for then there would be no difference, qua unity, between the thing as a whole and any one of its constituent parts. Heidegger nonetheless predicates unity in all three contexts. Given such predication, the same series of questions arises here as in the case of *Wesen* discussed above.[15]

Regardless whether or not any textual evidence in Heidegger's vast corpus can be drawn on to solve this interpretive dilemma, the question of the status of types remains important for understanding the structure of the fourfold. Thus, when Heidegger says that the jug is a thing when it gathers the sectors of the fourfold into a unity, does he mean that this *type* of being that is called a jug will be capable of such gathering, or only that this *particular* jug before me now will so gather—leaving it open perhaps that no other particular jug will? Does the qualification "in its own way" refer to individuation between the type of thing that is a jug and the type of thing that is a bridge, or does it refer only to the individuation between a particular jug and a particular bridge? My own belief is that Heidegger intends to ascribe the possibility of thinghood only to particular things, and not to types of things (assuming, of course, that there are types). However, I do not want to discount the subtle textual indications in "*Das Ding*" that types do in fact exist. Therefore, I would like to conclude the critical portion of this chapter by showing some of the consequences that ensue for each possibility. These consequences are important regardless whether the ontology of the fourfold does or does not admit types.

For Heidegger, the most fundamental question for thinking concerns the meaning of Being, particularly with respect to the ontological difference between Being and beings. In the doctrine of the fourfold, Heidegger has been thinking about beings insofar as they are things. It is not clear whether the ontological mode of existence of things is such that it can be divided into types. The question now becomes whether the notion of beings as an essential part of Heidegger's ontological problematic can itself be classified as a type. We shall consider the consequences in both cases: (1) if beings cannot be represented as a type and (2) if beings can be represented as a type.

*If beings cannot be represented as a type.* If all beings are different by virtue of their singularity, then it seems ontologically inappropriate to attempt to think this singularity by imposing a word such as "beings" on the set of all such particulars. For how can there be sufficient sameness among these particulars to warrant Heidegger himself designating one component of the fundamental question of ontology as "beings"? And if "beings" is just a word without any corresponding ontological substance, then Heidegger's own formulation has fallen prey to precisely the fallacy of misplaced representationalism that he so often and so vigorously condemns metaphysics for purveying. Heidegger the thinker would reduce to Heidegger the metaphysician.

*If beings can be represented as a type.* If the above conclusion is deemed at odds with Heidegger's intent, then it seems that the other alternative must be elected, i.e., that "beings" can be represented as a type, or something similar to a type. Notice, however, that if "beings" is a type, then Heidegger cannot consistently maintain *both* that the fundamental question for Denken is the ontological difference between Being and beings *and* that there are no types, for the very posing of that question assumes the existence of at least one type. But if there is at least one type then there may be other types. In fact, there may be many types. And if we continue to follow this line of interpretation, we will become more open to reading "*Das Ding*" as if the references to unity and to the jug, bridge, deer, etc., intend types and not particulars. Furthermore, if there are types of particulars, then there may also be types of types, e.g., artifact as including both (the type) jug and (the type) bridge, living being as including (the type) deer and (the type) bull, etc. But we need not compound our problems by introducing types of types. The relevant difficulties will emerge as long as types of particulars are allowed membership within the ontology of the fourfold.

It is important to keep in mind that what must be determined about types within Heidegger's own problematic is independent of the classical metaphysical dispute between realism and nominalism. For regardless whether the types in question are more on the order of one or the other of these venerable alternatives, the pertinent issue concerns how a type can be derived from the structure of the fourfold *at all*. How, first, could a type-distinction such as that between mortal and nonmortal be elicited from the fourfold as totality without destroying the quaternary character of that totality in order to establish the requisite difference and opposition? And a second problem concerns thinking the relation between beings as a type (i.e., in the Being/beings distinction) and those less inclusive types that designate specific sorts of beings. For while the Heideggerian might deny that there are types of types, the Heideggerian cannot deny that some kind of relation exists between beings as one type and the types of particular beings. It does not matter at this point how the various types of particular beings would be deployed, e.g., whether it be according to a genus/species arrangement or a division along entirely different lines. The important point concerns how to think the relation between beings (as a type) and a type of being, since beings must in one sense necessarily *include* all such types however these types may eventually be designated.

In conclusion, we may note that the problems introduced in this critique of thinghood revolve around the notions of negation and the correlative concepts of sameness and difference. This dependency may be sketched as follows: First, there is no readily available way to delimit the ontological boundary of a thing, that is, no limitation on what a thing is *not*. At precisely this point the Heideggerian principle that what determines a thing to be a thing is not itself a thing assumes paramount importance. Consider the jug as thing. What is "not" this jug? In one respect, everything other than the jug is not the jug. But how can we decide what in the class of everything other than the jug is relevant for determining the jug as thing? The range of such "otherness" is much too comprehensive—it in fact embraces a form of totality (the totality circumscribed by the dimensions of the fourfold) in order to provide conditions by which this particular thing is limited and individuated from that particular thing.

In a sense the problem of reducing the totality-condition of the fourfold so that things can become individuated is a direct consequence of Heidegger's more fundamental problems arising from the attempt to substantiate negation as such. We argued in chapter 2 that Heidegger's concern for situating nothingness on an ontological par with Being was such that no provision was made for the kind of otherness by which individual being A is *not* individual being B. Now if each being requires otherness to the limits of totality in order to become a thing, then nothingness (as such otherness) and everything are equivalent. But this equivalence is such that in the context of the fourfold each thing becomes virtually indistinguishable from everything else. And when each thing is everything then there is no distinction between anything and nothing. But if there is no limitation on what a thing is not, then all things are the same. And if all things are the same, then the very notion of sameness loses its significance since the essential opposition between sameness and difference can no longer be preserved.

In proposing the structure of the fourfold, Heidegger seems to be so intent on preserving all possible nuances of Being while he articulates the ontological character of things that he cannot account for differences between things of the same type, much less for differences between things of distinct types. The impetus compelling Heidegger to posit a sense of sameness so comprehensive in its inclusion of many forms of difference makes its presence felt here, when Heidegger eventually reaches the point of dealing with things in their own individuality. We examined this drive for an ontologically comprehensive sameness in chapter 3 and noted at the time some of the major problems that arose. These problems were located on a primarily abstract level. But if thinking the Being of beings as things necessarily results in losing the concrete particularity of beings within the scope of Being's comprehensive sameness, then one must wonder whether the way we are following is headed toward a feasible destination. For now, we shall leave the matter in a state of flux. Whether or not the fourfold can yield an intelligible sense of sameness and difference with respect to the individuation of things remains to be resolved by further thought.

# CHAPTER 6

# The Existence and Nature of Deity

IN *UNTERWEGS ZUR SPRACHE*, HEIDEGGER WROTE that without his own theological background, "I would never have arrived on the way of thinking" (*US*, 96). Heidegger's way has included frequent attempts to think about such traditional theological notions as the holy and the divine. But Heidegger's way has also included thinking about God, i.e., his existence, his knowableness, his death—or his "lack"—and his nature as a "lacking" deity. In this chapter we will examine Heidegger's position with respect to God—or to deity as one might put it in an attempt to suggest an appropriate ontological neutrality. The discussion will concentrate on various difficulties arising from an apparent conflating of logical principles in the nature of deity as developed in the account of the fourfold. And we shall see that the notion of thinghood defined in chapter 5 will become even more problematic once the particular relation between deity and the fourfold has been analyzed and assessed.[1]

It is important to separate the aspect of Heidegger's thought that is devoted to the existence and nature of deity from other aspects of his thought that have related but distinct theological overtones. Heidegger has generated considerable interest among theologians in these matters, especially in terms of the possibility that his thought can yield incisive reformulations and expressions of traditional theological doctrines. The radical character of Heidegger in this context appeals to the theological investigator in search of fresh ways to state venerable pronouncements; but it is precisely this radical quality that must be considered with care, especially with respect to the nature of deity. For Heidegger's thought about deity may, by implication, prove too radical for most, perhaps all, theological positions. Furthermore, this thinking may also have equivalently het-

erodox implications for any or all the related theological notions—
e.g., the holy—that have appeared so attractive to some theologically-oriented students of Heidegger. Both the substance and the implications of Heidegger's notion of deity must then be clearly developed before a decision can be reached concerning the nature and extent of the theological relevance of Heidegger's thought, regardless how fertile any one segment of that thought may appear at first glance.

*The Existence of Deity.* The claim that God exists logically precedes any claim about the nature of God. Although Heidegger's later thought develops a subtle theistic position, the early Heidegger emerged from an avowed agnosticism. This position was foreshadowed in several doctrines appearing in *Sein und Zeit.* There, for example, Heidegger stressed that his analysis of death as the "end" of Dasein concluded nothing either way on the possibility of life after death (*SZ,* 247-48); in addition, the account of consciousness offered in that work was not intended to be applied toward establishing a distinctive human consciousness of God (*SZ,* 269). Furthermore, in the essay "*Vom Wesen des Grundes*" (published in 1929, two years after the appearance of *Sein und Zeit*), Heidegger wrote that "through the ontological interpretation of Dasein as being-in-the-world, nothing positive nor negative is decided concerning a possible mode of being (*Sein*) toward God" (*WM,* 55). Heidegger did not deny that Dasein may be related to God, nor did he assert that it can or must be so related. The theoretical level on which he was working allowed him (or so he believed at that time) to maintain a neutral status on this important issue.[2]

But these early agnostic passages must be complemented with a number of other passages that seem to affirm the existence of a deity, or even deities. Thus, we read that "the gods have flown" (*G,* 31) and that modernity is an epoch characterized, in part, by the "deprivation of God's presence" (*Entgötterung—HO,* 70). But surely it must follow that flown gods are gods who once existed, and who may still exist, although not in the same way as present gods. Furthermore, when Heidegger endorses the Nietzschean slogan that "God is dead," he adds in commentary that the death of God does not imply that the deity represented by the name "God" and defined by certain metaphysical notions is impossible to resurrect by appropriate thinking (*HO,* 186). Heidegger nonetheless accepts the fact that God (as represented metaphysically) is dead and that this death was somehow necessitated by the interlocking traditions of secular theology as engendered by the Greeks and religious theology insofar as its proponents availed themselves of secular metaphysical notions and patterns of thought. That a God should be killed by mortals is, Heidegger asserts, simply unthinkable (*HO,* 240). Whatever may occasion a flown god to be "dead," that momentous event is not due to human agency.³

According to the poet Hölderlin, gods are gods and men are men, and each needs the other (*EH,* 69). Unfortunately, the "dark lack" of God affects all beings (*NII,* 394), mortals and nonmortals alike, in such a way that men and other beings are no longer gathered into harmony with one another and within the course of world history (*HO,* 248). However, God's lack is no "defect" (*Mangel—EH,* 28). Heidegger carefully defines what he means by "lack" (*Fehlen*): anything that is lacking "can be so only if it itself is 'there' (*da*), that is, it exists (*ist*)" (*WM,* 366). We may then take heart from the fact that although a lacking deity is, in a sense, dead, the epoch in which we presently live is a time of flown gods *and* of coming gods (*EH,* 47). Thus, even if the mode of existence of the deity is not what it once was, it does not follow that this absence will remain. A deity of some sort is coming just as certainly as another deity has flown.⁴

Can anything specifically ontological be said of this ambivalent deity? In his commentary on the Kantian notion of thinghood, Heidegger says that God is a thing (*Ding*) insofar as he is at all (*FD,* 4). And elsewhere, Heidegger has written that "God is, but does not exist" (*W,* 204). One might think there is a difference, a significant difference, between the being and the existence of God. Perhaps the attempt to think this distinction is difficult because "we today have not reflected on how the power of God rests in us" (*SG,* 88). And, even more bluntly, perhaps mortals are no longer able to seek God "because they do not think any more" (*HO,* 246). But why should mortals seek God in the first place unless there is a God to seek?

If taken as a unity, the above passages certainly display a theistic resonance, if not a theistic reverence. And the number of such passages could readily be multiplied. If, however, the passages are examined singly, and in context, then it is possible to argue that most, if not all, of them do not commit Heideggerian thinking to the real existence of a deity. The passages drawn from illuminations of poetry, for example, need not imply that Heidegger accepts as necessary for thinking what he says in illuminating a given poetic utterance.

All such passages may be prefaced with a tacit "the poet's language implies that . . . ", without Heidegger himself endorsing what the poet's language implies. In the same vein, claims about the place of God made from within the metaphysical tradition need not imply that Heidegger, in determining the hidden sense and direction of that tradition, would accept the consequences of these claims. It therefore seems prudent to maintain a certain skepticism with regard to attributing an existential sense to the deity based upon the types of passages illustrated above.

But notice the different substance and tone of the following remark in the first of the two Nietzsche volumes (a remark written in 1937, but not published in book form until 1961). Heidegger, discussing the possibility of proving the existence of God, maintains that this kind of demonstration "can be constructed with all the resources of the strictest formal logic, yet for all that it proves nothing, because a God who must allow his existence (*Existenz*) to be proved is in the end a very undivine God (*ungöttlicher Gott*) and the proof of his existence amounts to a blasphemy in the highest sense" (*NI*, 366). Heidegger vigorously denies that any proof purporting to show logically the existence of God is possible; furthermore, he affirms that the imposition of such a demonstration is, in fact, blasphemous.[5] But surely a proof for the existence of God would not be blasphemous if God did not exist—it would simply be a waste of time. One cannot prove the existence of something if that something does not exist. And to describe as undivine a God who must allow his existence to be proven suggests a great deal about the existence of God, the nature of God, and the place of reason in knowing God's existence and nature. It suggests that God exists, that God's existence is knowable according to an immediacy that grants direct awareness of this existence, and that reason—the calculative phase of human awareness—is neither necessary nor adequate as the medium for conveying this awareness.

Finally, consider this claim from *Identität und Differenz* (published in 1957): "The god-less (*gott-lose*) thinking which must abandon the God of philosophy, God as *causa sui*, is perhaps nearer to the divine deity (*göttlichen Gott*). Here this means only: god-less thinking is more open to him than Onto-Theo-Logy would like to admit" (*ID*, 141). The "God of philosophy" has gradually but inevitably become encrusted with two millenia of abstractions, such as "cause of himself." This is the God of metaphysics, that "onto-theological" (Heidegger's neologism) deity whose death was experienced and uttered, first in the thoughtful poetry of Friedrich Hölderlin, and second in the poetical thinking of Friedrich Nietzsche. Only this God is dead.

God as thought by traditional metaphysics is the "highest" (*höchste*) in the order of all beings—"the proper and highest being is that being which serves as the creative source of all being, the one personal God as spirit and creator" (*FD*, 84-85). When metaphysics attempts to think Being as a whole, then it becomes "logic as theologic" (*Theo-Logik*—*ID*, 139). God is the highest being in the order of beings; therefore, whatever logical principles and categories apply to that order must also apply to God. The highest level of being for the Greeks, Heidegger tells us, was Zeus (*ID*, 137). Apparently the Platonic demiurge and the Aristotelian unmoved mover are to be taken as metaphysical and representational approximations of the anthropomorphized individual who ruled Mt. Olympus. Be that as it may, the relevant point concerns the categorizing effect the introduction of logic had on thinking about Zeus or any other manifestation of God as the highest being. Heidegger contends that without "*legein* and its *logos*, there would not be the doctrine of the trinity of Christian faith, nor the theological interpretation of the concept (*Begriffs*) of the Second Person in God" (*Gottheit*—*WD*, 170). The same derivation from *logos* that resulted in the codification of a formal logic also served to ground the evocation of a distinctively categorical interpretation of that being which is called God. We have seen how logical principles have, for Heidegger, a distortional effect on Being as such; we should therefore anticipate that any theological utterances formally controlled by these principles will be similarly skewed from the true reality of that which they name.[6]

Heidegger's own thinking is god-less, not in the sense that it denies the existence of God, but in the sense that it proclaims a vast gulf separating the god of metaphysics and theology from the truly divine deity. Heidegger's phrase "the divine deity" appears redundant; however, the ascription of divinity to God serves an important purpose with respect to determining the ontological nature of God, as we shall see below. For now, however, the important point is that when Heidegger writes that "god-less thinking is more open to him," this openness must imply that there actually exists a being toward whom one can be directed. After all, can one be "nearer" and "more open" to the deity if the deity does not exist, or if the deity's existence is only in the mode of possibility? Surely not. Unlike Heidegger's earliest thinking, which situated mortals (as Dasein) in an agnostic universe, the later Heidegger is not reticent to assert that the right kind of thinking can and indeed must be prepared to experience a really existing deity.

Once thinking has been directed toward deity, then language can attempt to articulate in "saying" (*Sagen*) the "nearness of deity" (*Nähen des Gottes*—*US*, 219). One crucial issue is, of course, determining the appropriate words for this nearness. But this problem does not depend on the putative nonexistence of deity. As Heidegger puts it, God "is" and the world "is," but the "is" functions differently in each case (*PG*, 234). And since the "is" that properly belongs to deity remains problematic during our epoch, Heidegger concludes that God is only God "in what is unspoken in our language" (*MH*, 13). We shall now attempt to make this silence speak as much as possible—by implication if not directly—concerning the nature of this existing but currently lacking deity.[7]

*The Nature of Deity*. Heidegger makes clear the general ontological structure in which God is to be considered. The key to this structure is the relation between Being as such (*Sein*) and any particular being (*Seiendes*). For Heidegger, "Being (*Sein*) is wider (*weiter*) than every being and is at the same time nearer to man than every being, whether it be a rock, an animal, a work of art, a machine, whether it be an angel or God" (*Gott*—*WM*, 162). God is a being, and insofar as God is a being God is no different from any other being with respect to the relation between Being and beings. The pivotal word in this claim is "wider," for it is this word that must be questioned in order to reveal something of the connection between God and Being. Thus, if Being is wider than God, does this mean that Being is, perhaps, more powerful than God, or does it simply mean that Being can be predicated of any being whereas God cannot? Let us leave this question unanswered for the moment. We observe only that even the deity, "when he is a being," stands as "a being in Being" (*als Seienden im Sein*—*K*, 45). Therefore, we must grant that it is possible to open an ontological study of deity by noting that, at least initially, it might be determinate as a being in relation to Being. Once God has become determinate in this way, the problem becomes that of differentiating the being of God from the **being of everything other than God.**

Heidegger begins this differentiation, not by specifying properties unique to God, but by surrounding God with a penumbra through which deity can be experienced in relation to all things other than deity. This penumbra is named the divine (*das Göttliche*), one of the four sectors of the fourfold.[8] In the essay "*Bauen Wohnen Denken*," the sector of the divine is described thus: "The divine are the beckoning messengers of the deity. Out of the holy sway of the deity, the God appears in the present (*Gegenwart*) or withdraws into his concealment" (*VA*, 150). When mortals begin to dwell, they act in certain ways toward that sector of the fourfold which is the divine: "They wait for intimations of their coming and do not mistake the signs of this lack. They do not make their gods (*Götter*) for themselves and do not worship idols" (*Gotzen—VA*, 151). And in the essay "*Das Ding*," we find this important addition to the structure of the divine in relation to deity: "Out of the hidden sway of the divine the deity emerges as what he is, which removes him from any comparison with that which is in presence" (*VA*, 177). Finally, Heidegger clearly indicates that deity and the divine are not the same in all respects: "The divine (*Göttlichen*) are the beckoning messengers of the deity (*Gottheit*). From their hidden governance, (*Gott*) appears in his essence (*Wesen*)" (*VA*, 177). Although deity and the divine are distinct, they must nonetheless be essentially related to one another in order for what appears in the light of the divine to exhibit a truly "god-like" aura and to become expressible as such. Heidegger succinctly states this relation: "Only in the light of the nature of deity (*Gottheit*) can what the word 'God' ('*Gott*') should name be thought and said" (*WM*, 182). Since any word for deity ultimately depends on the divine, the divine must be sufficiently of or like the deity to reflect or to display those characteristics that properly belong to deity alone.[9]

We have just discussed a subtle and complex relation between deity and the divine. Yet this relation is little more than a chimera unless deity really exists. But does deity exist? Yes. In fact, the doctrine of the fourfold necessitates the real existence of deity. In this respect the fourfold epitomizes the theistic strain animating a number of other contexts in Heidegger's later thought. For although the structure of the fourfold may not permit distinguishing between the appearance of a sector and the sector "as such," the fourfold still requires the real existence of deity. This conclusion may be demonstrated by the following argument:

The earthly exists as one sector because there is an earth; the heavenly exists as one sector because there is a heavenly region; the mortal exists as one sector because there is a type of mortal that is human—therefore, the divine can exist as one sector different from the other three sectors if and only if it manifests a mode of being that cannot be reduced to anything in any of the other three sectors. Now the divine can be divine (and not something different from the divine) only if, in metaphysical language, it is related to, an instance of, or a manifestation of, the deity. For if there were no deity then the divine would be divine without the existence of anything by which it could derive the name "divine." In this circumstance such predication would surely be impossible. Therefore, if the deity did not exist, then it would be impossible for Heidegger to assert that the divine occupied its own unique place within the fourfold. However, the divine does occupy such a place. Therefore, the deity must exist in order that the divine be truly divine and the fourfold be truly four.[10]

God exists. But the mode of existence of deity is complex. It is complex because at the same time that God's existence is affirmed, this existence is qualified as "lacking." But what does "lacking" mean when predicated of an existing deity?

To be accurate, the deity has been described as lacking *in our time*, and this further qualification is of crucial importance. For unless deity is always lacking then it follows that in some other time deity was not lacking. The question then arises whether some account can be given to explain why the deity should be lacking at one point in time and not be lacking at another point in time. Now it is possible that this question cannot be answered. But even if it cannot be answered, this impossibility does not free us from assuming that the question is answerable and then proceeding accordingly, or exploring the question in order to know as precisely as possible why in principle an answer cannot be forthcoming.

We begin with a fundamental distinction: the lack of deity can be attributed either to deity as such, or to the relation between deity and that which is not deity. The latter alternative can be further subdivided, and we shall do so below. Let us now consider the former alternative.

A. *Lack of Deity.*

1. One way to understand deity as lacking is to think of deity as going in and out of existence. Thus, a lacking deity would be one who

does not exist. This would not be simply a "becoming" deity (as mentioned, for example, in the Schelling commentary—*S,* 131), but a deity who exists, then does not exist, then exists again.[11]

The problem with this interpretation is obvious. What could cause a deity to cease existing? And if a deity did cease to exist, who or what could cause it to regain existence? This interpretation surely is not the meaning Heidegger intends to convey by his notion of a lacking God.

2. Perhaps the lack in a lacking deity would not refer to deity *in toto,* but to some part or aspect of deity. Thus, even if some aspect of deity did cease to exist, another part (or parts) would remain intact, identical throughout time. This unaffected phase of deity may itself eventually become subject to some kind of alteration, but the point is that it does not cease to exist while the lacking part ceases to exist (for then deity would cease to exist altogether, and alternative 2 reduces to alternative 1).

According to this interpretation, the existence of deity continues throughout time, and thus precludes the type of objection raised with respect to alternative 1. However, this interpretation presupposes that deity is divisible into really distinct parts or phases. And this is a premise that runs counter to the traditional understanding of deity as perfectly self-identical in its simplicity. Here, for example, is Thomas Aquinas: "For since we cannot know Him naturally except by reaching Him from His effects, if follows that the terms by which we denote His perfection must be diverse, as also are its perfections which we find in things. If however we were able to understand His very essence as it is, and to give Him a proper name, we should express Him by one name only" (*SCG,* I, 31).

The ultimate simplicity of deity does, however, lead to apparently paradoxical consequences for this particular interpretation of the meaning of a lacking deity. One of the classical perfections attributed to deity is eternity. But it would follow that in a lacking deity, one part of deity *is* at the same time that another part of deity *is not.* Because different parts are involved, this consequence does not violate the principle of contradiction. But contradiction is avoided only because it is possible to attribute properties to deity for a certain definite period of time. However, these same properties then cease to belong to deity during another period of time (hence a "lacking" God). But if *all* perfections belong to God eternally, then to attempt to say of any one perfection that it was lacking would be to contradict the nature of deity—i.e., "God posseses perfection X and God does not possess perfection X." Furthermore, it follows that deity is as much composed of nothingness as of being, since it is part of deity's nature to lack perfections for certain durations of time. Here again, however, we must wonder who or what could dictate that God should oscillate between having and lacking properties. Can deity be constituted in this way? Surely not. We may conclude therefore that "a lacking God" refers neither to a nonexisting deity nor to a lack in any part of the nature of an existing deity.

B. *Lack in the Relation between Deity and what is not Deity.* We have already seen Heidegger vigorously deny even the possibility that mortals could have any effect on the existence of God. But mortals could effectively annihilate deity simply by ignoring the real appearances of deity's presence. And there are other possibilities as well, depending on how narrowly or widely that which is "not" deity is interpreted. Here we consider three possibilities. The lack of God could lie not in God as such, but in (1) mortals who fail to be receptive to the presence of God, (2) something lacking in the appearances of God, or (3) some other purely ontological factor.

1. By implication, this possibility bestows some considerable power on mortals, but in a sense no more power than does any religion that accords free will an essential role in human activity. However, even if there is no special theological problem here, there is definitely an ontological one. For the implications of such free choice would conflict with what Heidegger says elsewhere about the proper place of mortals, i.e., human beings, within the fourfold as an ontological totality.

If mortals freely choose to ignore deity, they cut themselves off from what makes the divine truly divine. But the divine is an integral component of the fourfold, i.e., of Being as such. Therefore, if mortals cut themselves off from the deity (and from the divine as the receptacle of the deity), then they cut themselves off from Being. How then can mortals be the instrument by which deity appears as lacking and at the same time properly exist as members of the fourfold? A paradox arises: If the lack of God results from willful human agency, then humans as mortals can no longer be an integral factor in the totality of the fourfold; and if humans as mortals do fulfill their place in the fourfold, then willful mortal agency cannot be the source of the lack in God. However, it does not appear that the structure of the fourfold can admit either possibility. We must therefore continue to think about the meaning of a lacking God.

2. If a lacking God results from something deficient in the appearances of God as mortals apprehend these appearances, then according to most forms of religious orthodoxy, mortals can do nothing other than wait—or, perhaps, pray—that the deity will transform lacking appearances into appearances sufficient for deity's presence. But surely the appearances of a deity can be altered only by the deity from which those appearances originate—and in no other manner. Yet this possible source of the lack introduces an unalterable passivity into the core of Being—the fourfold, and each sector in it, is ontologically defined by its manifestation of Being; but under this interpretation of lacking that sector of the fourfold inhabited by those mortals who are human would simply stand by and observe this lack. Furthermore, what does the possibility of such divine variation of appearance imply about the nature of deity as such? What kind of deity would appear fully in one period of time, then reserve part of that fullness during another period of time? These are questions not readily answered, but they are also questions that, on this interpretation, must eventually be addressed in order to clarify the implications of Heidegger's position.

3. We have briefly considered both end points in the relation between God and mortals as possible sources for the lack in God. But mortals are only one example of something that is not God. There is another relevant avenue of explanation apart from mortals. We have seen Heidegger postulate that Being is "wider" than any one determinate being and even all beings taken as one totality. It follows that if deity is to be thought as a being, then Being is wider than deity. Now Heidegger also explicitly affirms that Being is not God (*WM*, 162). The question then becomes whether anything can be said about the ontological relation between Being and deity. If, for example, Heidegger's intent is to maintain that Being somehow surpasses or even controls deity, then it is arguable that Being and deity are virtually indistinguishable on the theological premise that God, as omnipotent, cannot become subject to anything that is not God. If the deity is lacking or fully present by virtue of a "sending" (*Geschick*) emerging from Being as such (*EH*, 169), then what, if anything governs the manner in which Being functions in this regard?[12] Is Being sophisticated, malicious, or neutral?

Furthermore, the claim that Being and God are identical cannot be maintained for reasons other than Heidegger's own denial, since this identity would destroy the differentiation required by the fourfold. For if Being and deity were in some essential respects the same, then the fourfold would threaten to become only triune rather than quaternal. We are again confronted by questions that are difficult to formulate properly, much less to answer. But they are questions that appear unavoidable on the supposition that Being, insofar as it is wider than deity, is not deity. The burden rests on the Heideggerian to think this relation in such a way as to preserve the primacy of Being while concurrently delimiting the unique ontological character of the one being that is deity.[13]

C. *Being as Temporality and the lacking Deity*. Let us attempt to think through several possible interpretations of a lacking God based on Heideggerian principles. If Being is temporality and all beings are modalities of this temporality, then deity too is a modality of temporality. The sense of temporality introduced here, although provisional, is representative of the Heideggerian position on Being as the temporality of presence discussed in chapter 8 below, and is sufficiently developed in this context to make us aware of the type of difficulty the Heideggerian would confront in attempting to think the being of deity in accordance with Being in this sense.

The present appearance of deity is of a distinctive kind of lack. For whenever deity appears, he does so in a manner that, Heidegger asserts, withdraws him "from every comparison with that which is in presence" (*Anwesenden—VA*, 177). This crucial text admits two different interpretations. On the one hand, it could mean that God's mode of being is completely different from the modes of being of all things constituted through presence; thus, God cannot be compared with the presence of things other than God because a qualitative difference of considerable magnitude precludes even the possibility of such comparison. On the other hand, however, the text could mean that although the being of God is the same as the being of all other things in that both are constituted by presence, the being of God is different from all other beings by virtue of a complex structure such that its mode of temporality is unknown, or, at best, only partially discernible. According to this second interpretation, the presence of God cannot be compared with the presence of any thing other than God, not because of a generic or qualitative difference in ontological type, but because the status of God's presence—either for reasons of internal complexity or external lack of awareness on the part of mortals (or both)—cannot be compared with the more apparent modes of presence exhibited by things other than God.

The alternatives just outlined are decidedly distinct, so much so that it is necessary to suggest reasons for the alternative that seems to cohere more adequately with the general scope of Heidegger's thought. Let us first sketch some of the principal implications of each alternative.

1. *Deity as Temporally Ineffable.* If a qualitative difference exists between God's mode of being and the modes of being of all other things as constituted through presence, then the ineffability of deity's being is preserved. We know that the existence of deity is indubitable. But we also know that the nature of deity is not discernible in terms that apply to the nature of all things other than deity—hence, a "lacking" God. However, a problem emerges when this position is situated next to a fundamental Heideggerian premise. For if Being as such is wider than God, as Heidegger has maintained, then how can Heidegger claim that the structure of Being is the temporality of presence and at the same time claim that he does not know the structure of a particular being that is, by implication, "narrower" than that of Being as such? It seems that Heidegger must either retract the premise that Being is wider than deity or admit, by virtue of consistency, that the full nature of deity is also constituted by the temporality of presence just as all other beings are so constituted.

2. *Deity as Temporally Determinate.* If, on the other hand, there is no qualitative difference between the being of deity and the being of all other things, then Heidegger can maintain that Being is wider than deity, since deity as *one* being must be determined by the principles of Being that determine *all* beings. This particular fundamental premise can therefore be preserved. The problem now lies in the other direction. For if the being of deity is a modality of the temporality of presence, then deity's nature is necessarily temporal—and complex. Deity is in time because Being is presence and deity is a being existing in relation to Being; deity is complex because Being as temporality is complex in terms of its interplay of past, present, future. Although the death of God means that God has become distant from his presence (*Anwesenheit—HO,* 240), deity nonetheless remains determined as a being by this presence.

At this point, however, Heidegger would remind us that we should not attempt to think this presence according to traditional metaphysical patterns. Consider, for example, this assertion by St. Augustine: God "is in no interval nor extension of time but in His immutable eternity is older than all things because He is before all things and younger than all things because the same He is after all things" (*De Gen. ad Litt.*—8, 26, 48). For Heidegger, the "before" and "after" modes of temporality that Augustine employs are ontologically derivative and distortive as well. These properties cannot be proper to deity's nature because they are not proper to the structure of Being as such (as Heidegger attempts to show in "*Zeit und Sein*"). The being of deity must, by implication, be construed as a continuing reciprocal interaction among those phases of temporality that we now, misleadingly, represent as distinctly divisible past, present, and future.

If it is legitimate to infer that deity is constituted, in part, by its appearances throughout the passage of time, then unlike the mode of existence of, e.g., a number, that is instantiated in time but remains in itself independent of all temporal considerations, the being of deity changes inasmuch as the appearances of deity change through time.[14] But if deity becomes ontologically complex by virtue of participation in the temporality of presence, then deity may become subject to some form of change or alteration. If this consequence may also be properly inferred from the predication of temporality to the being of deity, it becomes all the more crucial to stipulate, if possible, the precise dimension of deity's "nature." We know that the nature of deity, whatever may be its proper structure, is essential to the divine. Therefore, let us approach this phase of the problem, not directly from the nature of deity as such, but indirectly from the relation between deity and the divine as one sector of the fourfold.

D. *Temporality and Divinity*. The following text is especially crucial in this regard. Heidegger has claimed that the absence (*Abwesenheit*) of deity and of the divine is no vacuum, but is rather the "appropriating presence (*Anwesenheit*) of the hidden fullness of what has been (*Gewesenen*) and thus collects the essence (*Wesenden*) of the divine in the Hellenic age, in the Judaic-prophecies, in the preaching of Jesus" (*VA*, 183). Thus, God is present now, in his absence, in the sense that the divine manifests what was essential to three different examples of religious experience—Greek polytheism, Judaism in the prophetic age, and the Christianity of the New Testament. Presumably the fact that God is still absent, or lacking, in the midst of these present modalities implies that no one or all of these three religions can support the full reality of deity's presence. We shall return to the primarily theological aspects of this consequence shortly. The problem now is to determine, from the standpoint of temporality rather than theological orthodoxy, what seems to be entailed by Heidegger's claim that the "essence of the divine" includes appearances drawn from the Hellenic age, the Judaic prophesies, and the preaching of Jesus.

This sequence suggests that the divine is, in part, especially historical. Now if this feature of the divine is also a necessary characteristic of deity, then it would follow that God *is* Zeus, *is* Yahweh, and *is* Jesus. In fact, if Zeus was essential to the divine appearances of the deity in Homer's day, and if what has been divine in that epoch is still present now, then deity *is still* Zeus (to some degree) at the same time that deity is both Yahweh and Jesus. But does Heidegger mean that the essence of the divine will include every appearance of the deity in these three religions, or does he mean that this essence will emerge from one (or more than one) of the various epochs in the history of these religions to the exclusion of those manifestations occuring in all other epochs (not to mention all other religions, whether organized or "primitive")?

This particular ambivalence in Heideggerian Denken produces a number of paradoxes, both ontological and theological. The essence of the divine, we are told, includes the appearances of Zeus, Yahweh, and Jesus. Now among many other pastimes, Zeus was instrumental in the mortal business of waging war; but Jesus was a man of peace. Depending on the precise mode of its formulation, this confluence of differences could be an example of either a logical contrary or a logical contradictory. This particular instance is readily derived from cursory inspection of the divine aspects of the figures specified. But of course such logical tension could be considerably amplified, both quantitatively and substantively, once the complete spectrum of theological dogma for all relevant divine manifestations is taken into account. Thus, unless distinctions are introduced in order to provide some kind of standard for determining what aspects of Zeus, Jesus, etc., belong to the essence of the divine, the attempt to think the divine will continually be threatened by logical impossibility.

Furthermore, these logical considerations have significant theological repercussions. The Jews or Christians who care about what philosophers say will, on Heideggerian principles, have to accommodate their respective notions of deity with the peculiarly finite and flawed characteristics of Zeus, the highest form of divinity conceived by the Greeks. In addition, the many references to the conjunction "God and the gods" in Heidegger's writings seem to imply that his claim about the essence of the divine is indeed intended to cover the complete historical sweep of religions—Greek polytheism, Judaism, Christianity, and perhaps all others as well.[15] But if the essence of the divine is to be "collected" from these historical religions and this collection is then to be incorporated back into the essence of deity whenever deity becomes fully present in presence, then it will follow that this presence will include references to Zeus, Yahweh, and Jesus, all at the same time.

One could attempt to defend Heidegger's position on the intimate historical relation between deity and the divine by distinguishing between, say, Zeus as anthropomorphic phenomenon and Zeus as divine in a more traditional theological sense, and then claim that Zeus will be part of the divine because he shares traits with Yahweh and Jesus. But the problem with this line of defense is its reductionism—for if Zeus is the same as Yahweh in that both, as foundational elements in deity, are the highest divinity recognized by their respective religions, then there is no real distinction in this respect between Zeus and Yahweh. As a result, Heidegger would lose that apparently necessary historical period that was peculiarly Greek. Thus, at some point the Heideggerian must be able to indicate an attribute of Zeus that is the same as one belonging to all other deities specified and that also establishes a sense in which Zeus differs from all these deities. This specification is necessary in order to preserve the identity of Zeus within the complete cycle of historical sequence essential to the divine.

Now if no ontological ground for deity can be determined, then there is no possibility of securing a standard for differentiating between those appearances proper to deity and those appearances not proper to deity. Without this standard all appearances taken by some mortals to be emblematic of deity have equal claim to veridical status. As a consequence no religion can assert that its dogma with respect to divine revelation is more accurate than any other religion, an implication that includes religions that are contemporary with one another (e.g., Judaism and Christianity) and also religions that **are or become related to one another by historical succession (e.g.,**

Greek polytheism and Christianity). And without a standard to discriminate between what is essential and what is not essential to the divine and, by implication, to deity, it is impossible to determine whether Zeus can properly be said to belong to deity and, if he does so belong, which properties in deity are Zeus-like and which are not.[16]

Furthermore, it also follows that no one religion ever receives the manifestations of deity in their entirety, since deity is always appearing in a different form throughout the passage of time.[17] All formulations of dogma with respect to the nature of deity are therefore necessarily incomplete, pending the next appearance of deity—a process that seems to be without an omega point. We seem forced to conclude that the essence of the divine is defined simply by the fact that deity is manifested differently in different historical epochs. In short, the fact of difference itself rather than the specification of any one manifestation of deity as the same throughout history is the only necessary element in the notion of the divine.

Another alternative in interpreting the relation between deity and the historical appearances of the divine is to assume that a fundamental difference exists between the two. If, however, the appearances of deity are distinct from deity, then Heidegger must specify how deity as such is related to its divine appearances, particularly in terms of that aspect of the being of deity that differs from the appearances of deity. For if the being of deity is completely manifested in its appearances, or is even capable of complete manifestation, then there is no aspect of deity that is hidden from those to whom deity appears. One might then contend, however, that such a deity becomes virtually pantheistic, at least if the being of deity is in some respect the same as the being of the appearances of deity as reflected in the mirroring of the nondivine sectors of the fourfold. But if, on the other hand, the being of deity does remain hidden in some respect, then, again Heidegger cannot give a comprehensive account of Being, since the aspect of Being that is the being of God is not accessible in all respect to thoughtful expression. The hypothetical positing of a difference between deity and divine appearances thus also terminates in paradox.

E. *Divinity and Thinghood.* Whatever may be its precise character, there must be some kind of relation between that sector of the fourfold that is the divine and the unique member of that sector that is deity. It is therefore essential to take into account the ontological character of things (in the technical sense discussed in chapter 5) with respect to their distinctive function regarding the determination of the "divine" essence of deity. For as we have seen, the divine points to deity from within an ontological setting defined by the limits of a thing constituted as such by the fourfold. Now Heidegger has stressed that things are "small in number" (*VA*, 181). Therefore, since not all beings are things, those beings that are things will in fact exhibit the divine and those beings that are not things might not exhibit the divine.

This crucial ontological restriction results in additional difficulties with respect to certain theological considerations pertaining to the relation between deity and the world. First, if not all beings are things or are capable of becoming things, then what standard excludes those beings from possessing this capacity? Does Heidegger want to claim that some type or types of being can become things but that other types of beings are disallowed from possessing thinghood? No answer is given to this question. And the question is important. For if there is no way of determining which beings will or will not become things, then we may think we are in the presence of the divine when in fact we are not, and we may not think we are in the presence of the divine when in fact we are.

A second issue points to an even more crucial problem. Assume that we can specify a standard for distinguishing between those entities that are capable of becoming things and those beings that are not so capable. This standard will allow us to recognize those beings that are things. But how can things be divine unless that aspect of the thing that is divine points to something in the nature of deity which guarantees that the divine is veridical and not false? Heidegger himself says that mortals, when they await the divine, must not "make gods (*Götter*) for themselves," nor should they worship "idols" (*Götzen*—*VA*, 151). For, in general, man can never put himself in the place of God (*HO*, 235), and the nature of man is also other than it would be if God does not reveal himself (*S*, 198).

Heidegger recognizes the problem. Contemporary mortals are just as prone to worship idols as mortals were in the days of the Old Testament. The contemporary idols might not take the form of a gilded calf, but a sophisticated idol is no less false than a primitive one. If mortals are "awaiting" (*erwarten*) the divinely beckoning messengers of deity, how will they know if a given messenger beckons to deity or to an idol? Heidegger's notion of the divine may thus be accused of an empty formalism, since it does not seem possible to determine when the divine is spurious, an idol's penumbra, and when it is authentic, the proper radiance of deity. And, in fact, if Heidegger were to attempt to answer this question, he would face another internal inconsistency. For if he describes a property of the divine that could serve as the required standard, then it would no longer be possible to maintain that God was lacking, at least not entirely, for deity would manifest the one essential characteristic that allows mortals to distinguish between the truly divine deity and all idols.

Additional problems with respect to deity arise from the distinctive ontological structure of the fourfold. As we have seen, deity is different from the divine, just as the divine is different from the other three sectors of the fourfold. But at the same time, the divine is necessarily interrelated to each of these three sectors by virtue of the contextual demands of the fourfold as unity. If the divine must be defined ontologically in relation to the other sectors of the fourfold, then those properties of deity through which the divine is determined as a distinct sector must also be definable in terms of these three sectors. Thus, each property of the divine must be recognizably derivable from the nature of deity at the same time that that property is recognizably related to all beings other than deity insofar as these beings exists as things within the fourfold. Now if there is some measure of sameness between the deity and the divine, and if the divine is essentially constituted by its relation to all that is nondivine, then the ontological continuum that includes the deity, the divine, and the nondivine seems to possess at least some properties shared by all three components. It follows that Heidegger's notion of the divine entails a pantheistic perimeter in order that it, as part of a whole, can accommodate the contextual demands of that whole. Therefore, even if (contrary to what we argued earlier) deity is not itself pantheistic, it seems difficult to avoid the implication that the medium through which mortals experience deity—the divine—is animated by a pantheistic dimension.

Stated abstractly, all these difficulties involve preserving sameness and difference at this fundamental ontological level. The doctrine of the fourfold seems to imply that the being of deity is irreducibly different from all other instances of beings as things. But Heidegger nonetheless wants to maintain that all beings as things are ontologically the same in that each thing gathers all four sectors

THE EXISTENCE AND NATURE OF DEITY    147

of the fourfold. But if there is a real difference between the appearances of deity within the divine and the appearances of all other beings as things, then how can the divine be understood ontologically only in relation to the three other stipulated sectors?

Quite apart from any theological problems that may arise, this aspect of Heidegger's thinking definitely leads to ontological difficulties. For example, the nature of the relation connecting the divine to the other sectors of the fourfold as parts of a whole must be given further thought. Does the relation simply preserve the sameness of each sector as such? If so, then the putative unity underlying the four sectors when they determine a being to be a thing is only apparent and cannot explain how any one appearance of the divine is actively joined with any one phase of any other sector. And if, in the process of merging the four sectors into an ontological unity, the relation somehow represents a dissolution of the strict integrity of each sector, then the fact of difference is threatened. If, for example, deity and earth share all essential properties at some point beyond the level of perceptual immediacy where such differences are manifest, then there is no real ontological difference between deity and earth. In this case and at this level, it would make just as much sense to call deity the earth as it would to call the earth deity.

It is the historical dimension grounding the diversity of divine appearances that permits Heidegger to incorporate all of the major forms of religious manifestation into his notion of deity. As a result this notion, at least by intent, exhibits universality on an order that cannot be superceded by any instance of a determinate divinity that has made its presence felt at any moment within history. However, it is precisely the temporality of these continual historical changes that results in logical problems with a theological cast. As we have seen, the omnipresence of temporality as historical is such that deity can be self-contradictory—i.e., when deity both possesses and does not possess the same property at the same time; and pantheistic—i.e., when there is no apparent distinction between deity and what is not deity. The distinctive temporality that grounds the Heideggerian notion of history must therefore be questioned in order to determine whether consequences such as these—whether in matters theological or in any other context—can somehow be avoided.

In view of the objections sketched in the critical section of this chapter, we seem justified in concluding that the metaphysical import of logical principles results in significant difficulties with respect to the function of deity as an integral aspect of Heidegger's own Denken. Therefore, whether the principles that ground Heidegger's thinking—and which have instigated this portion of our critique—can be integrated into a theological approach to the nature of deity remains to be seen. The more that contemporary theologians follow the letter of Heidegger's thinking about deity, the greater will be the need to solve the problems raised above. For if these problems are not solved, either by theologians or by philosophers concerned with theological matters, then the ultimate theological implications of Heidegger's thought remain distant, regardless how immediately attractive the near periphery of that thought may appear.[18]

The unique difficulty in determining deity's nature is in a sense only a secondary problem, at least from the standpoint of Heidegger's own concern for the meaning of Being. After all, the more fundamental question for Denken is determining the destined structure of Being in relation to beings, an ontological priority that Heidegger explicitly asserts (*NII,* 396). Thus, "whether God is God is a matter appropriated from the constellation of Being" (*Konstellation des Seins*—*K,* 46). If the ontological priority of Being to deity is indeed the pivotal aspect of the issue, then the Heideggerian must think through the nature of Being—to the extent that such thinking is possible at present—before turning attention to the more restricted problem of describing the nature of deity with respect to Being. Heidegger has claimed that the unity (*Einheit*) in which theology and ontology are joined and yet distinguished still remains "unthought" (*ungedacht*—*ID,* 128), and that the relation between man and deity, since it is "higher and more difficult" than any other relation, cannot be determined with the available terminology of traditional metaphysics (*HE,* 181). Whether the theologian can wait for the right thinking and the right language on these fundamental questions is a matter that must eventually be confronted before Heidegger's overall position in this context can be accurately assessed.[19]

# CHAPTER 7
# History and Being

HEIDEGGER'S THINKING ON HISTORY IS IN MANY WAYS no less involuted than his thinking on Being. This similarity should not be unexpected given that, for Heidegger, Being *is* history in some essential sense. This sameness between Being and history can nonetheless be divided into different ontological domains, and it will be part of the burden of this chapter to distinguish several senses of history as they appear in Heidegger's discussions of metaphysics in general and of the relation between metaphysics and Denken. These accounts are as problematic as they are provocative. Furthermore, it will become apparent that many of the questions that arise in the context of Heidegger's thinking on history will emerge again, in virtually the same form, in the context of Heidegger's thinking on Being as such. This chapter will therefore serve a dual purpose—it will offer a direct confrontation with the historical factor in Heidegger's thought on Being, as well as an indirect introduction to the type of critical approach developed in chapter 8 concerning the doctrine of Being as presence.

The structure of this chapter reflects the complexity of its subject matter. Sections A through F outline Heidegger's general position on history. A critique (Critique I) concerning this position follows this exposition. Section G is a more detailed discussion of one seminal aspect of Heidegger's attempt to think Being in its historical relation to beings—the epochal character of the ontological difference. This attempt is sufficiently important and intricate to warrant a separate critical analysis (Critique II). The chapter closes with a brief conclusion, Section H.

A. *The Dimensions of History*. Heidegger has stated as an ontological principle that all history is sustained by one fundamental difference—i.e., that between Being and beings (*EM*, 156). However, it is not immediately obvious how this difference performs such a mammoth task. The engines that drive human affairs seem, at least on the surface, to be many and diverse. Heidegger has reduced all these forces to one, and one of such abstract character that it scarely seems to have an influence on historical complexities as normally understood. What then does Heidegger mean by history?

In *Sein und Zeit*, the introduction of history as a thematic concern follows directly upon Heidegger's thinking about Dasein and its distinctive mode of temporality; in several respects this account grounds all attempts to reveal the relation between Being and history in Heidegger's subsequent thought. Heidegger calls the temporal motion of Dasein its "historizing" (*Geschehen*), "the specific movement in which Dasein is *stretched along and stretches* itself along" (*SZ*, 374—italics in text). For our purposes we do not need to consider at this point how Heidegger then attempts to describe the complex structure of this temporality in terms of an interplay of past, present, and future. What is important, however, is that the temporality of Dasein becomes the underlying basis for the possibility of "history" (*Historie*—*SZ*, 397) understood in the usual sense— i.e., as dates, facts, and causal relations about various forms of human activity. For Heidegger, this dimension of history proceeds from a purely representational endeavor consequent upon Dasein's more fundamental historical character as a being determined by temporality. It is because Dasein possesses this distinctive property of "stretching out" through its own time that Dasein can then establish an inquiry into that past which stretches beyond the immediate past of any one instance of Dasein. Thus, Heidegger is not doing "philosophy of history" in the grand speculative manner of his Germanic predecessors. He is, in fact, attempting to think the ontological ground for both the possibility of this particular branch of the philosophical enterprise and also the more recognized sense of history as practiced by historians. His intention is to establish the derivative character of such endeavors by pointing to a dimension of temporality proper only to human beings.[1]

The historizing (*Geschehen*) of Dasein serves as a clue to the origin of history proper (*Geschichte*). According to Heidegger history as *Geschichte* began when questions were first asked about the meaning of Being (*EM*, 109). In fact, that particular ontological question concerned with determining the Being of human beings with respect to temporality is so fundamental that Heidegger asserts that "this question first creates history" (*Geschichte*—*EM*, 109). It becomes evident from such passages that Heidegger's understanding of history as *Geschichte* is stipulative. For Heidegger, there was considerable human activity long before there was history in the sense he intends. Thus, only after a certain event does history in the Heideggerian sense begin—and that event was the questioning thought of the pre-Socratics (*EM*, 96).

We may note at the outset that this fundamental alliance between certain events in history and the meaning of Being as uttered during those events renders Heidegger's position susceptible to the charge of historicism. But in *Sein und Zeit*, Heidegger claims that "the emergence of a problem of 'historicism' (*'Historismus'*)" occurs only when history in the sense of *Historie* has "alienated Dasein from its authentic historical nature" (*SZ*, 396). The implication is clearly that Heidegger's own position is not historicist for this particular reason. Historical truth is never arbitrary, Heidegger maintains (*HO*, 62), and he denies that his own account of the place of history in thinking results in "relativizing" ontological standpoints (*SZ*, 22).[2] However, since Heidegger does not elaborate his understanding of historicism, it becomes difficult to show precisely how he is attempting to safeguard his own thinking in this regard. We may nonetheless conclude, at least provisionally, that the Heideggerian doctrine of the ontological function of history is not, at least by intent, beset by factors that would render self-destructive this particular thoughtful attempt to integrate history with ontology. If Heidegger's thinking is indeed weakened or even vitiated by virtue of its historical structure, the appropriate criticisms can be formulated only after taking into account the complete panorama of that thinking.

Apart from possible historicist problems, however, one might initially object to Heidegger's approach to history simply because it seems arbitrary. Why contort the meaning of the word "history" by limiting its scope so that its technical sense excludes many patently historical events? But this objection has force only if events occurring prior to the emergence of the pre-Socratics are related to what happens during and after the pre-Socratics in such a way that the course of events specifically included in Heidegger's own stipulation of history would be significantly altered. Without demonstrating this relevance, the Heideggerian can admit that much transpires prior to circa 600 B.C., but then deny that whatever did happen had any bearing on the meaning of the sequence of events originating in

600 B.C. and continuing into the present. This response may or may not be persuasive, but this particular aspect of Heidegger's position will not be pursued here.

For present purposes we shall grant Heidegger's distinction between two dimensions of history. The first dimension is ontological—history as *Geschichte*; the second phase is representational—history as *Historie*. All events considered and brought to consciousness by history in the latter sense depend on the ontological possibilities grounded in history thought in the former sense; all events falling under the rubric of history stipulated in the former sense will be far fewer in number than those events that can be made subject to the type of scrutiny denoted by history in the latter sense. But this quantitative dominance is, for Heidegger, not a significant statistic once the ontological level has been achieved. For, in fact, it is history as *Geschichte* that allows history as *Historie* to date the onset of history as *Geschichte* as "circa 600 B.C." As Heidegger tersely puts it, history as *Geschichte* is a "history to which no *Historie* extends" (*HE*, 242).

It is essential to keep in mind throughout our discussion that Heidegger's approach to history has become, at this point, philosophical rather than empirical. Therefore, once Heidegger is permitted to develop a purely philosophical notion of history as *Geschichte*, then that notion becomes subject to purely philosophical means of assessment. The following outline sketches the essential structure of Heidegger's teaching on history as a prerequisite for this kind of assessment.

B. *Thinking and the Historical Origin of Metaphysics.* History began when mortals sought to inquire concerning the meaning of Being. There were three "originary" (*anfängliche*) thinkers—Anaximander, Parmenides, and Heraclitus (*HE*, 4). Nevertheless, for all the greatness manifested in these three exemplars of pre-Socratic thinking, the beginning of history was characterized by the "forgetting" (*Vergessenheit*) of Being (*HO*, 243). In general, the Greeks did not reflect on the fundamental meaning of *logos* (*HE*, 382) and the meaning of *logos* was hidden to them because of the forgetfulness of Being that, in fact, characterized this entire epoch (*HE*, 323). In particular, the Greeks divined nothing of the time-problematic (*L*, 193), i.e., the privileged access to the fundamental nature of Being that was only grasped in its fullness later, by Heidegger himself, in *Sein und Zeit*.

There was nonetheless an essential gap between the initial forgetting of Being found in the seminal utterances of the pre-Socratics and that continuum of forgetfulness that for Heidegger, embodies the tradition of Western metaphysics. Metaphysics proper began with Socrates and Plato (*HO,* 162). Heidegger's reasons for making this judgment are developed primarily in the essay "*Platons Lehre von der Wahrheit*" and their plausibility need not detain us now.[3] Suffice it to say that it was Plato who stilled the fundamental movement of temporality by hypostatizing Being as a world of timeless Forms. And what Plato began in Greek metaphysics, Aristotle completed inasmuch as Aristotle was the "last Greek thinker" (*HE,* 75).[4] For Heidegger, the metaphysical tradition originated with Socrates, Plato and Aristotle and has lasted until "now," although the originary thinkers cited above remain apart from that tradition, at least to some degree (*HE,* 57). However, since they too were subject to that forgetfulness of Being that later defined the entire metaphysical tradition, what the pre-Socratics said about *logos* can only be thought metaphysically (*HE,* 258). The problem for the contemporary thinker is a recovery of the original vision that remains in the hints left to us in the appropriate pre-Socratic texts to be accomplished by thinking behind, as it were, both the surface meaning and the original meaning of those texts.

C. *The Structure of Antiquity as a Metaphysical Epoch.* Heidegger claims that we barely know the nature (*Wesen*) of metaphysics (*HO,* 254). However, we do know metaphysics sufficiently well to divide it into several epochs. There are, apparently, a series of such epochs, for Heidegger tells us that the number of "great" (*gross*) epochs in the history of thought is "rare" (*einzig*) and of "brief" (*sehr kurz*) duration (*NI,* 36-37). Now if there are "great" epochs then there are also epochs that are not great (since if all epochs are great, then the predication of greatness loses its significance). And we may note that Heidegger does not specify at this point, or anywhere else for that matter, either how many epochs there are altogether or which ones are great and which ones are not.

We do know, however, that antiquity was an epoch of greatness. There was, in fact, a "destiny of Being" (*Seinsgeschick*) that resulted in a unity of thought among all Greeks from Anaximander to Aristotle (*SG,* 176). This unity possesses a structure that may, without undue distortion, be described as organic in character; thus, Heidegger infers that what is great can only have begun with greatness

(*EM*, 12).⁵ As a prerequisite for establishing this point, Heidegger carefully distinguishes between a beginning (*Anfang*) and a startingpoint (*Beginn*—*HG*, 3-4): a starting-point "disappears in the advance of history" (*Geschehens*): a beginning, on the other hand, "comes first of all to appearance and is complete (*voll*)only in its end" (*HG*, 3). Antiquity was a great epoch not because of Plato and Aristotle, but because of Anaximander, Parmenides, and Heraclitus. However, the beginning of Greek thinking can only be understood when it is seized in its completion (*EM*, 137) because the beginning of an epoch already contains the completion in it (*HO*,63). It seems therefore that even if Plato and Aristotle are seen as the progenitors of metaphysics, the pre-Socratics themselves must be taken as the ultimate source of the metaphysical approach to Being since they sowed the seeds that became Plato and Aristotle. Although this continuum effect permeates the entirety of Greek thought, Heidegger nonetheless speaks of gradations of greatness within the epoch as a whole. Thus, Aristotle was more truly Greek (*griechischer*) than Plato (*NII*, 409), and Heraclitus and Parmenides were "*greater*" ("*grösser*"—italics in text) than Socrates and Plato (*WP*, 52). Presumably these determinations are based on the extent to which each thinker either did or did not contribute to the concealment of Being, both for the Greeks themselves and for all subsequent epochs throughout the metaphysical tradition. It is not clear whether such levels of greatness can also be determined within the other epochs occurring in the history of metaphysics.⁶

D. *The Structure of Modernity as a Metaphysical Epoch.* Modernity represents the end, or completion (*Vollendung*), of metaphysics as a philosophical enterprise.⁷ By completion in this sense, Heidegger means that period when the "essential possibilities" (*Wesensmöglichkeiten*) of metaphysics have been exhausted (*NII*, 201). The "beginning" of this completion of philosophy may be dated as 1600-1900 (*NI*, 477), and Heidegger describes the "today" (*Heute*) of modernity as including all of the nineteenth and twentieth centuries (*S*, 27). The historical figure who marks off the initial phases of the beginning of the completion of metaphysics is Leibniz (1646-1716—*NII*, 298) and the figure acting as the spokesman for the completion of metaphysics is Nietzsche (1844-1900—*NI*, 464). The essence of modern metaphysics is the thinking of Being as will (*HO*, 225)—thus, Leibniz thinks it as the *Drang* in his notion of the monad, and Nietzsche thinks it as the will to power. For Heidegger, these two versions represent the same fundamental understanding of Being, and, as such, this understanding denotes the completion of metaphysics.[8] Although what we refer to as metaphysics continues to be practiced, both now and doubtless into the future, for Heidegger it is philosophical endeavor that has already said all that it can say about Being—what continues to be said and what will be said under the rubric of metaphysics are only variations on already stated themes.[9]

E. *The Epochal Structure of Metaphysics.*

1. *The Circularity of Metaphysics.* According to Heidegger, the last epoch in metaphysics is, in an ontological sense, also the first with respect to completion (*NII*, 178). Thus, the completion of metaphysics "*is*" (*ist*—italics in text) as the whole course of the history of philosophy (*WM*, 261). This unique existential sense follows from the fact that the entire history of philosophy is, as it were, always present all the time. Or, as Heidegger even more tersely puts the point, philosophy ends at its beginning (*Anfang*—*S*, 118).

An essential and important historical circularity arises from this omnipresence. In view of the ontological sameness displayed by the history of philosophy taken as a unity, Heidegger can infer the continual existence of products of thinking by philosophers at opposite historical poles of the metaphysical continuum. And it follows from such historical omnipresence that what happens between the fourth century B.C. and the onset of the twentieth century is, in a sense, happening throughout that entire period. Even the notion of the absolute as developed in German Idealism, that pinnacle of Western speculation from which Nietzsche desires to outdistance himself, was "already in Plato and Aristotle" (*HE*, 346). In general, therefore, all Western philosophy, all metaphysics "is Platonism" (*NII*, 220).[10] And since "logic" originates with Plato, all metaphysics is essentially "logic" (*HE*, 236). Furthermore, since Nietzsche is the last metaphysician, he is also "a Platonist" (*WM*, 133), despite any disclaimers on this point we may read in Nietzsche himself.

Metaphysics ends with the Nietzschean view of a worldwide nihilism; therefore, metaphysics itself is the "proper nihilism" (*NII*, 350). In fact, since metaphysics is necessitated by history, it follows that nihilism *is* history (*Geschichte*—*NII*, 91). And perhaps even more striking is Heidegger's inference that Platonic metaphysics is "no less nihilistic than the metaphysics of Nietzsche" (*NII*, 343). According to Heidegger, nihilism is that unique feature of the history of metaphysics such that Being is *not* what it has been thought to be throughout the various epochal phases of that history, and Heidegger develops a purely ontological sense of this negation in many of his works. This special sense of nihilism somewhat softens the claim about Plato, although it still rings harshly for anyone unaccustomed to thinking of metaphysics as a singular nihilistic continuum bounded by antiquity and Nietzsche. And, in a sense, it follows from Heidegger's injunction that "perhaps a thinker thinks more than he knows" (*HE*, 307).[11] For although Plato could hardly have intended to beget a legacy ending in Nietzsche, on Heidegger's view of history all of the thinking that followed Plato was already latent in the Platonic dialogues. And if, at the opposite pole of the metaphysical continuum, Heidegger has revived the original but still fragmentary insight of the pre-Socratics with respect to Being thought as unhiddenness, then the Greeks too must have known of such unhiddenness; however, they did so "indistinctly," as Heidegger himself adds (*NII*, 138).

2. *The Relativity of Metaphysics.* If we continue to think the history of metaphysics according to a figure of circularity, then it will follow that "the modern age is no more correct than the Greek" (*HO*, 71) in its metaphysical assertions, just as one arc of a circle is no more or less circular than any other arc. Nonetheless, such uniformity is diversified by the fact that each step in the history of philosophy has its own laws (*EM*, 7). The uniqueness of the law binding each epoch in the history of philosophy means, for Heidegger, how the thinker for that epoch is "claimed by Being for history" (*NII*, 484). (Whether or not this position should be understood as historicist in a detrimental sense is a matter to be discussed in Critique II below.)[12]

3. *The Possibilities of Metaphysics.* Although Heidegger tells us that the history of metaphysics has, in general, developed into a "pile of distortions" (*Anhäufung von Verdeckungen*—*NII*, 415), it cannot simply be jettisoned as a farrago of philosophical errors. For, in fact, the essential nature of metaphysics is "still unthought" (*NII*, 386). If this nature is still unthought now, then it could hardly have been thought by any figure who flourished before its completion. Thus, neither Nietzsche nor Hegel came into the original beginning of history (*NI*, 469), nor was it possible for them to do so. Furthermore, neither Nietzsche nor philosophy as such could have unfolded the meaning of beings as a whole (*NI*, 365), a possibility that de-

pends upon thinking the meaning of Being in an ontologically proper way.

The possibilities running through the history of metaphysics are important because, as Heidegger disclosed already in *Sein und Zeit*, an authentic understanding of history will take into account the emergence of possibilities present in history (*SZ*, 392). It is from this store of possibilities that mortals will learn what tasks are demanded of them (*SZ*, 394). In a sense, therefore, ethical imperatives are derived from, if not reduced to, historical possibilities.[13] In order to become fully aware of these possibilities, it will follow that everything great in the history of metaphysics must be thought again (*FD*, 62). In this way the "greatness" of an epoch—i.e., what is accessible in it as preserved for posterity (*SG*, 107—may make its presence felt to the contemporary thinker. For Heidegger assures us that every genuine philosophy has the power to be repeated by later thinking (*HP*, 105). As a result of this capacity and the ontological need to realize this capacity, history as a whole should not be construed as movement from a beginning (*Anfang*) to an end, but rather as a return backwards, as it were, to its moment of origin (*HE*, 288). Thus, for example, Aristotelian philosophy is still "there" (*da*) even now (*AM*, 70), and this enduring mode of existence is why Heidegger does not simply play the schoolmaster when he cautions prospective students of Nietzsche that they should first study Aristotle for ten or fifteen years (*WD*, 70).

Every epoch throughout the history of metaphysics shows something of Being (*HO*, 193). Therefore, every metaphysical epoch must be taken into account when considering the history of metaphysics as a whole and in its relation to Being. However, Heidegger also insists that the history of Being is not a representable process (*SG*, 157-8), and consequently we must anticipate problems as we attempt to understand how the various epochs of metaphysics are related to one another. For example, Heidegger denies that the epochs are connected with each other like so many beads on a string; in fact, it is even misleading to think of the epochs as succeeding one another serially. Nor are the epochs juxtaposed in any kind of necessary dialectic with one another (*WP*, 62). Heidegger does tell us, however, that the epochs are related in "the nearness of the same" (*HO*, 196), although the precise sense of nearness in this important context is left undeveloped. Finally, it is also important to note that, for Heidegger, the totality of metaphysics is itself an epoch (*HO*,

245). Thus, Nietzsche as the spokesman for the completion of the modernity of metaphysics also speaks as the destiny of two thousand years of metaphysical reflection (*HO*, 196-97).[14] The notion of epoch is therefore predicated of both part (each epoch in the history of metaphysics) and whole (the history of metaphysics as such). This part/whole equivalency becomes important once we take into account the possibility that metaphysics as an epochal whole may itself be cyclical; consequently, no one knows whether it will return (*H*, 124).

F. *History as Destiny*. The early Greek thinkers determined Being as the temporality of presence (*Anwesen*), a determination that has remained binding throughout the subsequent tradition of metaphysics (*NI*, 655). And Heidegger also insists that it was "no accident" that the pre-Socratics experience of Being was oriented toward temporality in this sense (*HG*, 430). What grounds this necessity? It is destiny (*Geschick*)—for Heidegger, Being "always speaks as destined" (*geschicklich*—*ID*, 117). And Heidegger frequently appeals to destiny as the ultimate origin of the course of history and the manifestations of Being within history. For example, the Greeks were bound eventually to suggest conceptual ideas in an attempt to explain their experience of Being (*WD*, 129); it was no accident that church language is "dead" (*PG*, 386); ;and it is destiny that holds the sectors of the fourfold into a unity (*EH*, 171). These three instances could readily be multiplied,[15] and the diversified contexts in which destiny is found follows upon the ontological possibility that the whole history of metaphysics stands under a single "*Geschick*" (*HE*, 296). If, therefore, the entire history of metaphysics has been guided by a stroke of destiny, then the essence of nihilism is what has been destined by Being itself (*NII*, 369); and Nietzsche's thought, the culmination of this nihilism, is what it is, not because of Nietzsche's unique genius, but because of the essence of Being (*NII*, 239).

For Heidegger, one of the preeminent facets of nihilism in this historical sense is the existence of man defined throughout this tradition as rational or calculative (*rechnende*—*SG*, 210). Now we might think of the history of metaphysics as a record of attempts by mortals to express their rational visions of reality. But Heidegger denies that metaphysics was produced by men (*NII*, 489). Thus, the destiny of metaphysics insofar as it produced a sequence of distortions does not rest on a failure of human thinking (*WM*, 160). It does not do so because the history of Being is neither the history of man in itself nor the history of man in relation to Being (*NII,* 489). If, therefore, the history of Being is a process grounded in something beyond human control, then it follows that metaphysics leaves the essence of Being undecided (*NII,* 459). Two important consequences emerge from this distinction: first, since Heidegger's own thinking takes shape from within a predominantly metaphysical frame, the time is not yet ripe to reveal properly how, e.g., a principle (*Satz*) serves as the ground of sufficient reason (*SG,* 15). In short, even Heidegger himself is subject to destiny, and there is only so much open for him to see and say. And second, it also follows that there is no rescue from destiny, or at least none Heidegger knows of (*WM,* 253), since there could be no possible agent of sufficient ontological dimension to effect a rescue by altering the course of Being.

What then is destiny? Does Heidegger offer any clues to its nature? Heidegger says, "When we say the word 'destiny' of Being, then we mean that Being addresses (*zuspricht*) itself to us and lights itself and so lighting, grants (*einräumt*) the play of space-time (*Zeit-Spiel-Raum*) in which beings can appear" (*SG,* 109).[16] Furthermore, when Being is thought as destiny, the lighting proper to Being both gives itself and refuses itself at the same time (*WM,* 166). This conjunction of opposite ontological functions seems to suggest that an important and indeed obvious question should not be asked—i.e., are all events destined? Now one might question whether Being is deterministic, since if Being is not deterministic, then some events are destined and some events are not destined. However, Heidegger asserts that events should not be distinguished into those that are destined according to an incomprehensible fate and those that are comprehensible and thus removed from destiny (*WD,* 103). On the contrary, what is destined is always what must be thought—and presumably we can always recognize such destined events in this way. The thinking behind this claim is not elaborated, but it apparently follows from the fact that Being, as unhidden, is still concealed to some degree. For if Being were wholly revealed, then it would seem to be possible to discover whether or not all events were destined; and if all events are not destined, it would also seem possible to determine the difference between destined and nondestined events. The presently concealed character of Being seems to provide Heidegger with a rationale of sorts for refusing to consider the possibility of speaking to this most important matter.

*Critique I.* Although Heidegger's approach to history is, at least by intent, ontological in character, his account of history includes a number of notions that have their own metaphysical heritage. We may begin to clarify our understanding of this account by studying the apparent implications of such classical metaphysical terminology. How, for example, is one epoch in metaphysics the same as and different from any other epoch? And what distinguishes the unity of metaphysics as itself part of that whole?

Heidegger claims that the epochs constituting the history of metaphysics have exhausted the possibilities in metaphysics with respect to its unconcealment of Being. One especially pivotal notion in this claim is that of possibility. This element of Heidegger's thinking possesses a particularly rich metaphysical tradition, a fact that will doubtless complicate any attempt to understand its present ontological function. Thus, is possibility to be understood in such a way that its fruition must be an actuality? And, if actualized, are the possibilities then joined to one another in some kind of serial order, or are they related in something like an organic manner? If the former, then it seems that the notion of possibility is predicated only analogically, and must therefore be clarified; and if the latter, then the actualization of these possibilities may be progressive, as the oak from the acorn, or regressive, as a tumor from a malignant cell. But can the mode of actualization be specified further in this regard?

The boundaries of Critique I will be circumscribed by the notion of possibility, in particular through an examination of some of the principal implications that seem to follow from its function within Heidegger's position on history as a whole. The notion of possibility is a fundamental aspect of the epochal structure of history, and it is this aspect of history that, as we shall see, establishes an important link between Critique I and the more specifically ontological problems considered in Critique II.

We should perhaps remind ourselves at this point that these critical remarks are intended only to suggest that certain problems must be considered in greater detail before the direction of Denken can be properly assessed. It should also be mentioned, however, that these problems could doubtless be multiplied once the complete range of Heidegger's own dependency on metaphysics has been unearthed and analyzed. The following critique serves only as an introduction to this important and difficult task.

*Possibility with respect to one epoch within metaphysics.*

1. If the philosophical statements defining one epoch are diverse in content, then on what ground can Heidegger select one of them—e.g., temporality—as *the* decisive factor for that epoch? For example, the Parmenidean poem contains many utterances that seem to be concerned with nontemporal matters—why should the contemporary student reduce these utterances to only one ontological dimension? Why must time and only time determine the nature of Being?

2. It seems clear that the completion of an epoch must be realized, and therefore discussed, in the arena of concrete human conduct, not just among the fairly rarified stratum of humanity comprising that epoch's philosophers. To demonstrate the real efficacy of the notion of epochal completion, the Heideggerian must be able to show how the possibilities latent in philosophical positions have affected all phases of mortal life. Without such a demonstration, there is no reason to believe that philosophy has had more than a marginal affect on human affairs. Heidegger's concern for technology and its potential for worldwide good and evil is a relevant step in this regard, but until the underlying structure of technology is more clearly related to the epochal nature of metaphysics, this concern cannot by itself establish the requisite connection.[17] Furthermore, there are many social and political problems that beset our time, and on these Heidegger is virtually silent.

3. If a given philosophical position is in fact refuted (e.g., Aristotle's critique of Plato's Forms), does it follow that the refuted position continues to influence all succeeding epochs? And if all possible interpretations of a given position could be refuted, how would such refutation pertain to the reputed "inexhaustibility" of that position? Should the notion of possibility be thought without any limits whatsoever in this regard?

*Possibility with respect to metaphysics as itself one epoch.*

4. The first thinkers were decisive for all of subsequent metaphysics. Authentic history is an attempt to return to the ontological lucidity of that thinking, and then to transcend even its limitations. But why must the first thinkers play such an overwhelmingly definitive role in this particular phase of the human drama? Heidegger seems to assume that the first thinkers are at least as important for the fact of being first as they are for what they said as thinkers. But

how decisive is this factor? Why must what happened first be the most important, the most true, the most decisive?

5. Of all the great possibilities at the origin of thinking, why was it necessary that one end, represented by Nietzsche, had to be the one destined to be actualized? Could it not be the case that there are more possibilities within the history of metaphysics than the one that has been actualized? If Heidegger admits, as he has, that metaphysics as a whole has yet to be thought fully, then how can he proclaim that metaphysics "ended" with Nietzsche? The unthought whole may contain an unseen part, one that may not be actualized until some unknown moment in the future of metaphysics.

6. Which figures in the history of metaphysics are epochal and which are not? For Heidegger, it is clear that Aristotle and Kant are manifestly epochal. But, for example, is Spinoza's thought (on which Heidegger published very little) definitively epochal? Or is it only marginal and in subservience to some other epochal figure? Or is it, as Megarian logic, destined to be forgotten by history? Thus, how are we to determine the difference between epochal thinkers and nonepochal thinkers? Surely we must know this difference in order to direct our energies to thinking the relevant historical possibilities that Heidegger contends are present in the truly epochal thinkers. Are all philosophers capable of being rethought in this sense or only some of them?[18]

7. Even if it is possible to determine the identity of those philosophers who are truly epochal, there is an additional problem—what precisely is to be repeated from a possibility latent in any one figure from a given metaphysical epoch? Thus, for example, is everything Nietzsche or Aristotle said capable of repetition or only part of what they said? If the latter, how can the relevant portions of their teachings be determined?[19]

8. Heidegger has designated the whole of metaphysics as one epoch. And he has also depicted each part of metaphysics as one epoch. But if the notion of possibility predicated of one epoch as part of metaphysics can also be predicated of metaphysics as a whole, then the notion of possibility in this historical context is such that it cannot preclude the production of contradictions. Consider: If thinking must repeat all epochally definitive philosophers, then thinking must repeat both Plato and Aristotle. But if metaphysics is itself one unity, then it must be possible to repeat the thinking of Plato and Aristotle simultaneously as a process within that unity. Plato

maintained that self-existent Forms are necessary to explain the intelligibility of particulars; however, Aristotle argued that self-existent Forms are not necessary to explain the intelligibility of particulars. To rethink the conjunction of these two views is to posit a contradiction. And the completion of such thinking would seemingly be self-contradictory. Therefore, if possibility extends over metaphysics as a whole, then possibility as an ontological notion endorses—or at least cannot deny—different philosophers holding views that, conjoined, become self-contradictory.

If such instances can only give rise to self-contradictions, then it would seem that the principle of contradiction itself becomes dependent on the sense in which "unity" is predicated of metaphysics as a whole. But surely the principle of contradiction cannot be dependent in this sense. Therefore, either metaphysics cannot be considered a unity, or, at the very least, the predication of unity must be rethought. For if the notion of possibility includes the whole of metaphysics, then if parts of that whole produce contradictions, then the notion of possibility itself cannot avoid being self-contradictory.

9. The crucial notion of destiny in Heidegger's account of history invites a number of questions. Must the concealment of Being have happened the way that it did and when it did? What transpired between the relatively undistorted thinking of the last pre-Socratic and the representationally biased notions first promulgated by Socrates and brought to fruition in Plato and Aristotle? For if we must understand the concealment of Being to have been destined, then metaphysics necessarily concealed Being. But how then can such necessity be made subject to any form of thoughtful criticism? Metaphysics was simply and irremediably destined to be—there were and could have been no alternatives. The destiny of Being must have determined not only each epochal difference throughout the history of metaphysics, but also its beginnings, end, and duration. And, in view of such necessity, how can the notion of possibility be introduced at all? For if the history of metaphysics was destined to happen, both as a unity and in terms of its parts, then there was no possibility for metaphysics to be anything other than what it in fact turned out to be. If destiny is indeed the driving force within history, then the notion of possibility seems devoid of any substantial ontological significance.

This statement of the problematic implications in the relation between possibility and destiny concludes Critique I. We shall now resume our summary of Heidegger's program for thinking history by considering the notion of the ontological difference—i.e., the difference between Being and beings—with respect to its various historical determinations.

G. *Thinking of Being as Historical.* Heidegger has admitted that metaphysics both "helps and hinders" Denken (*NI*, 397). This ambivalence also applies to Heidegger's own thinking, since it too has been shaped by the past even while it is in the process of pointing toward a new and thoughtful future. It therefore becomes essential to consider how Heidegger himself attempted to think the historical phase of ontology. As we have seen, Heidegger contends that each epoch in metaphysics has glimpsed something of Being. Thus, each epoch in metaphysics must be taken into account in the attempt to think Being. In this regard the metaphysical notion of sameness and difference again assumes considerable importance; for if Being is the same throughout the history of metaphysics, then how can the difference between metaphysical epochs be preserved while attempting to think the difference between Being and beings? And if metaphysics itself is one epoch, then how can it maintain its sameness throughout its history of very different epochal manifestations of Being? An inquiry according to these guidelines may throw some light on the apparently impenetrable power of destiny to control the manifestation of Being into "great" epochs and epochs that are not "great." And, finally, the attempt to think the sequential aspect of the epochal history of metaphysics prefigures the complexities in thinking the tripartite structure of Being as the temporality of presence (see chapter 8).

The following interpretation of the implications of Heidegger's position on the ontological structure of history is limited to the pertinent principles developed in the essay "*Die Onto-Theo Logische Verfassung der Metaphysik*" (The Onto-Theo-Logical Constitution of Metaphysics), the second of the two essays in Heidegger's important opusculum *Identität und Differenz*. This essay is sufficiently complex to stand as an approximation of Heidegger's complete position on the essential historical factor proper to Being and to the thinking of Being. As we shall see, the major strands of Heidegger's reflections on history as outlined in Sections A through F above are gathered together in this essay, and the resulting account possesses a relatively clear thematic unity. A brief outline of the relevant portions of this essay will therefore be advanced in preparation for the analysis of that position argued in Critique II.

In contrast to Hegel, for whom the matter of thinking is the idea as the absolute concept, Heidegger asserts that for him "the matter of thinking is the difference *as* difference"—i.e., thinking "Being with respect to its difference from beings" (*ID*, 113—italics in text). To think the difference as difference is not an exercise in timeless abstractions, but requires thinking through the entire variegated history of metaphysics and its respective representations of this distinction. In order to guide this inquiry, Heidegger discusses the "criterion" (*Massgabe*) for thinking about, or conversing with, the history of metaphysical thought in this regard. The criterion involves seeking something in the history of metaphysics "that has not been thought" (*ID*, 114). We shall consider the implications of the "not" in this claim below. The relevant point here is Heidegger's insistence that, again in contrast to Hegel: "The criterion of what has not been thought does not lead to the inclusion of previous thought into a still higher development and systematization that surpass it. Rather, the criterion demands that traditional thinking be set free into its essential past which is still preserved" (*ID*, 114).

The notion of that "essential past" still somehow "preserved" for us today thus provides both substance and direction to the matter of thinking. But how does this preservation of the past relate to the ontological difference between Being and beings? The linking concept is that of "the step back" (*Schritt zurück*): "We speak of the *difference* between Being and beings. The step back goes from what is unthought, from the difference as such, into what gives us thought" (*ID*, 116—italics in text). It is the step back that "determines the character of our conversation with the history of Western thinking" (*ID*, 116). Thus, the "step back" may be taken as a reformulation of the well-known strategy of "destroying" the history of ontology as advanced in *Sein und Zeit* (e.g., p. 22). In the conversation Heidegger now proposes, one must think through the history of metaphysics in order to show how the ontological difference has become subject to that forgetfulness (*Vergessenheit*) proper to "Western thinking in its entire nature" (*Wesens*). The essential negational aspect of the subject matter of the step back—i.e., what has been "unthought"—should be kept in mind throughout the following discussion.

Heidegger has carefully integrated the notion of the step back into the structure required for thinking the ontological difference. The step back is not merely a device to aid in thinking about the ontological difference. It is essential to such thinking, reflecting the fact that the content of the ontological difference must be defined not by the difference between Being and beings taken in some abstract sense, but by the difference between the Being/beings relation determined in one epoch as compared to the Being/beings relation determined in another epoch. And if the epochal succession is of finite duration, then clearly the content given to the ontological difference by thought must be drawn from within that succession in its entirety, however many epochs that totality may encompass.

*Critique II.* The development of the notion of the ontological difference represents one especially crucial grounding element in Heidegger's middle and late thinking. And the aspect of that notion perhaps most open to criticism is its inherent reliance on historical succession. The appropriate line of criticism for our purposes concerns a confluence of distinctions that, at a certain level of high metaphysical generality, renders the very possibility of asserting "the" ontological difference extremely problematic. Thus, the critical standpoint adopted here does not address the nature of Being as specified from one epoch to the next; rather, it addresses the very possibility of undertaking the thinking of the ontological difference regardless of the diverse epochal content of Being and its relation to beings.[20]

Let us assume that each epochal Being/beings difference must be taken as a unity of sorts, so that the ontological difference as such—i.e., taken as a transepochal totality—concerns a relation connecting a sequence of complex unities. The latent historicist character of the ontological difference then becomes more manifest. Heidegger's position may be schematized as follows: Being (and, necessarily, beings) has been made determinate in one epoch. But in the next epoch, Being has made determinate in another way. The process of epochal determination continues in this manner, ceasing only when the number of epochs has been exhausted and the number of metaphysical possibilities has been exhausted. From the fact that such differentiation pervades the whole history of metaphysics, Heidegger infers that Being is identical to itself in each of its epochal manifestations and yet in an essential ontological sense is not identical to itself in that Being will become different in the next epoch. Stated abstractly and in classically metaphysical terminology, Being is as much not-Being as it is Being, with the "not" referring both to what Being "will be" in subsequent epochs and to what Being "has been" in previous epochs (assuming that there is at least residual sense in speaking of a "first" epoch and that the epochs continue to maintain some form of existence as they succeed one another.) And it is important to note that this paradoxical consequence holds no matter what the specific determination of the Being/beings relation might be.

A similar conclusion can be reached by following a different series of implications. According to Heidegger metaphysics itself can be construed as a single epoch. Therefore, unless Being exhausted itself at some point within metaphysics, there had to have been a single *Seinsgeschick* underlying the alteration of Being throughout metaphysics. It is a fact that Being has assumed different configurations within the history of Being. Therefore, Being was destined to be both itself throughout the history of metaphysics and also not itself, i.e., to be one form in one epoch and a different (and perhaps incompatible) form in another epoch. Thus, Being both is itself and is not itself at any given epochal point within the total historical continuum of metaphysics. But what could the notion of "not" mean at this most fundamental ontological level? For what could be other than Being than something that itself has being by virtue of Being? The fatefulness of that one stroke of destiny must be thought in such a way as to grasp how it can withdraw Being into a wavering kind of nonexistence at the same time that it grants Being a certain epochal determination. On the surface at least, the matter is not at all one with a readily comprehensible solution.

If the above summary approximates the epochal character and implicit reliance on negation in Heidegger's thinking on the basic structure of the ontological difference, then we must question the results of that thinking. To begin, the mere transition from metaphysical epoch to metaphysical epoch need not imply that Being, the subject of metaphysics, is itself necessarily epochal in its structure. An alternative interpretation is that the manifestations of Being are liable to variation simply and solely because of individual differences in the metaphysicians who have enunciated their reflections. Thus, metaphysicians vary in their attempts to describe Being—but Being itself does not vary. Heidegger seems to assume that Being is and must be identical to whatever all major metaphysicians have said about it, and since there has undoubtedly been a history of metaphysics then it follows that Being itself is, and necessarily is, identical to the totality of that history. But why must this inference be drawn?

Let us briefly explore the alternative just presented. If Being is not identical to the history of attempts by metaphysicians to represent it, then either Being has already been approximated somewhere within that history or it has not been approximated at all. If the latter, then of course the accurate description of Being still awaits its spokesman—an accomplishment that, if ever realized, will require energy and insight on an order equalling if not surpassing that already visible in the lengthy history of philosophy's most elegant and abstract discipline. If the former, then the problem is to determine the true approximation and to defend it against competing accounts. But in either case, one need not conclude, with Heidegger, that Being must somehow be identified with all the successive statements about Being found in the history of metaphysics.

In fact, such an identification becomes readily paradoxical. Now within any given epoch, it is not difficult to appreciate that a difference of sorts may obtain between Being and beings. But how can Being as determined in one epoch fundamentally differ from Being as determined in a prior, succeeding, or any other epoch?

Consider any two examples of the manifestations of Being cited by Heidegger.[21] Call them X and Y. The paradox resulting from the historicist character of the ontological difference in its epochal phase may be thus stated: If X and Y are in some essential sense different from one another and if X, as Being, connotes a principle of totality, then if X does not incorporate Y it follows that X is not really Being, since X does not include an aspect of totality. But if X and Y are the same insofar as each designates Being as totality, then regardless of possible divergent linguistic formulations there is no real difference between them. And without this difference, Being cannot be said to be historical in character, an implication that in turn collapses the sense in which the ontological difference itself necessarily displays historicism. Thus, if Heidegger maintains that Being is different in different epochs, then he must forgo the possibility that Being can manifest itself as totality in any one epoch; if he maintains the epochal identity of Being, then he loses an essential feature of one of his cardinal ontological notions. And if he insists that the identity / difference rubric can still apply despite this apparent paradox, then the burden rests on the Heideggerian to provide criteria for understanding how identity and difference are to be thought in this crucial context. As we have seen in chapters 3 and 4, however, these criteria may not be as readily available as the present need would seem to demand.

Will there be an ontological difference of some sort if and when the Heideggerian Denken has properly enunciated Being? We would intuitively expect the answer to be in the affirmative. But such intuition may be rooted in metaphysical habit, so it will be necessary to substantiate this conviction from Heidegger's own texts. And reasons can indeed be found, or at least derived, from those texts.

Consider the crucial premise that Being is essentially historical by virtue of its epochal manifestations. This claim is what might be called a transepochal assertion, since this kind of claim presupposes that one can be outside the complete set of epochs in order to recognize that these epochs are both different (in one sense) and identical (in another sense). For if Heidegger's view of Being depended on what could be discerned about Being solely from within whatever historical moment he himself occupied, then there would be no grounds for asserting that Being *must* be *other than* what became manifest to Heidegger as a spokesman for that moment.

It is part of the province of Denken to think the ontological difference. But if Denken receives either its structure or its content (or both) from sources partially rooted in the portion of the history of metaphysics that is the "essential past," then the proper evocation of Being within the ontological difference must retain some essential vestige of that history in order to connect metaphysics with Denken. As a result the transepochal character of Heidegger's own assertions about the history of metaphysics must merge with the products of Denken, whatever those products may be. An historicist continuum of sorts thus joins the history of metaphysics—itself an integrated whole composed of distinct epochs as parts—with the process of thinking Being according to the strict guidelines of Denken.

If this interpretation is sound, then a paradox also arises here, in that Denken would constitute yet another essential phase in this historicist continuum. Furthermore, it should be noted that this paradox appears even if Heidegger's claims about the ontological difference are only heuristic—i.e., necessary to instigate an experience with Being and beings because the sway of history of metaphysics still conceals the proper character of that relation from anyone who attempts to think it. In this case the paradox becomes circumscribed by the fact that the position producing it is only a heuristic stance—thus, the paradox need not pertain to Being once Being has been properly thought. But if the heuristic position is itself beset with paradox, then it will surely be difficult to know how to proceed toward an appropriate experience of Being, given that stable guidelines for measuring the adequacy of that experience will be available only if the heuristic aspect of the paradox is somehow resolved, or at least shown to be capable of resolution.

Let us outline this paradox:

For Heidegger, Being is historical because it is manifested differently in different epochs in the history of metaphysics. We have offered reasons to justify the view that the history of metaphysics and Denken form a continuum of sorts. The question then arises whether the epochal manifestation of Being throughout the history of metaphysics will continue on and into the attempt by Denken to think Being.

If the epochal character of Being continues into the history of Denken, then whatever Denken says about Being will be no less epochally finite than what has been said by all the great evocations of Being contained in the history of metaphysics. Denken will obviously have an essential role to play in the epochal manifestation of Being, but that role is no more (or less) privileged than has been the role of every other epochal manifestation. And when Denken has had its day, then something else may replace it. If, however, the epochal character of Being ceases at some point during the career of Denken, then the products of Denken will not become susceptible to such finitude. But given the epochal structure of the history of metaphysics, how could the epochal character Heidegger finds so essential to metaphysics cease to be essential for Denken?

Two approaches to the resolution of this dilemma appear readily at hand (there may, of course, be others). First, the Heideggerian could maintain that Denken has elicited, or will elicit, the structure of Being at a trans-epochal level. But if the properties of this structure are ascribed to Being, as surely they must, then at least some phase of Being ceases to be epochal—otherwise these properties would have no necessary grounding in Being itself. And if all or even part of Being is nonepochal for Denken, how can Denken be necessarily epochal for metaphysics? Even if the defender of the powers of Denken can show that Denken is somehow more attuned to Being than metaphysical reflection, that defender must still account for this fundamental fluctuation in the structure of Being.

The second approach concerns the sequential aspect of the epochal character of Being. Heidegger has told us that Being always speaks as destiny (*ID*, 117). But are there discernible properties pertaining to the sequential aspect of destiny? In particular, is the sequence necessarily epochal or only contingently epochal? Now if destiny speaks contingently, then it is possible for Being to cease its epochal manifestations and for the results of Denken to avoid epochal variation. Denken would thereby be safeguarded from the vitiating affects of ontological historicism—but at what cost? For if destiny dictates the epochal character of Being only contingently, then Being is not now and never has been *necessarily* epochal. And if Being is destined to cease being epochal for Denken, then why would it not have ceased being epochal for, say, the account of Being presented in the Platonic dialogues? In fact, if the process of destiny is only contingently epochal, then it would have been possible for Being to have become solidified in some determinate and unchanging form at *any* point along the continuum—now a continuum only by accident—of the history of metaphysics.

In order to preserve the epochal character of Being, it seems essential to assume that destiny allows Being to manifest itself as necessarily epochal. If therefore the ontological difference as such is also necessarily epochal, then the necessity generates a form of sameness between the history of metaphysics and Being as thought by Denken. But this sameness in turn establishes a dimension of the ontological difference by which Being displays properties cutting across the continuous epochal shifting of metaphysical utterances. Now these properties cannot be unique to Being in the sense that they are entirely hidden from us; the continuum aspect of the historicist metaphysics of Being requires that at least some part of the "essential past" of metaphysics be preserved in the structure of the ontological difference properly thought. But surely repeating the same moment in the history of metaphysics must result in damaging if not destroying the essential historicist character of Being. Thus, the sameness of the nonhistoricist element of Being seems to admit the possibility that the ontological difference may not be any different from some moment in the continuum of historicist metaphysics. And if part of the history of metaphysics is repeated in this way, then there is no reason why all of that process could not be repeated.

Furthermore, if Being is necessarily epochal throughout the history of metaphysics, then there is no reason to think that it will not also be necessarily epochal for all possible modes of apprehension—including Denken. As a result, the transient character of Denken's own pronouncements about Being in relation to the "true" structure of Being reemerges as a problem of some consequence.

The paradox of the ontological difference with respect to Denken may be summarized as follows: If destiny dictates that Being is necessarily epochal, then Denken is no less epochal than any and all moments in the history of metaphysics; if destiny dictates that Being is only contingently epochal, then it is entirely possible that the "true" character of Being has appeared somewhere in the sequence of epochs constituting the history of metaphysics. If Heidegger preserves the modality of necessity for the epochal character of Being, then this historicism vitiates the products of Denken; if he preserves the products of Denken against such historicism, then he can assert the necessary historicism of Being only by remaining oblivious to the grave internal inconsistency that results. The Heideggerian might object that the application of the contingent/necessary distinction to the notion of destiny in this fundamental ontological sense unavoidably distorts the structure of that notion.[22] But if so, then here again, as in the predication of the notions of identity and difference discussed above, the burden is on the Heideggerian to provide a coherent analysis of the notion of destiny. The paradoxical consequences just sketched seem to compel such an analysis.

H. *Conclusion.* Heidegger's discussion of the ontological difference appears readily susceptible to the generation of paradoxes. But it should be pointed out that Heidegger has anticipated consequences along these lines. At the conclusion of "*Die Onto-Theo-Logisches Verfassung der Metaphysik*," he notes that "everything that results by way of the step back may merely be exploited and absorbed by metaphysics in its own way" (*ID,* 141). Presumably the codification of a string of paradoxes at a high level of generality would exemplify such metaphysical "exploitation."

Despite this real possibility, Heidegger holds out hope that the results of taking the step back will not necessarily be nullified by the pervasive influence of metaphysics. The articulation of that hope will, however, face severe problems. "The difficulty lies in language," Heidegger insists, since "our Western languages are languages of metaphysical thinking, each in its own way" (*ID*, 141). Thus, "the little word 'is,' which speaks everywhere in our language, and tells of Being even where It does not appear expressly, contains the whole destiny of Being" (*ID*, 141). The Heideggerian thinker must somehow become fitted to the destiny of Being by eliciting the structure of the ontological difference from within a medium, language, made recalcitrant by the fact that its origin and development have occurred in the forgetfulness marking Western metaphysics.

But is an appropriate evocation of the ontological difference just a problem of language? Is the Heideggerian project of thinking bedeviled in its own way by the tyranny of language over ontology? The suspicion lingers that it is a matter not simply of locating, or creating, the proper terminology, but of dislodging the entire metaphysical framework that has grounded our various attempts to transcribe reality into coherent and stable conceptual patterns. For surely it is not mere obduracy to maintain that the paradoxes outlined above will and must remain regardless how thoughtfully innovative our language may become. If, therefore, the problem lies elsewhere than in the domain of language (however far-reaching that domain may be understood according to the Heideggerian manner of thinking), then the question becomes whether or not the ontological difference —and, in turn, the entire Heideggerian approach to Being as the temporality of presence—can continue as a legitimate perspective for describing the general features of reality.

However, even if we agree that the complex structure of the Heideggerian ontology must eventually be made to confront some form of metaphysically motivated criticism, we need not insist that the relevant considerations have been accurately detailed in the paradoxes offered in Critique II of this chapter. Yet it is probable that something like this line of scrutiny must be directed at Heidegger's notion of the ontological difference before that notion can assume a status of importance commensurate with the various epochally definitive moments still living in the history of Western metaphysics. We should note at this point that the relatively abstract considerations pertaining to the epochal structure of Being will become more concrete when they reappear in the next and final step on our traversal of Heidegger's ontological way—an interpretation and critique of his one concentrated attempt to thing Being as the temporality of presence. Whether or not a transition from the abstract to the concrete will obviate the difficulties already described remains to be seen.

# CHAPTER 8

# The Structure of Being as Presence (Anwesen)

MARTIN HEIDEGGER DIED IN 1976. IN 1969 A SMALL VOLume entitled *Zur Sache des Denkens* was published. The lead essay in this work was "*Zeit und Sein*" (Time and Being). This essay, twenty-five pages in length, is an expansion of a lecture, and in it Heidegger carries Denken as far as it can go in terms of thinking Being as the temporality of presence. We shall now attempt to analyze and assess this condensed and difficult essay.

This chapter is divided into two sections. Section I is devoted to a fairly detailed reconstruction of the progression of thought throughout the essay. Each of the discussions in Section I begins with an exposition and concludes, whenever appropriate, with brief critical remarks. Section II is an extended commentary focusing on the principal logical and metaphysical factors in the essay's approach to Being as presence. Supplementary passages from other works will be introduced in both Sections when they may assist in clarifying the direction of Heidegger's thinking.

## I

1. "*Zeit und Sein*" begins with a short introduction. Heidegger mentions two pictures by Paul Klee, a poem by Georg Trakl, and some thoughts on theoretical physics by Werner Heisenberg. He then contends that although we would not expect immediate understanding when confronted with these artistic and scientific works, we frequently expect philosophy to provide "useful, practical wisdom." The implication is that this essay will not be useful in any

practical sense; however, it may well be necessary in some more fundamental sense.

This essay is also described as "inevitable but preliminary"; it is an indication of guideposts for further thinking rather than a finalized position. Heidegger's intent is "to say something about the attempt to think Being without regard to its being grounded in terms of beings" (*SD*, 2).[1] For Heidegger, Being is ontologically prior to beings, and he goes so far as to assert that Being may exist without beings, but not vice versa (*WM*, 102). The thinking of Being as separated in this sense is necessitated both by the current status of Being and for determining the unique relation of man—one kind of being—to Being as such. The ontological implications of the distinction between Being and beings in the statement of this attempt are of considerable importance, and they will be examined in Section II. For now, we only note the appearance of the statement in the introduction of the essay.

The introduction concludes with Heidegger insisting that the point of the essay will be understood only if we do not "listen to a series of propositions" but rather follow "the movement of showing (*Zeigen*)."[2] This warning is echoed at the end of the essay. After an extremely condensed development of the notion of appropriation (*Ereignis*), Heidegger concludes by claiming that this notion must not be construed according to canons of metaphysical rightness. In fact since the very intention to overcome metaphysics presupposes a concern for metaphysics, Heidegger asserts that "our task is to cease all overcoming and leave metaphysics to itself." To think about Being in the format Heidegger has just offered his audience "remains itself an obstacle" because "the lecture has spoken merely in propositional statements" (*SD*, 25). And on this somewhat apocalyptic note, the essay ends.

It is important to note that Heidegger has admitted the unavoidable metaphysical residues to be found in what he has attempted to say about Being. Thus, we should appreciate his insistence on the need to follow the "showing" connoted by these propositions rather than their literal—and presumably metaphysical—denotation. If there is some essential difference between these two realms of expression—what can be shown in proper thinking insofar as it can appear through what must be said in discursive language—and if the destination of thinking cannot be expressed in propositional forms, then the most we can expect from this essay is to discern the appropriate ontological direction from the literal character of Heidegger's language.

2. Heidegger asks why time (*Zeit*) and Being (*Sein*) are named together. He indirectly answers this question—the point will be addressed more fully later—by stating that Being has meant "presencing" (*Anwesen*—*SD*, 2) since the dawn of Western thinking until today. Even beings not "in time" exist only in relation to time and are thus made determinate by temporality (*MA*, 182). But how at this ultimate level can the relation between Being and time be thought? Any attempt at such thinking immediately results in a "hopeless tangle of relations." This hopelessness is why Heidegger warns against construing Being as a concept or a category (*SZ*, 3-4).[3] However, Heidegger does admit that, in Being, all relations are other than they are in the region of beings (*HE*, 379); it is vital therefore to keep in mind that Being as such does have relations within it. The problem, of course, will be to approximate the thinking of these relations in a manner different from the ways in which relations have been thought throughout the history of metaphysics.

Heidegger then illustrates some aspects of this tangle. For example, it seems intuitively clear that everything has a time allotted to it. And every thing *is*. But is Being as such a thing? Heidegger states categorically that "Being is not a thing, is not in time," even though "every thing has its time." Similarly, although it is in the nature of time to pass away, time remains as time in the very process of this passing away. Heidegger then states that "to remain means: not to disappear, thus to presence." In general, "Being is not a thing, thus nothing 'temporal'" and "time is not a thing, thus nothing which is."

We should note the sustained use of negation in this initial formulation of the problem. The meaningfulness of the twin denials of thinghood to both Being and time depend implicitly on what "not" is taken to imply. Is Heidegger using "not" in a manner consonant with the sense analyzed in his own earlier thinking on the notion of negation (as discussed in chapter 2 above) or is "not" to be understood in a more thoughtful sense—i.e., less beholden to metaphysical bias? The question is significant at this point in that the precise sense of negation intended here, although not made explicit, will direct our own reflection in determining the difference between time and Being, as well as their mutual determination.

The importance of logical considerations in this regard becomes evident when Heidegger asserts that Being and time determine each other reciprocally, and that Being cannot be spoken of as temporal nor can time be spoken of as a being. For, as thinking reflects on these assertions, "we find ourselves adrift in contradictions" (*widersprechenden Aussagen—SD,* 3). The initial statement of the premises grounding the relation between Being and time seems sound. And yet these premises produce contradictions. If we grant that contradictions should be avoided, the upshot is that the original premises must be reconsidered, assuming that such reconsideration is possible. The air of paradox surrounding the problematic relation is bounded by the notions and principles of logic.

3. What mode of existence should be granted to Being and time if they are fundamentally in question? Being and time are "matters" (*Sache*), Heidegger asserts, as long as "matter" is not understood to mean "something existing" (*Seiendes—SD,* 4). Presumably the denial of existence to both Being and time is intended to safeguard subsequent assertions concerning Being and time from the threat of certain paradoxes, e.g., of the third man sort—self-referential objections based on the fact that Heidegger must assume some sort of ontological character for Being in the very attempt to make claims about what Being "really" is. Whether or not he succeeds in this attempt to disassociate the matters of Being and time from all possible meanings of "is" will be discussed in Section II. The relevant point now is that Heidegger appears to be aware of this kind of difficulty, and has attempted to deflect thinking away from these classically metaphysical objections.

Thinking about Being and thinking about time are, Heidegger says, "presumably" (*vermütlich*) *the* matters of thinking. But it is the relation between these two matters that "holds both issues toward each other." This situation is described as "Being *and* time, time *and* Being" (*SD,* 4—italics in text). Thus, "*Sein und Zeit*" names a task to be thought, not a solution in a book (*HP,* 212). And the alternation between "Being" and "time" emphasizes the essential reversibility of the relation between these two fundamental matters. However, the alternation also illustrates that the possibility of producing such reversibility depends on the principle of commutation, a form of metaphysical rightness proper to that particular logical axiom.

4. In addition to emphasizing the logical reversibility of the Being-time relation, Heidegger also introduces a linguistic consideration to ground his claim that Being and time should not be

construed according to metaphysical standards. Instead of saying "Being is" and "time is," Heidegger suggests that we recall the literalness of the (German) idiom "there is" or "it gives" (*es gibt*—SD, 6). The giving indicated by this idiom is this "unconcealing" (*Entbergen*) in which the "presencing" of Being comes into the open. The metaphysically neutral "it" in this idiom is intended to represent the as yet undetermined nature of Being in relation to temporality. In trying "to bring the It and its giving into view," we shall at least minimize the distortions of metaphysics by allowing the hiddenness of this "it" to emerge as something that "gives" (*gibt*). This appeal to the hidden significance in ordinary language hints at the fact, which Heidegger announces shortly, that authentic Being and time are no more remote from everyday experience than is this idiom. The problem is to attend in the appropriately thoughtful manner to what this language says.

5. Once one has examined the structure of the essay, it becomes clear that at this point Heidegger begins the first of the three phases that comprise the rest of the essay. In the first part, "We shall think Being in order to think It itself into its own element." And in the second part, "We shall think time in order to think it itself into its own element." The third part concerns the relation between Being and time. In a brief paragraph introducing this part, Heidegger states that "in this giving, it becomes apparent how that giving is to be determined which, as a relation (*Verhältnis*), first holds the two toward each other and produces (*er-gibt*) them." This indication points to the third component in the problematic relation, the giving itself, the analysis of which occupies approximately the last fifth of the essay. This analysis is based on the discussion of "appropriation" (*Ereignis*). These three parts are not specifically designated as such in the text, yet the progression of the narrative definitely reveals this pattern of organization.

6. Heidegger now asserts that even in this reformulation of the problem, the giving and the "it" remain "obscure" (*dunkel*—SD, 5). Nonetheless, Heidegger frequently maintains that we never completely lose sight of Being.[4] As an initial step in attempting to think this matter, Heidegger supposes that the "it gives" might emerge more clearly if we consider the transformation of Being found throughout the history of metaphysics (the abstract pinnacle of which is reached in Hegel's *Science of Logic*). But, it might be asked, why should we accept Heidegger's conviction in this regard? Why

must the history of metaphysics be seen as a set of variations on the theme of Being as presence?

7. Heidegger recognizes the problem. He asks: "What gives us the right (*Recht*) to characterize Being as presence?" The answer: It is "too late" (*zu spät*) to ask this question—"The character of Being has long since been decided without our contribution, let alone our merit" (*SD*, 6).[5] The current manifestation of Being—although with a fundamentally hidden significance—occurs most predominantly in modern technology and industry, which, Heidegger asserts, jointly rule the whole earth. And the ontological character of this rule is such that whatever Being may be determined as, man had no say in defining its essential nature. As we shall see, however, man does play a crucial if not decisive role in the specification of Being insofar as Being is presence. Therefore, the sense in which Being can be thought as including a human element must remain an open question at this point.

One problem that should be raised now is why it is "too late" to question whether or not Being is presence. Also, is it meaningful to ask by whom, or by what, Being has been so ordained? If not, then the origin of Being—and, on Heideggerian principles, the nature of Being as well—would verge on the unsayable. We could not know why Being took the form of presence—in fact, we could not even ask why. The question has already been decided by something other than human agency.

The issue here is one of ontological ultimates. As such, this question could be circumvented by affirming that Heidegger can only discern—but cannot demonstrate in any sense—the true nature of Being. The capacity for recognition is controlled by what might be called ontological sensibility, and the results of its exercise should not be assessed according to criteria that can be properly applied only to derivative metaphysical concerns. Notice, however, that even if we assume that Heidegger's sensibilities concerning the peculiar unthought character of Being as a type of temporality are correct, it need not follow that what was determined about Being at the origin of Western metaphysics must hold throughout all epochs of the subsequent history of metaphysics. In order to maintain that contemporary thinking is bound to the origin of Being as presence, the Heideggerian must show that what was revealed about Being at one point in the historical continuum will obtain throughout that continuum. And this premise concerns not only Being as such, but the pervasiveness of Being within history. In short the premise concerns the existence of a mode of sameness defining the entire history of metaphysics.

8. We have been assured that Being as presence appears within and throughout the history of metaphysics. But Being as presence is encountered elsewhere as well. As Heidegger once put the point, we should not separate the content of time from its form ($H$, 61), and in this context he insists that "we perceive (*vernehmen*) presencing in every simply, sufficiently unprejudiced reflection on things of nature and artifacts" (*Vorhandenheit und Zuhandenheit des Seienden* —*SD*, 7). One might question at this point whether Heidegger has strayed beyond the self-imposed limits of his subject matter in this essay, since the types of things just specified are beings and not Being. The point seems to be, however, not *whether* Being is accessible but rather *how* it is accessible, i.e., how the human observer can approach what is "there" in order to experience the authentic Being of this or that particular being.

Heidegger now introduces the important point that absence (*Abwesen*), the ontological counterpart to presence insofar as it refers to the sense in which something is not there, is nonetheless determined by presencing, at times in an uncanny or "unearthly" (*unheimliche*) manner. Here again it will become essential to determine at some point the function of the negational factors at this fundamental ontological level. For if absence is, in fact, the opposite of presence, then how can something be both not present (in absence) and present (in presence) at the same time?

Heidegger's appeal to the notions of "*vorhanden*" and "*zuhanden*," terminology used forty years earlier in *Sein und Zeit*, indicates that he is not entirely displeased with the temporal evocations connoted by these words. However, the relevant point for thinking the structure of Being concerns the proper translation of *vernehmen*. Does it mean "perceive" as a primarily perceptual activity, or should it include an essential mental quality as well? If the former, then Being is bounded by the particularity of individual beings, and Heidegger's anticonceptualism remains consistent with his implicit rejection of types as discussed in chapter 5. If the latter, however, then Being will possess properties that can only be discerned by thinking when its object transcends the particularity of individual beings. In this regard the inclusion of absencing within presencing would seem to imply that *vernehmen* cannot mean just perceiving, for we cannot perceive what is not present to be perceived. This inference may not be conclusive, but it is a sufficient reason to interpret *vernehmen* as at least partially determined by an activity other than perception as normally understood.[6]

Of course, from a more fundamental ontological perspective—and quite apart from the specific function of perceiving—the problem with the close juxtaposition of presencing and absencing is that of preserving the differences between the two, and of recognizing the nature of the element of negation as it pertains to absencing as such. This issue will be addressed in Section II below.

9. In an early work, Heidegger once remarked that we must experience time in order to experience history (*HG*, 110), and the intimacy between time and history is a primary concern in "*Zeit und Sein.*" The historical character of presencing is now recalled as Heidegger lists a series of the ultimate names for Being found throughout the history of metaphysics. Parmenides is again given special attention, just as he was in *Identität und Differenz*. And Heidegger cites his own claim, made in the "Letter on Humanism" (1947), that the "it is" (*esti*) in Parmenides' dictum that "for Being is" remains unthought to this day. Heidegger then reminds us of the essential historical factor involved in the thinking of Being, and the inclusion of a reference to an earlier work of his own indirectly points to the fact that he himself has his own history within the much vaster historical continuum. The origin of thinking in Parmenides and the return to thinking in Heidegger are thus joined in common concern for determining the meaning of Being.

It is essential to note in this regard that although the history of thinking has indicated that the meaning of Being is the meaning of Being thought as presence, Heidegger insists in other works that it would be erroneous to think that Being must *always* be meaningful as presence. It is therefore possible that in the future Being could *not* be presence. This possibility is of considerable importance, and we shall examine some of its implications in Section II below.[7]

10. At this point the actual attempt to think Being begins. The "it gives" (*es gibt*) bestows a giving that Heidegger names "sending" (*schicken*), a term reserved for the kind of giving that is both an extending and a withdrawing. And furthermore, Heidegger claims

that the self-withdrawal and self-bestowal of the giving of Being are "one and the same" (*Ein und das Selbe*—*SG,* 109).[8]

Each of the transformations of Being appearing throughout the history of metaphysics is "destined" (*geschickt*) according to this mode of ontological giving. The history of Being is thus an epochal history, i.e., Being is both held back as well as manifested during a succession of given periods of time. In this ontological and historical oscillation, "the sequence of epochs in the destiny of Being is not accidental, nor can it be calculated as necessary." In fact, the epochs "overlap each other (*überdecken sich*) in their sequence so that the original sending of Being as presence is more and more obscured in different ways" (*SD,* 9). We have examined the sequential aspect of the history of Being already in chapter 7. The point now is that despite the seemingly regressive character of this history, any attempt to think the meaning of Being always "remains bound to the tradition of the epochs of the destiny of Being." Thus, Denken rests within history even as it attempts to move beyond history.

The distinction between necessary and accidental is of venerable metaphysical parentage, and Heidegger's denial of both in this context is an attempt to drive a wedge between these two jointly exhaustive alternatives. Notice, however, that the force of his denial depends on predicating negation of their conjunction—the sequence of epochs is *not* accidental and it is *not* necessary. What then is the relation among the various epochal phases of this sequence, an especially pressing matter when Heidegger himself does not address the issue. Is it possible to think this denial in a meaningful manner?

11. Being has been characterized by its relation to time. Let us now attempt to think time. We can no longer employ the characterizations of time as represented by traditional metaphysics. For example, the present cannot be understood as a "now," with the succession from past through present into future being reduced to a series of evervanishing nows. This approach to thinking time began with Aristotle and remained constant up to and through Kant.[9] Heidegger insists, however, that "the present (*Gegenwart*) in the sense of presence differs so vastly from the present in the sense of the now that the present as presence can in no way be determined in terms of the present as now."[10] Thus, authentic time is "earlier than" every possible "earlier" (*MA,* 184)—the problem is to think

this relation in a manner that, apparently, preserves the relational character of "earlier" and "later" but yet reorients the substance of what is so related.

12. What then is the present as presence? Heidegger says that "to presence means to last (*währen*)." However, lasting is not the same as "mere duration" (*blösses dauern*).[11] At this point Heidegger notes that it is man who perceives a lasting that is characteristic of presence. Only man is "himself present in his own way for everything presencing and absencing" (*allem an- und abwesenden*—SD, 12). In fact, Heidegger insists, man would not be man without the giving of Being as presence.

The distinction between the temporality of presence as lasting and temporality as duration thus depends on the existence of man, who experiences and defines his nature by what is present and what is absent. It seems therefore that the essential ontological contrast between presence and absence depends, at least in part, on the one kind of being that is man. And yet man is himself defined by presence "in his own way" (*auf seine Weise*—SD, 12). At some point, therefore, the joint presence and absence that characterizes Being as such must be differentiated from that one instance of presence on which the distinction between presence and absence depends. Thus, the potential threat posed by the self-referential character of presence reappears when the human element in Being is introduced.

13. Presencing as such always concerns man. And Heidegger contends that even "that which is no longer present presences immediately in its absence" regardless whether that absence is the "not yet present" of the future or the "no longer present" of the past. Presencing comes to us in this way because it is "in itself a reaching" (*in sich ein Reichen*). This reaching possesses a "unity" (*Einheit*), but it is not the unity of bare simultaneity.[12] The unity of presence derives from the sense in which past, present, and future "belong together in the way they offer themselves to one another" (*SD*, 14). What do they offer?—"nothing other than themselves," i.e., the presence that is in each of them. Furthermore, Heidegger adds almost immediately that this unity "opens up what we call time-space" (*Zeit-Raum*), an opening from which "space" (*Raum*) as we usually know it must be thought.

When, in analyzing the notion of time, Heidegger says paradoxically that "time itself is nothing temporal," he is, perhaps, again anticipating objections of a third-man sort. For how can the being of time be temporal in a way such that time and Being are and remain different from one another? Be that as it may, the problem remains of determining sameness and difference with respect to past, present, future—how they are all the same as divisions of temporality and how they are different as distinct phases of a temporality which also, we are now told, grounds space as well. (The sense in which space is related to, or emerges from, the temporality of presence is not developed in the essay, and we shall therefore concentrate our attention on the manifestly temporal features of space-time.)

14. The unity of the three phases of temporality thus continues to require thought, and Heidegger says that the presencing to be thought cannot be attributed to any one of the three temporal dimensions. In fact, "true time is four-dimensional" (*vierdimensional*—*SD*, 16). However, this fourth dimension—the "interplay" (*Zuspiel*) of the three dimensions—is, in the nature of the matter (*Sache*) really the first dimension in that it allows the "nearness" (*Nähe*) of past, present, and future to remain open to one another in the appropriate withdrawal and denial. In a word, "time is not" (*Die Zeit ist nicht*), with the "not" apparently referring to the fact that what grounds the unity and reality of time is a dimension of temporality that cannot be reduced to any one or a combination of the classical divisions of time.[13]

15. Heidegger affirms that "there is no time without man." But then he adds immediately that "time is not the product of man, man is not the product of time."[14] Once again, we note the double use of negation to separate different ontological domains, in this case man and time. But Heidegger is aware that by so divorcing the two, he risks the charge that "It" of the "It gives" (*es gibt*) will be understood as an arbitrary and mysterious source. The nature of the "It" must continue to be thought.[15]

16. At this point in the essay, Heidegger offers an extended discussion, not given in the original lecture, on the problem of discovering language appropriate for such a fundamental ontological inquiry. Thus, if the "It" is thought of as a propositional subject, then the It is "a Being" (*ein Sein*). But then if Being is substituted for It, "It gives Being" becomes "Being gives Being." This substitution reduces to a tautology and therefore is uninformative, at least according to formal logic. However, Heidegger's objection to "Being gives Being" is not that it is tautologous, but that it says that "Being is," and thus returns thinking to the beginning of the lecture.[16] The

appropriate thinking must contend with the possibility that "It gives Being" and "It gives time" are not expressible ontologically in a subject-predicate linguistic form.[17]

17. This linguistic preface clears the way for a development of one of Heidegger's must diffuse notions, a development as important in intent as it is sparse in detail. What determines both, Being and time, in their own nature and as they properly belong together is "appropriation" (*Ereignis*). Now if appropriation is construed as occupying a mode of existence for purposes of grounding Being and time, then, Heidegger claims, we are misrepresenting appropriation. Therefore, Heidegger tells us the way in which appropriation is *not* to be thought. First, it is not an event, distinct from other events, for it is what grounds the possibility of events in the first place; second, it is not a genus of which Being and time are species. For Heidegger, such a conceptual move is "cheap" (*billig*), and he emphasizes that "logical classifications say (*sagen*) nothing here."[18]

18. What then is appropriation? Heidegger offers, "briefly and inadequately," a pair of characterizations peculiar to appropriation. First, appropriation is that which "withdraws what is most fully its own from boundless unconcealedness." Here Heidegger attempts to capture the oscillation essential to Being and time as they both merge and yet remain distinct from one another. Second, in presencing there is the concern which, in "perceiving" (*vernehmen*) and "receiving" (*übernehmen*) it, grants to us "the distinction of being human." And as an important corollary, Heidegger notes that the relation of space to appropriation can only be thought by way of the notion of "place" (*Ort*) as that notion has been developed within the thinking of the fourfold. (Heidegger here cites the essay "*Bauen Wohnen Denken*," one of the principal sources discussed in chapter 5.)[19]

19. But the last word on appropriation has hardly been uttered. Heidegger says that "appropriation neither *is*, nor is appropriation *there*" (*SD*, 24—italics in text). What then can be said? Heidegger puts what can be said as follows: "Appropriation appropriates" (*Das Ereignis ereignet*). To say this is to say "the same in terms of the same about the same." Heidegger readily admits that he is offering, again, a tautologous dictum and that, as such, it will continue to say nothing if "cross-examined by logic." If, however, it is used as a guide for further thinking, then it will be possible to think the "ancient something" that is concealed in the Greek "aletheia" and that

will provide the key to the thinking of authentic temporality and thus of Being as such.[20]

20. Finally, Heidegger repeats that the purpose of the essay has been an attempt to think Being without regard to beings by looking through "authentic" (*eigentliche*) time. To think Being without beings is to think without taking metaphysics into account, which now no longer need be overcome, but can be left to itself. For metaphysics has left unthought its own grounding in time (*WD,* 40), and thus offers no guidance in determining the thinking of the Being of beings as Being is in itself. To think Being properly, we must think the appropriation of Being and time. Heidegger has started us on the way toward such thinking through the hints offered in "*Zeit und Sein.*"

II

Many themes worthy of thoughtful consideration are introduced in "*Zeit und Sein.*" However, some of these themes are more fundamental than others, especially when considered from the standpoint established by the ontological concern for thinking the meaning of Being as the temporality of presence. And, as we shall see, it is precisely the most fundamental matters that are the most problematic. The questions raised in the following critique are based on the supposition that the thinking Heidegger offers in this essay must eventually be placed in apposition to a number of classic metaphysical issues. In this respect the interpretive strategy here at the close of our traversal of Heidegger's way mirrors the critical stance adopted at the beginning of our investigation. We argued there that the notions and principles of formal logic must be examined with special care in order to sanction the possibility that Denken may penetrate this formality and glimpse a more basic ontological dimension. We now have reached a similar point in our attempt to understand Heidegger's own thinking on Being. For until that thinking has been confronted with metaphysical notions of similar or equivalent generality, it will not be possible to determine the extent to which the position Heidegger develops in "*Zeit und Sein*" can be considered the same as and different from metaphysical thought.

The themes to be discussed in Section II revolve around the notions of unity, negation, and simultaneity, the latter as a kind of sameness. The relevance of these notions for metaphysics and logic may be outlined as follows: A being must have unity before it can be differentiated as possessing properties and thereby be made determinate. Furthermore, a propositional form (e.g., 'S is P') must allow for the possibility that a given instantiation of that form will possess one and only one meaning; for if all instances of a propositional form are intrinsically ambiguous, then the distinction between propositional truth and falsity is eliminated and contradiction, which depends on this distinction, is impossible. Once unified, a being is the metaphysical product of negation by virtue of the fact that it has been made determinate as this being and not that being; analogously, a proposition must be capable of being negated in order to reflect the fundamental difference between what the proposition refers to and what it does not refer to. Finally, the possibility that two beings or events can coexist and yet be different from one another implies that these beings or events are simultaneous. The interrelation of beings in this respect suggest that simultaneity as such must be defined (an especially crucial factor if the ontology in question is based on temporality). Similarly, the assertion that a given determinate being cannot both possess and not possess the same property "at the same time" presupposes that the notion of simultaneity as it relates to distinct beings can also apply to any one being with respect to contradictory propositions about that being.

A careful examination of *"Zeit und Sein"* reveals that a critical application of this three-fold interpretive perspective would include a minimal imposition of metaphysical categories, since all three notions implicitly ground what is explicitly said in the essay—and none of the three is mentioned as itself problematic.[21] Furthermore, although this implicit grounding is concerned more with Being than with language about Being, we shall nonetheless see the linguistic dimension enter the discussion at several key junctures.

  a. *Unity.* There is unity in Being as such, in contradistinction to the unity of the class of beings, and there is unity in Being as opposed to the unity of time. The "It" of the "It gives" in Heidegger's reformulation of the approach to Being must also have unity, otherwise it could not give Being in a sense that would allow Being to be thought as one. There is unity in the appearances of Being throughout the history of metaphysics, for if there were not, then it would not be possible for Heidegger to assert that Being is one as the temporality of presence throughout this history. There is also unity in temporality insofar as Heidegger can predicate "lasting," "lingering," "preserving," etc., of temporality as such; the fact that the process factor of temporality is emphasized does not obviate the need to think accurately the unity of that process. And finally, there must be a kind of unity in the process whereby "Appropriation appropriates" in order to guarantee that appropriation cannot be reduced to something other than itself.

b. *Negation.* We have already noted in Section I Heidegger's frequent use of negation as a guideline for indicating the direction of thinking. Thus, Being is not a thing, nor is time something temporal; the sequence of metaphysical epochs is neither necessary nor contingent; and absencing involves an essential "not yet" and "no longer." But there are also more muted introductions of negation, no less important for being understated. We are told, for example, that to think appropriation is not something expressible in propositional forms; and, perhaps most decisively of all, that Being may not always be the temporality of presence, a possibility that implies as much about negation as it does about Being.

c. *Simultaneity.* If Being remains the same throughout the history of metaphysics, then from the standpoint of temporality the unity of Being becomes a kind of simultaneity. Furthermore, the unity of the three standard divisions of time as given by the fourth dimension results in a simultaneity that gathers all four dimensions into one. Finally, insofar as Being is instantiated in a being perceived as *vorhanden* or *zuhanden*, then the confluence of the four dimensions of time must again result in a type of simultaneity, both within any one individual being and also between that being and every other coexisting being.

The fact that Heidegger himself does not dwell upon any of these three notions does not tell against our present concern; what is relevant is the fact that any attempt to rethink the Heideggerian approach to Being will entail the introduction of these notions as a constitutive phase of the process of rethinking. This task will be taken up in the following critical discussion, which analyzes the main aspects of the structure of Being as presence. And this discussion should not be looked on as an illicit resumption of biased metaphysics; it contains thinking that is in fact directed more toward the complexities of the matters at hand than is the literal expression of that thinking found in the text of "*Zeit und Sein.*"

The analyses of Section II are divided into three parts: The Appropriation of Being and Time, Being as Presence, and The Ontological Difference between Being and beings.

## THE APPROPRIATION OF BEING AND TIME

In "*Zeit und Sein,*" Heidegger concludes his brief discussion of the substantive character of appropriation by affirming that all that can be said is "Appropriation appropriates." If considered formally this claim seems redundant. But its apparent redundancy exists only as long as we linger within sterile logical notions of identity. In fact, we have seen that in a part of the essay not included in the original lecture, Heidegger himself offers a tentative characterization of appropriation in terms of the self-withdrawal and self-revelation of time and the concern for time by man as a self-defining activity for man. Heidegger also lists the various elements constituting appropriation—Being, time, man, and the distinctive and elusive "belonging" that unites all these elements into something of absolutely fundamental character. The unity of appropriation remains to be discovered in a way which guarantees that the various differences among its constitutive elements may be preserved—e.g., so we can understand how Being is *not* time even while each element remains a matter nonetheless made proper only in relation to one another.

If, however, the elements of appropriation are themselves subjected to critical scrutiny according to the guidelines already suggested, then it may be possible to indicate, at least provisionally, how the structure of appropriation must be thought in order to accomodate the complexities intrinsic to these elements. We have seen Heidegger assert that to say "Appropriation appropriates" is to say "the same in terms of the same about the same." But if, as Heidegger maintains elsewhere, sameness holds apart differences as widely as possible, then we can initiate at least one essential phase of the thinking of the sameness proper to appropriation by analyzing its various parts in terms of the differences they bear to one another from within the sameness of appropriation. In this way we could make a start toward determining the proper structure of the unity, negation, and simultaneity that appropriation will doubtless manifest once it is a matter properly thought.

In view of Heidegger's concerted emphasis on the importance of appropriation in this essay, the conclusion just reached—i.e., the need to think further about the elements of appropriation rather than about appropriation as such—may appear somewhat anticlimactic. But if we examine what Heidegger himself has provided in the essay, then it seems that the burden is more on the Heideggerian to develop the notion of appropriation than it is on the student of

Heidegger to question how such development is possible, given the stipulated ontological comprehensiveness of appropriation. Thus, will concurrent self-revealing and self-concealing assume a form within appropriation that is totally distinct from any other sense in which it is currently possible to formulate such properties? And must the concernful activity of human nature within appropriation be defined in a totally different way from concern that is thought in any other context? If the answer to these questions is only a qualified yes, then the problem of thinking these elements within that more inclusive whole that is appropriation will require—but of course will not be restricted to—the type of preliminary analysis undertaken in this critique. It seems, therefore, that even appropriation, the speculative apex of the Heideggerian ontology, cannot be completely severed from its metaphysical heritage. Only by determining the significance of the constituted parts of appropriation as they have been presented already in "*Zeit und Sein*" can we be led into a measure of awareness for thinking the structure of the notion as a whole.

BEING AS PRESENCE

1. Can Being be stipulated as temporality? The answer to this question is of considerable importance in terms of directing an assessment of the most fundamental level of Heidegger's ontology. We may begin by recalling Aristotle's claim in the *Metaphysics* that "being falls immediately into genera" (1004a5). These genera differ from one another, and in several important senses they are not reducible to one another. With this essential differentiation of Being in mind, we must ask how Being can be *exhaustively* described by notions of temporality. Heidegger has insisted that all principles of ontology are temporal (*GP*, 460). It seems then that the Heideggerian must either deny that there are any ontological properties other than those defined by Being as temporality, or be able to show how all apparently nontemporal predicates of extreme generality (e.g., living and nonliving, potential and actual, etc.) are reducible to and explainable by the tripartite structure of temporality.

2. Let us assume that Being can in fact be exhaustively described by temporality understood in Heidegger's sense. This temporality includes a sameness derived from its tripartite structure. Now if such sameness follows the technical sense of sameness that Heidegger has himself put forth elsewhere, then there is necessarily

difference within sameness. And, as we have seen, there is difference within Being—Being is tripartite, or, perhaps more accurately, quaternal. But if there is difference at this fundamental level, how can there also be unity? To what common aspect of the divisions of Being as temporality could the Heideggerian appeal to justify the claim that Being as such has unity ascribable in one specific sense?

Heidegger's difficulties in expressing that unity may be stated as follows: He has appealed to a "lighting" and to a "reaching" and to a "giving" in his explanations for the dynamic quality proper to Being as such. But it is difficult to construe these terms as anything other than metaphors to suggest how, in more traditional terminology, the many are one.[22] Heidegger has also appealed to the notion of "preserving." But, again, to state that what is essential to temporality represented as past-present-future must be preserved in presence does not reveal the difference between a metaphysical formulation and Heidegger's ontological reformulation. For example, if time as presence "preserves" time as past by allowing the past to "light" and "reach" its way into the present, then how does the pastness of past time become the present of present time? To pose the problem in this way prejudges the matter in a sense, for it suggests that the difference between past and present may be expressible by reference to something like a point in what is apparently a flux-like continuum, but the general shape of the problem is at least made visible by setting it up in this fashion. The same question can be brought to bear on that property of presence Heidegger names as "lingering" (*Weilen*). "Lingering" has a certain quality of temporal indefiniteness that Heidegger seems to find relevant to the nature of presence, but once again its strength in this respect is its weakness as far as providing guidelines that distinguish among the various divisions of temporality.

3. One might further argue that Heidegger's derivation of the essential phase of Being—its concurrent self-revealing and self-concealing—ultimately depends on the "givenness" of the fact that the history of metaphysics is marked by profound diversification. In a situation lacking this rich differentiation in metaphysical positions, there would be no reason to think that some one given destined revelation of Being could not completely exhaust Being. Thus, the question is whether the differences found within the history of metaphysics eventuate from a legitimate ontological source or whether they are derived from the simple fact that great philos-

ophers have different perspectives on the beings they are attempting to think. Has Heidegger given sufficient reasons to justify the belief in a destiny as the source of Being's diverse manifestations? If not, then Heidegger has generated a property—simultaneous self-revealing and self-concealing—that need not be thought as part of the appropriation of Being for the simple reason that it is a contingent consequence of the activity of that one being who is the spokesman of Being.

4. Let us assume that the differentiation of Being as presence can yield a comprehensible sense of unity. If Being, as unified, is temporally conditioned, then the unity of Being as such may be described as a form of simultaneity. But if simultaneity belongs to Being, then Being is always simultaneous insofar as it is always presence. However, Heidegger has admitted that it is possible for Being as such to change, i.e., to become something other than the temporality of presence. Now if Being can become something other than presence, then Being could, as one possibility, be atemporal. But now can Being both be presence and not be presence? Only if Being is itself historical, i.e., changing through history. Notice, however, that whatever its specification may be as determined through the passing of history, Being must still evidence some mode of existence. Therefore, the real burden of Denken would be not, as Heidegger maintains throughout his entire corpus, to think Being as presence. The real burden would be to think that even more fundamental ontological dimension which grounds *both* the reality of Being as presence *and* the possibility that Being may not be presence. The notion of possibility thus becomes just as important in our discussion concerning Being as presence as it was, in chapter 7, for Heidegger's understanding of the epochal manifestations of Being in history. Furthermore, the nature of the negation that underlies the possibility that Being may not be presence must be given additional consideration in order that the evident historical character of Being as a medley of differences can be thought according to ontological propriety.

THE ONTOLOGICAL DIFFERENCE BETWEEN BEING AND BEINGS

Even if Heidegger is correct in asserting that temporality of a distinctive sort is the fundamental ground of Being, it remains to be seen whether this ground can be differentiated in a manner responsive to the multiform phenomena that are determined, as beings, by their relation to Being. Ontological vision of considerable penetration is required to discern the nature of Being as such; however, the matter of distinguishing between Being and beings, as well as distinguishing between different beings, is no less essential to an ontology and no less a product of correct vision.

Issues derived from the latter concerns are not addressed in "*Zeit und Sein*," and in a sense they need not be, given the explicitly circumscribed scope of Heidegger's ontological inquiry. However, at some point the implications of Heidegger's thinking on Being as such must be considered as they pertain to beings, since the ontological difference requires something on the order of mutual entailment in this regard. And, after all, Heidegger himself has introduced the distinction between *zuhanden* and *vorhanden*, characteristics that, although referring ultimately to beings in their Being, nonetheless incorporate the ontological level of beings. Heidegger once described the phrase "the presence of something" as "empty and abstract;"—but then he quickly added—"and yet not" (*AM*, 179). In our attempt to think presence with respect to individuated beings, we will perhaps gain some insight into either the sense in which presence is indeed "empty and abstract" or the way in which such an approach to Being offers new and vital insights into the nature of beings.

We shall now trace in detail some of the relevant implications concerning unity, negation, and simultaneity as they pertain to the structure of the ontological difference.

*Unity.* If Being is presence and if presence is irreducibly tripartite, then it seems that unity can be predicated of Being only if this tripartite characteristic is itself subjected to a form of abstraction. And the same kind of abstraction must apply to the ascription of unity to a given being, for in its own way each being is made determinate by its relation to Being as such. Accordingly, when unity is predicated of a being, then unity must refer to the being's distinctive interplay among the three principal dimensions of presence—past, present, future—and to the grounding fourth dimension that allows them to play into one another. The unity of a determinate being, therefore, must be understood not as a mere synonym for undifferentiated oneness, but as a gathering of different temporal dimensions into *one* whole.

The necessary ontological condition for the predication of unity to an individuated being is that a being must exist in presence. Now all beings will either exist in the present or in relation to the present. A being may exist in the past but not in the present, just as a being may exist neither in the past nor in the present but be quite real in its futurity. But a being that once existed in the past still exists as past even if it does not exist in the present. And insofar as it *is* as past, it is determinate and thus unity is predicable of it. The same considerations hold for a being that does not exist in the present but that will exist in the future. Beings presently existing exhibit all three dimensions of temporality, since the present is continuously becoming the past and anticipating the future. Therefore, in this context the notion of unity must be interpreted on the basis of the ontological fact that an existing being is differentiated within the interplay of the three dimensions of presence.

Unity cannot be simply a function of presence insofar as presence is in flux in the present, for this appeal to a single temporal dimension would exclude past and future beings not existent in the present. We have inferred that such beings are still determinate, and can have unity predicated of them by virtue of the primordially tripartite character of presence. In sum, unity may be understood as that ontological property which designates whatever mode of temporality determines the being with respect to the present. Unity then becomes a relational notion, an ontological consequence entailed by the essential differentiation in Being itself. If we grant for the moment that this kind of relation can serve as a ground for unity, then the question becomes whether this approach to unity can be maintained once we continue to think other notions of equivalent generality.

*Negation.* Perhaps the most distinctive feature of this notion of unity is that its predication presupposes a certain differentiation derived from the primordially tripartite character of Being as presence. Thus, in the ontology of presence, unity will always mean three-in-one rather than a bare indeterminate oneness. An analogous differentiation must be proper to negation insofar as negation is part of the structure of Being. We see this differentiation become essential to negation if we assume, with Heidegger, that at some point Being and beings are interdependent, and that a determinate being both *is* and *is not*. Now if all properties of a being derive from

Being, then Being itself must contain the principles of differentiation by which any given being is what it is and is not what it is not. But Being is the temporality of presence. It follows that negation as such cannot be sheer otherness, a neutral and unspecified difference between beings. Negation is and must be defined in relation to Being as the temporality of presence.

The most promising direction for such specification lies in the necessary difference between any two dimensions of presence—the past is *not* the present, the present is *not* the future, the future is *not* the past. This series of related differences, essential to the structure of Being as presence, must also belong to the determination of any given being in relation to Being. Therefore, let us posit that negation is difference determined by that otherness constituted within the interplay of the dimensions of presence.

But if this introductory analysis is aimed in the right direction, then it is difficult to see how this specification of negation can avoid a crucial difficulty. The difficulty emerges from the lack of appropriate reference points within the flux of time as the totality of time determines beings to be what they are. If each individual being is determined by a distinctive past-present-future mode of temporality, then such reference points become necessary in order to mark the limits between different beings. Without these points of reference, all beings are the same because of the sense in which each is determined as a being within the temporal flux of the totality of Being as such. Heidegger himself has said that not everything comes to presence in the same way (*WD*, 143). How then can individual beings constituted as such by presence be said to differ from one another?

Let us illustrate this objection with two examples. First, if being A is in presence only by virtue of its pastness (i.e., it no longer presently exists) and being B is in presence only by virtue of its futurity (i.e., it does not yet exist in the present), then A and B may be said to be distinct by virtue of the negation which has been generated from the fact that pastness is not futurity and the fact that neither the past nor the future is the present. In this case negation defined by the interplay of the three dimensions of presence seems, at first glance, to provide for the differentiation of beings that are distinct from one another in the sense just stipulated.

But, it can be shown, this differentiation is only apparent. Being A can be said to be past and not present only if that being as such and in its entirety is past and not present. For if some part of A is both past and present, then it is false to say that A as a whole is past and not present. The problem arises when we ask whether A as a whole (i.e., as past) can be made determinate *solely* by virtue of temporality as that temporality is differentiated within the domain of beings. But it seems that A cannot be made determinate in this way. For how can A be defined as past and not present if its pastness is not designated in relation to something other than itself? How can B be defined as futural and not present unless its futurity is designated in relation to something other than itself? Without such additional designation, how could the ascription of pastness and futurity be meaningful? How can pastness—or any other temporal dimension of presence— be designated as *the* ontological source of the determination of something unless that something is also defined in relation to something other than itself on the same ontological level, i.e., to something from which pastness can be generated as a temporal dimension distinctively different from the present and from futurity?

Furthermore, if it is the case that one temporal dimension of a (putatively) determinate being does require additional specification in terms of something other than that dimension, it is evident that this requirement obtains for all three temporal dimensions. For the significance of any one temporal dimension with respect to a determinate being depends on the relation between that dimension and the other two (or three) dimensions.

For example, the meaning of predicating pastness to a being depends on how that being exists in relation to that pastness. Is it past and no longer present or is it both past and present? Thus, there is a necessary interdependence between the past as such and something other than the past. What is this something other? The required specification cannot be generated simply by appealing to additional temporal discriminations; i.e., it will not be sufficient to assert that the difference between pastness and futurity is the temporal distance, so to speak, between these two dimensions. This assertion is unpersuasive because there would be no reason to suspect that, in fact, there *is* a difference between pastness as such and futurity as such unless these two ontological specifications are located within a region of being that would permit the recognition of such a difference. And clearly this region of being must itself be other than the region that grounds pastness and futurity, for if it is the same, then there can be no real difference between this proposed region of being and that region of being exemplified by pastness and futurity. Therefore, it seems that the "something other than itself" required to differentiate any one temporal dimension from any other temporal dimension must be itself nontemporal.

The first example considered the possibility that negation could be generated from the fact that two beings were determined by two different dimensions of presence. It has been argued that it could not be so generated. The second example also illustrates this impossibility, perhaps even more vividly. In this case consider two different beings, C and D, which both exist within the same dimension of presence, e.g., the present. Negation is obviously essential here in order to indicate that C is not D. But if negation is defined by otherness between or among temporal dimensions *as such*, then it is impossible to say that C is not D. The "not" in this case refers to a difference obtaining within one and the same temporal dimension. And in order to show difference between beings that have been determined by the same temporal dimension, negation must be defined by some kind of differentiation proper to the temporality of that dimension as such. If this differentiation is itself of temporal specification, then we are compelled to maintain apparently contradictory claims, e.g., that the present is both present to itself and not present to itself. In this context such a conjunction could mean only that the present, since it must be the source of otherness, is both past and future at the same time that it is the present. However, if we make such claims with a view toward preserving relevant aspects of negation, then all differences between and among the dimensions of the present, the past, and the future would be lost. In general, therefore, all attempts at locating the required source of differentiation for negation from within the structure of temporality are seemingly impossible, not merely because they are logically incompatible, but because they violate the explicitly stated principles of the ontology of presence.

Nevertheless, negation must be preserved; without negation there can be no differentiation of beings and no contradiction in propositions about beings. Since the negation required for differentiation between beings in the same temporal dimension (our second example) cannot be defined in terms of temporality, it must be defined in terms of nontemporal factors. Only with such a definition will it be possible to distinguish by negation between two beings that are different but that also exist in the same dimension of presence. Thus, both the first and the second examples point the same way. We may conclude, at least provisionally, that negation defined strictly by the principles of Being as presence does not appear to possess the proper range of differentiation for performing the functions that it must perform in both ontology and logic.

*Simultaneity.* As we have seen, the qualification "at the same time" is essential to both the formal and material formulations of the principle of contradiction. But the notion of simultaneity is complex and problematic. Heidegger himself once questioned how it is possible for two beings to exist at the same time (*GP,* 335). Simultaneity is therefore an essentially crucial pivot for the ontology of presence insofar as it provides the ground for logical principles. We shall see, however, that this notion will be just as difficult to define satisfactorily as is the notion of negation. Since the source of the requisite sameness must be located purely in terms of temporality, it might be suggested that simultaneity refers to the sameness that is found *within any one* of the three dimensions of presence. Simultaneity can then be predicated of two beings whenever they are each determined within the same dimension of presence; for example, two beings will be simultaneous if they coexist in the past even if either or both beings no longer exist in the present. Furthermore, since one dimension is different from another dimension, it follows that the simultaneity of two past beings no longer present is not the same as the simultaneity of two present beings. In general, then, simultaneity may always be specified with respect to one of the three dimensions of presence.

Further reflection reveals, however, that simultaneity understood from this perspective requires the articulation of an additional property within the structure of each such dimension. Let us recall that each dimension must itself be construed as a sort of continuum in order to allow the differentiation required for simultaneity to occur within that temporal sameness. Thus, the past has a continuum proper to itself as past and distinct from the continuum of the present. Earlier we attempted to define negation by appealing to differentiation occurring *between* any two dimensions of presence; now, however, we are attempting to define simultaneity by the sameness and difference found *within* the continuum proper to any one dimension of presence. However, the problems that arose concerning the specification of negation also occur, *mutatis mutandis*, with respect to simultaneity.

In this case the problems derive from the continuum factor within each temporal dimension. If simultaneity is based on the fact that each dimension is a continuum somehow different from the continua of the other two dimensions, then the three dimensions *qua* continua must nonetheless interrelate in order to constitute presence as such. But how is the continuum-aspect of each dimension to be construed in order that any one continuum provide the requisite source of differentiation? If we adhere strictly to the principles of Being as presence, the answer must be specified in terms of temporal properties. However, such strict adherence leads directly to problems of a self-referential sort. For if each dimension is itself a continuum of unique duration, and if this duration is temporal according to the only discriminations available—past, present, future —then the duration of any one dimension is constituted by the same temporal triplicity proper to the totality of presence. Thus, the properties that belong to presence as the unity of three distinct temporal dimensions become indistinguishable from the properties that belong to each of these three dimensions taken separately. What then is the difference between the lingering proper to any one dimension and the lingering of Being as such?

Furthermore, if the ontology of presence does admit types into its structure, this additional factor merely compounds the problem. For what then would account for the difference between the presence of an instance of a type and the presence of the type as such? And, in the same vein, what would account for the difference between the presence of one type and the presence of another type? We have inferred that each continuum must somehow produce the source of a temporal sameness and difference in order to ground the notion of simultaneity with respect to that continuum. But if Being as such is the interplay of the past, the present, and the future, and if each member of this triplet is itself an interplay of past-present-future, then what is the difference between that pastness which, as a single dimension, is a constituent of Being and the secondary but nonetheless essential pastness that is itself part of that dimension?

The self-referential aspects of the problem may be illustrated as follows. The sameness and difference proper to each dimension as such will be either identical to or other than the sameness and difference proper to presence as a whole. If the sameness and difference proper to the continuum of each dimension as part of presence is itself identical to the sameness and difference proper to presence as such, then there is no real distinction between the lingering of any one dimension and the lingering of presence (the putative unity of all dimensions). Notice also that the introduction of a fourth dimension again only compounds the problem; for if the fourth dimension is itself temporal in some sense of temporality specified by the past-present-future rubric, then the fact that there are four parts and not three is not decisive and the same question can be asked. The number of temporal differentiations does not matter—what matters is how any one dimension can be part of a whole and yet, somehow, also incorporate the totality of that whole within itself.

Without appropriate differentiation between the lingering of dimension as part and the lingering of presence as whole, the implication is either that all beings are always simultaneous or that simultaneity can never legitimately be predicated of any two beings. Both conclusions are untenable, for each in its own way destroys the meaning of simultaneity. If, on the other hand, there is a distinction between the sameness and difference of a given continuum and the sameness and difference of presence as such, then this distinction must be accounted for by temporal differentiations for which the vocabulary has yet to be articulated. We seem faced with a serious dilemma: If simultaneity is to be preserved, then the principles of Being as presence have been inadequately stated; if these principles have been adequately stated, then to all appearances simultaneity cannot be formulated on the basis of these principles.

A second problem also concerns the differentiation of simultaneous beings. In general, two beings are said to be simultaneous if, regardless of the extent to which they differ from one another, they are the same with respect to coexistence on one temporal plane. To say that two beings are simultaneous is not to say that these two beings are identical, but only that they share the same temporal specification. Therefore, the predication of simultaneity presupposes that the two simultaneous beings are different from one another. Simultaneity can be predicated of two beings only on condition that there is at least one property, a property necessarily other than that of simultaneity itself, that distinguishes the two beings from one another.

If this argument is sound, then its conclusion poses a serious objection to the ontology of presence. Put bluntly, it seems impossible for the Heideggerian to maintain that different beings can be simultaneous. First, if two beings are said to be different from one another, and if each being is determined by its own distinctive interplay of past-present-future, then the ground of their differentiation depends on a difference in their respective exemplifications of temporality. How then can beings determined as different by virtue of temporality also be said to be the same (i.e., simultaneous) by virtue of temporality? If, second, two beings are said to be simultaneous, then the additional property that specifies their difference will be either temporal or nontemporal in character. If that property turns out to be nontemporal, then of course simultaneity cannot be defined in conjunction with that property, for definitional conjunction of this sort would violate the temporality that exclusively constitutes Being as presence. The other alternative must therefore be adopted. One might then attempt to argue that two simultaneous beings could be determined as different from one another by virtue of a difference in the duration of their pasts—e.g., two beings can still be simultaneous when one being has existed longer in the past than the other being. On this interpretation a locus of differentiation would have been specified within the structure of Being as presence.

But it is not difficult to show that this attempt is also inadequate. First, if this characteristic of temporality were claimed as a sufficient condition for differentiation, then in fact there would be no differentiation between two distinct beings which are simultaneous in that case where both beings originated at the same time, for their respective pasts would be identical in duration. And, second, even if two beings do have different temporal points of origin, then one being cannot be specified simply as "older than" the other without also and necessarily determining the respect in which this specification has been determined, i.e., by indicating whatever in the older being generates the possibility of discerning that it is older than something other than itself. This respect cannot be defined purely in temporal terms, for such definition would be logically circular. Therefore, this respect must be specified in terms of a nontemporal property. But, again, nontemporal specification of this sort is incompatible with the principles of the ontology of presence. It seems then that simultaneity cannot be adequately formulated. For two beings that coexist "at the same time" will become indistinguishable from one another if the sameness of this time cannot be specified in relation to something other than that sameness, i.e., to something nontemporal.

A brief recapitulation. We allowed the three-in-one aspect of the temporality of presence to signify an intelligible sense of unity. However, we then saw that bringing this sense to bear on negation and simultaneity, notions of equivalent generality and of commensurate importance, resulted in a series of problems and paradoxes. The implication is that the unity of Being has not yet been thought properly in relation to the explicit structure of Being.

What lesson can be learned from this implication? At *Parmenides* 135e, Socrates is advised to undergo severe training in what the world calls "idle talk" and condemns as "useless." His mentor, Parmenides, then launches into what is arguably the most searching analysis of unity ever thought in Western metaphysics. The Heideggerian may consider such thinking "idle talk" and condemn it as "useless." Such talk is, after all, merely metaphysics. But the discussion in this chapter has indicated that perhaps there remains more to this kind of thinking than one might initially suspect. The point is not that Plato bests Heidegger in the arena of ontology. The point is simply that Plato as a metaphysician, and also metaphysics in general, may dwell on the same ontological heights as the thinking of the temporality of presence. If so, then our brief journey through the speculative terrain of unity, negation, and simultaneity may perhaps have been something more than idle talk.

Part I of this study was devoted to a critical exposition of Heidegger's ontological approach to logic, and we may conclude this chapter by restating those results within the more expansive ontological context established by the inquiries pursued in Part II of the study.

We have seen how Aristotle formulated the principle of contradiction without reference to the temporality of Being as presented through the original meaning of *logos*. The subsequent history of metaphysics, to the extent that it took notice of the presuppositions of logical principles, perpetuated this Aristotelian exclusion in different ways. The contemporary proliferation of forms of metaphysics executed within the framework of a purely formal symbolic logic merely adds to the concealment of Being as presence. For Heidegger, the very structure of Being has dictated that logical principles are necessarily ontological and that the structure of that ontology depends on the construal of Being as the temporality of presence. If the principles of logic are not explicitly articulated in light of this fundamental ontological vision, then these principles remain separated from that vision, inhabiting a purely regulative and formal domain.

But if Heidegger is correct in his exclusive designation of Being, i.e., if the formal character of contradiction and all other logical principles can be substantiated only by the ontology of presence, then all philosophers who abide by the principle of contradiction should also endorse that ontology. Presumably all philosophers do so abide; therefore, all philosophers—including all formal logicians—are fundamentally Heideggerians, whether they know it or not, whether they would or would not be happy with this very definite description. For if Being must be univocally described by a single property or by attributes grounded in that property—and, on Heidegger's account, all derived from the temporality of presence—then logical principles that, by virtue of a putative formality, are compatible with alternative accounts of Being will tend to obscure the essential nature of Being. The more intransigently one holds to the belief that the processes of philosophical thought are guided by a purely formal conception of contradiction, the more likely that one's pursuit of philosophy will become less ontologically rigorous precisely because the essential property of Being will disappear within the universal indifference of this most crucial logical principle.

However, the radical character of Heidegger's ontological position compels questioning. It is a fact, and perhaps not an accidental fact, that ontological visions differ in content. If Heidegger's concerns with logic were to be adopted by other protagonists of ontology, then the resulting different visions would substantiate the principles of logic in different ways. Furthermore, at least some ontologies would elect to leave logic precisely as a set of formal axioms completely indifferent to the substance of those ontologies. Now if it is true that no discernible standard can be agreed on for deciding whether any one ontology is more adequate than any other, then there is good pragmatic reason to allow logical principles to remain purely formal, and without specific ontological substance. Therefore, it seems that Heidegger's first claim, that logical principles are necessarily ontological, need not be granted. But even if it is granted, we need not admit that the first claim must be followed by Heidegger's second claim, that the nature of this ontology must be grounded in the temporality of presence. For the adequacy of the second claim rests both on the correctness of Heidegger's reading of early Greek language and thought, and, more importantly, on the truth of the premise that the contemporary nature of Being is necessarily whatever was spoken about Being at the origin of reflective attempts to discern that nature. Finally, even if the Heideggerian stipulation of Being as presence does prove to be impervious to these potential criticisms, the problems that emerged in the analyses of notions fundamental to the differentiation of presence—those notions studied in chapters 5 through 7 above—raise serious internal difficulties as far as adopting that position is concerned.

Heidegger never ceased to maintain that the *question* of the meaning of Being is the most fundamental and most important philosophical problem. Therefore, if contradiction and all other logical principles do have ontological significance, then it seems incumbent on the philosopher to continue questioning the substantiation of the principles of logic even beyond the point at which these principles can be accurately specified through Heidegger's own statement of the ontology of presence. For we may assume that any attempt at the articulation of Being carries with it an awareness that the profundity of this particular subject matter will surpass the results of what we have learned about Being from that attempt. If this attitude of thoughtful humility is appropriate in these matters, then Heidegger's stipulation that Being is the temporality of presence represents the locus for further questioning rather than an omega point at which both the adequate substantiation of the principles of formal logic and the answers to all other ontological problems are readily at hand.

# Conclusion

OUR AGE FINDS ITSELF SWIRLING IN FREELY BESTOWED superlatives. Evaluations of all sorts punctuate a variety of human endeavors, and those so caught up in the times may therefore be tempted to accord to Heidegger the epithet "the most important philosopher of the century." In the end, of course, the putative winner of such a contest will depend on one's philosophical preferences, and it would doubtless be possible to nominate several other individuals for this lofty position. But surely all such evaluations are of little worth, since the real significance of a philosopher can be determined only by the extent to which that philosopher influences philosophers, and the current of life in general, in subsequent ages. And no philosophical figure who has flourished in this century, regardless of present status, can be judged as incontestably preeminent in this regard for the simple reason that the future is not the present.

Heidegger's place in such a hierarchical ranking may nonetheless be privileged precisely because of his concern to show how our fundamental nature is permeated, if not defined, by historical considerations. As the awareness of our historical character deepens and becomes more refined and more articulated, one might expect that the various Heideggerian insights into history will solidify his own importance as a truly epochal thinker in this regard. It may, after all, be possible to reorient our rational sensibilities so that the ontological demands of thinking Being as presence can displace whatever has been distorted by the representational rightness of logical principles. If so, then a claim supporting Heidegger's eminence as *the* thinker of our century, and perhaps of modernity as a whole, becomes all the more viable. For it is a fact about the philosophical activity of our time that it considers the canons of formal logic to be inviolate in themselves and independent of all substantive considerations. Heidegger has challenged both of these assumptions. Should his challenge be accepted and the direction of his thinking carried through to a successful conclusion, then not only will Heidegger's own apparent ambiguousness and "irrationality" be seen in a new light, but all other forms of philosophical activity will also have to be recognized as to some degree naive in their unreflective acceptance of logical principles. Heideggerian Denken would therefore warrant elevation above its philosophical peers precisely because it laid the groundwork for showing that all other types of philosophy depended on logic in ways that were not ontologically justified. The extent to which any style of philosophizing rests on the unquestioned apodicticity of logic is the extent to which Denken must be judged superior to all those styles because the results of their inquiries ultimately rely on a metaphysical formality that renders those results ontologically suspect, however precise and profound they may initially appear.

However, the resident rightness we feel to be inherent in the notions and principles of logic stands as a unique obstacle for this kind of thoughtful approach to ontology. The elements of logic appear to be essential to thinking—at least any kind of ordered thinking—in a way that places them outside of history and outside of temporality. If, therefore, human nature is defined, in part, by the limiting conditions of this ahistorical phenomenon, then human nature is, precisely to that extent, itself ahistorical. Now Heidegger has challenged us to think through the metaphysical presuppositions of logic in light of our ontological nature as historical beings. We must therefore begin to question whether we accede to the apodictic character of logical principles because they themselves have been historically conditioned—just as mortals have been—or because of some intrinsic necessity displayed by these principles and apart from any historical considerations that may pertain to them. This question is absolutely fundamental to the Heideggerian project for thinking as the overcoming of metaphysics. For if the correctness bestowed on discourse by logical principles is based on a metaphysical framework that is, at some point, in conflict with the Heideggerian version of the meaning of Being, then Denken cannot escape the fact that it must proceed in a tense alliance with that other form of thinking. Although we have been assured that metaphysics has been overcome, we must nonetheless wonder whether that dimension of metaphysics represented by logic has also been overcome as well. Perhaps it has not been. Perhaps it cannot be.

But Heidegger has done his work well, at least to the extent of establishing the ontological possibility for such a revisionist program. For the more we allow the pressure of our nature as historical to permeate the supposedly secure formality of logical principles, the more we will be open to the kind of ontological inquiry originating in and exemplified by Heideggerian Denken. The problems and paradoxes outlined in this study may recede in seriousness, if not fade away altogether, once we embrace the thesis that our acceptance of the formal rightness of logic is guaranteed only by the fact of a certain historical mode of existence—one that, apparently, could have and perhaps even should have been other than it was.

To realize fully the historical and therefore in some sense derivative character of logic is a project that will assume proportions of considerable magnitude. Our daily existence is, or seems to be, thoroughly impregnated with the relevance of logical patterns—e.g., the need to be consistent, the need to preserve some kind of difference between true and false, the need to maintain a vibrant distinction between what in fact appears and what does not appear in our experience of the world. We must cope with the existential pressure of logic, as one might call it, while, as prospective Heideggerians, we at the same time confront this pressure in the attempt to think through to its ontological source. And this is not the only difficulty. For if we are as determined by the totality of history as Heidegger maintains, then we must not only exist "logically" in the present but also attempt to recoup all of the pastness that has been lost by millenia of unreflective acceptance of "logic" and to incorporate that pastness into our present mode of existence. Hence the need arises to rethink all of the fateful moments throughout the history of metaphysics, an epic endeavor that, we may hope, will grant us insight into those structures of temporality presently blocking our awareness that logical notions and principles are indeed derivative and distortive.

But the challenge Heidegger has proposed will still place a considerable strain on the traditional avenues of consciousness. One could plausibly maintain that it is virtually impossible, at least in our present situation, even to attempt to think in a manner following Heidegger's own example. And the reason is precisely the quandry in which we find ourselves once the logical difficulties implied by Denken have been forced into the open. Thus, how can we think that the apparent omnipresence of Heidegger's notion of temporality will have any effect on the notion of simultaneity integral to the principle of contradiction? How can we merge the distinctive mood of anxiety with the formal "otherness" that seems sufficient to account for the function of negation in propositions of the form "X is not Y"? How can we balance a genuine philosophical concern for totality with the Heideggerian approach to sameness, so wavering in its establishment of difference that it becomes difficult to determine where and how difference appears within that quest for totality? These are problems that must eventually be examined further in order that thinking in accordance with Heideggerian standards can assume its rightful place as a counterpart to, if not an improvement on, the primarily ratiocinative processes found in classical metaphysics. Only when these abstract matters have been carefully and consistently thought through would it be possible to apply the Heideggerian approach toward ontology to such themes as the individuation of things, the nature of deity, the structure of history, the constitution of time and other practical concerns requiring such fundamental consideration.

These concluding remarks have, in a sense, oscillated between recognizing the value of Heidegger's questioning and questioning the value of his thinking in terms of its implications on logic as the ordering schematic for our knowledge of self as "rational." In this respect the conclusion has mirrored the oscillating structure of this study as a whole. One may nonetheless infer that the extent to which we feel that Heidegger's questioning of Being has legitimately thrown into doubt the traditional understanding of logic is the extent to which we will acquit Heidegger of being arbitrary in his own ontological assumptions. Thus, those who wholly embrace the Heideggerian approach will see only a marginal need for human beings to exercise rationality through logic, since for them our true ontological nature is not defined by the display of reason.

Yet is human nature related to logic in this accidental sense? This is the question that must be answered—and it is, again, testament to Heidegger's greatness as a thinker that he forces us to think this question to the very limits of our understanding of self and our relation to history and to time. The answer must delimit the extent to which human nature is essentially defined by an adherence to logic and its rules. This issue is fundamental; thus, it is difficult in principle to do more here than point out some of the competing alternatives rather than to offer a summary judgment at this time on the "truth" of any one of these alternatives. In fairness to the Heideggerian approach, such a judgment would presuppose a more evident revealment of Being than Heidegger believed to be accessible in our epoch. Nonetheless, one could contend that, in the mere attempt to question Heideggerian Denken according to guidelines provided by logic and the history of metaphysics, this study depends on at least a tacit endorsement of the supremacy of logic and metaphysics. If so, then so be it. My own belief is that whether in the end a coherent account of human nature can be rendered from within the Heideggerian assumption of the primordiality of time and history will depend, in large measure, on the capacity of Denken to elicit a structure faithful to the demands of the human need to speak with meaning, with order, and with conviction that reaches to the heart.

One final thought. Socrates, on the verge of death, counseled his audience to do their best, in thought and action, to acquire virtue and wisdom, "for the prize is fair and the hope great." The array of arguments examined in the *Phaedo* for purposes of establishing this end had been long and intricate. Heidegger's way into the ontological core of logic, to the extent that this way has been traversed, is also long and intricate. It seems reasonable to conclude that the limitless energy Heidegger himself expended in this regard holds out the hope that this core can be reached. But whether or not the prize is fair can be determined only when the Heideggerian thinker has penetrated this core and spoken of its substance, both with respect to its ontological unity and in relation to the metaphysical structures that surround and, at present, obscure that unity.

# Notes

## Introduction

1. See John Caputo's review of David A. White, *Heidegger and the Language of Poetry* (Lincoln: University of Nebraska Press, 1978) in *Review of Metaphysics* 33 (1980): 811-13. And for remarks in a similar vein, see also Karsten Harries's review of the same book in *Philosophy and Literature* 4 (1980): 132-33.

2. Caputo, p. 812.

3. See *US*, 16, 18, 26. All citations of Heidegger's works are to the German editions as listed in the Bibliography (Part I). The translations generally follow the English translations currently available, although these translations have frequently been modified whenever necessary. All other translations are my own. See Part II of the Bibliography for references to the available English translations.

4. See *WM*, 237; *SG*, 69. Cf. also the discussions of Schelling as a mystic (*S*, 141) and Nietzsche as a mystic (*WD*, 47). For interpretations asserting or suggesting that Heidegger is in fact a mystic, see Bernd Magnus, *Heidegger's Metahistory of Philosophy* (The Hague: Martinus Nijhoff, 1970), p. 141; Leon Rosenstein, "Mysticism as Preontology: A Note on the Heideggerian Connection," *Philosophy and Phenomenological Research* 39 (1978): 57-73; and Clarence W. Richey, "On the Intentional Ambiguity of Heidegger's Metaphysics," *Journal of Philosophy* 55 (1958): 1144-148. For an extended discussion denying that Heidegger is a mystic, see John D. Caputo, *The Mystical Element in Heidegger's Thought* (Athens: Ohio University Press, 1978). See also the number "Heidegger and Eastern Thought" in *Philosophy East and West* 20 (1970), and Peter Kreeft, "Zen in Heidegger's Gelassenheit," *International Philosophical Quarterly* 11 (1971): 521-45.

5. On the need to keep *Denken* and *Dichten* distinct from one another, see the typical discussion at *WD*, 8ff. For an extended account of this fundamental Heideggerian distinction, see *Heidegger and the Language of Poetry* (hereafter abbreviated *HLP*): esp., pp. 143-67. See also David Halliburton, *Poetic Thinking; an Approach to Heidegger* (Chicago: University of Chicago Press, 1982).

6. *US*, 94; *WM*, 96; *AM*, 39.

7. Consider, in this regard, Heidegger's remark, "Only a free nature (*Wesen*) can be unfree" (*MA*, 247). Opposition in this context need not imply opposition in the context of truth, but Heidegger's implicit appeal to this classic metaphysical distinction is worth noting.

8. Thomas A. Fay, *Heidegger: The Critique of Logic* (The Hague: Martinus Nijhoff, 1977): p. 111.

9. Fay, p. 112.

10. Fay, p. 119—italics in text.

11. For a concise restatement of the same criticisms of Fay's book, see the review by J. N. Mohanty in the *Southwestern Journal of Philosophy* 11 (1980): esp., pp.

175, 177. The most useful article on Heidegger and logic is by Albert Borgmann, "Heidegger and Symbolic Logic," in *Heidegger and the Quest for Truth*, Manfred S. Frings, ed. (Chicago: Quadrangle Books, 1968): pp. 139-62. See also Walter Bröcker, "*Heidegger und die Logik*," *Philosophische Rundschau* 1 (1953/54): 48-56. This article also appears in *Heidegger: Perspektiven zur Deutung seines Werkes*, ed. Otto Pöggeler (Cologne: Kiepenheuer & Witsch, 1970), pp. 298-304. In this article Bröcker maintains that "Heidegger does not see that the formal logical structure of thinking depends not at all on either the richness or the poverty of the world as thought about and of the human reference to that world" (p. 303). This, of course, is precisely the unquestioned formalistic view of logical principles that Heidegger intends to scrutinize. See also Rolf-Dieter Hermann, "*Heidegger und Logik*," *Sophia* 29 (1961): 353-57.

12. See *HLP*, pp. 200-208. This problem will be taken up again in chapter 5 below.

13. See, for example, *SZ*, 11, 27, 35; *KP*, 13; *MA*, 195; *GP*, 319.

14. Cf. also the view of Otto Pöggeler that Heidegger should be considered as an integral part of Western philosophy. Pöggeler develops this view in his essay "Heidegger Today" in Edward G. Ballard and Charles E. Scott, eds., *Martin Heidegger: In Europe and America* (The Hague: Martinus Nijhoff, 1973): pp. 1-36. And Werner Marx has contended that Heidegger thought in "categories," although they were "more original" categories for the being of man and things than those present in the tradition. See Werner Marx, *Heidegger and the Tradition*, translated by Theodore Kisiel and Murray Greene (Evanston: Northwestern University Press, 1971), p. 85. If Marx's view is correct, then the question becomes whether "more original" categories must nonetheless obey rules of formal correctness. See also Walter Biemel, "Heidegger and Metaphysics" in *Heidegger: The Man and the Thinker*, ed. Thomas Sheehan (Chicago: Precedent Publications, 1981): 163-72.

15. The more prominent works on this vexed point include: Otto Pöggeler, *Philosophie und Politik bei Heidegger* (Freiburg/Munich: Verlag Karl Alber, 1972); Karsten Harries, "Heidegger as a Political Thinker," *Review of Metaphysics* 29 (1976): 642-69; and the chapter entitled "National Socialism, Voluntarism, and Authenticity" in Michael E. Zimmerman, *Eclipse of the Self; The Development of Heidegger's Concept of Authenticity* (Athens: Ohio University Press, 1981), pp. 169-97. For an extended study of the early Heidegger in this context, see Mark Blitz, *Heidegger's Being and Time and the Possibility of Political Philosophy* (Ithaca: Cornell University Press, 1981). See also Heidegger's personal statement on the matter in *Der Spiegel*, 31 May 1976, pp. 193-219. This interview, entitled "Only a God can save us," can be read in translation in *Philosophy Today* 20 (1976): 267-84.

## Chapter 1

1. Heidegger's device of referring to a certain interpretation of logic as "logic" occurs frequently. See for example: *SZ*, 165; *EM*, 18-19, 92, 102; *WM*, 5, 103, 105, 146-47, 177, 179, 220, 228; *KP*, 44, 220; *FD*, 122; *WD*, 10, 99, 145; *US*, 116; *NI*, 92, 147; *NII*, 52, 54; *VA*, 234; *S*, 127; *MA*, 1, 128, 132; *A*, 143, 154. This list is only representative.

2. *WM*, 104-5—italics in text. Cf. also *HE*, 70.

3. Cf. also *HO*, 297.

4. Cf. 287, 325.

5. Heidegger asserts that logic is substantive rather than formal in a variety of contexts. See *SC*, 437; *EM*, 91-92, 142-44; *KP*, 136; *WD*, 61; *MA*, 25, 27, 126, 128; *ID*, 138-39. In fact, for Heidegger, even logical connectives possess ontological significance. See *WM*, 283; *S*, 187; *MA*, 29, 39; *PG*, 413.

6. Heidegger is not alone in seeking to determine the substantive principles underlying the "formality" of logical notions and axioms. For a different phenomenological approach to this problem, see Robert S. Tragesser, *Phenomenology and Logic* (Ithaca: Cornell University Press, 1977), esp. pp. 92-111. And Henry Veatch argues for a reconsideration of the Aristotelian schema of logical categories in lieu of metaphysically neutral symbolic notation in his *Two Logics: The Conflict between Classical and Neo-Analytic Philosophy* (Evanston: Northwestern University Press, 1969). As a foil to such attempts at the "metaphysics of logic," see Ernest Nagel's eloquent and carefully reasoned appeal for "Logic without Ontology" in *Naturalism and the Human Spirit*, ed. Yervant Hovhannes Krikorian (New York: Columbia University Press, 1944), pp. 210-41. For additional discussion of the need for a type of thinking "stricter" than formal logic, see *EM*, 94; *NI*, 59; *S*, 177; *WM*, 228; *HE*, 372, 399.

7. The three quotations are from, respectively, *WM*, 251; *VA*, 184; *EM*, 18.

8. For additional passages on the importance of the correctness or rightness of logical thinking, see *L*, 37, 54; *PI*, 189, 191.

9. Heidegger carries this radical line of thought to the point of asserting that, from the standpoint of fundamental ontology, the principle of contradiction is subservient to the need to having to give any kind of reason (*MA*, 66). Presumably language could speak without presupposing any need to justify what was said even in the purely formal sense governed by the principle of contradiction. In this regard Heidegger asks—in, one suspects, only apparent rhetorical guise—what right does reason have to make itself ruler of philosophy (*WP*, 5)? An appeal to the supposed fact that the use of reason is essential to preserve intelligibility would seemingly be rejected as derivative and unthoughtful. Heidegger thus questions whether Aristotle is justified in using the notion of *paideia* to deflect inquiry from the supposedly self-evident status of the principle of contradiction—see, *SG*, 29.

10. To assume the primordial formal character of contradiction without such questioning is, for Heidegger, to fall under the pedagogically rote spell of "school logic" (*Schullogik*), an intellectual malady against which Heidegger frequently complains: see *L*, 4, 12-3; *NI*, 552; *HP*, 150; *GP*, 253; *AM*, 221; *GM*, 52-56. One cannot learn to think by construing logic at this level—*L*, 15; *HE*, 156. If, however, we assume that logical principles are purely formal, then one would be unlikely to assert that such formality could, by itself alone, yield substantive ontological results.

11. For additional discussion asserting the substantive character of the principle of contradiction, see *EM*, 19-20, 66; *SG*, 201; *L*, 39; *WM*, 69.

12. For further examples of Heideggerian contradictions, see *US*, 150; *S*, 135, 137, 183; *L*, 21, 45; *HG*, 57; *HE*, 110, 111, 125.

13. See *GP*, 314, 315 for the same point made with respect to mathematical propositions of the "self-evidently" certain form of 2+2=4.

14. For additional commentary on Hegel and the principle of contradiction, see *HE*, 125; for an interesting remark on the relation between Kierkegaard and Hegel in this regard, see *HE*, 126; and for Kant's special relation to the principle of contradiction, see *FD*, 133-40; *KP*, 167, 176-77; *L*, 336.

15. We should also note the passage in *HE*, 239, where Heidegger wonders

whether "logic" had "neither father nor mother." The point seems to be that dropping the genetic metaphor will compel the prospective thinker to trace the ontological roots of logic beyond that of its original historical spokesman. Cf. also in this regard *GP*, 254.

16. Cf. also *HE*, 199, 232, 398.

17. For an earlier formulation of the fundamental meaning of *logos*, see *SZ*, 32-34.

18. The point seems to be that if *logos* took a form other than that defined by the proposition, then the principle of contradiction may no longer be applicable to that linguistic form. How such discourse is possible in anything like the standard modes of language remains difficult to understand.

19. P. F. Strawson, *Introduction to Logical Theory* (London: Methuen, 1964), p. 3—italics in text.

20. For additional passages discussing Aristotle on the principle of contradiction, see: *EM*, 143; *FD*, 134-35; *NI*, 602-6; *PG*, 3, 87; *L*, 129, 135, 164, 166, 171, 191.

21. For a brief discussion of the Platonic separation of time from the noun through the grammatical distinction between verb and noun, see *WD*, 134.

22. For additional discussion of this "ontological" interpretation of Aristotle's distinction, see *L*, 135, 136-37, 141, 163; *GP*, 298; *MA*, 125; *HE*, 384; *AM*, 65-66.

23. For two different yet related approaches to the ontological significance of the principle of contradiction, see Carol A. Kates, "An Intentional Analysis of the Law of Contradiction," *Research in Phenomenology* 9 (1979): 108-26; and Karl Heinz Volkman-Schluck, "*Der Satz vom Widerspruch als Anfang der Philosophie*," *Martin Heidegger zum Siebsigsten Geburtstag* (Pfullingen: Neske, 1959), pp. 134-50.

## CHAPTER 2

1. For Heidegger, the Kantian analysis of negation in the first *Critique* is inadequate precisely because Kant did not deal with nothingness as such, but with the "concept" (*Begriff*) of nothingness (*PI*, 204).

2. Heidegger describes falsehood as "*verstellend*" throughout his discussion of the topic in *L*; see especially pp. 132, 169, 182, 189, 190.

3. For additional discussion of the relation between anxiety and nothingness as developed in *Sein und Zeit*, see *SZ*, 187, 188, 266, 343. It is also interesting to note that in *Sein und Zeit*, Heidegger did not restrict his attention to locating the ontological ground of negation. He suggested at one point that the conditional (if .-. . then) structure so pervasive to contemporary logic is derived from the "deliberative . . . circumspective" complexus of feelings unique to Dasein (*SZ*, 359). As far as I know, this intriguing hypothesis was never developed in any of Heidegger's subsequent works.

4. Heidegger does not intend the analysis of anxiety developed in this fundamental ontological context to be confused with a "philosophy of feeling." See in this regard his extended quotation from Kant against *Gefühlsphilosophie* cited at *GP*, 468-69.

5. Cf. also *HG*, 62.

6. Heidegger affirms the inclusive relation between nothingness and Being in numerous contexts, but without sustained development of the sense in which the

inclusion should be understood. See *SZ*, 285; *EM*, 85; *HO*, 104; *WM*, 190-91, 240-42; *NI*, 277, 456, 541; *NII*, 50; *S*, 122; *US*, 108-9; and *HE*, 58. At *GP*, 433, Heidegger tells us that Hegel's correlation of Being and Nothing is "on the right track," but he does not detail precisely how Hegel was right and how he erred. The literature on Hegel and Heidegger in this regard is worth considering. See Jan Van der Meulen, *Heidegger und Hegel, oder Widerstreit und Widerspruch* (Meisenheim: Hain, 1953), esp. chapters 13 and 14, pp. 61-79, and Ernst Tugendhat, "*Das Sein und das Nichts*," in *Durchblicke Martin Heidegger zum 80. Geburtstag* (Frankfurt am Main: Vittorio Klostermann, 1970), pp. 132-60. Tugendhat also provides useful historical background on Parmenides' "two ways" as a precursor of the approach toward negation taken by Hegel and Heidegger. Both Van der Meulen and Tugendhat raise their own significant criticisms of Heidegger's position. See also Christopher Smith, "Heidegger, Hegel, and the problem of *das Nichts*," *International Philosophical Quarterly* 8 (1968): 379-405.

7. The ontological priority of nihilation to the "not" found in negative utterances is also stated at *WM*, 190.

8. Alfred North Whitehead, *Process and Reality* (New York: Macmillan, 1929), p. 245.

9. The comparison between Plato and Heidegger in this context is apposite not only because of significant similarities in doctrine but also because Heidegger himself had very high regard for this work. The motto, inaugurating *Sein und Zeit* is taken from the *Sophist* (244A), and elsewhere Heidegger referred to the dialogue as a "most profound" work (*WD*, 134; *L*, 142). For additional commentary on Plato and Heidegger in this regard, see Stanley Rosen, "Thinking about Nothing," in Michael Murray, ed., *Heidegger and Modern Philosophy* (New Haven: Yale University Press, 1978), pp. 116-33, esp. pp. 133-37.

10. It must be mentioned at this point that Heidegger frequently cites Plato's tendency to refer to a particular being as *me on*, i.e., as a type of nonbeing. Cf. *WM*, 345; *NI*, 541; *NII*, 218; *GP*, 295. However, even if Heidegger's emphasis on this type of metaphysical negation is sound, it does not affect the fact that the *Sophist* develops a position on a type of negation that intersects the sense of negation Heidegger is attempting to describe. For Heidegger's understanding of the meaning of nonbeing for the Greeks in general, see *EM*, 49, 78. And for a balanced scholarly commentary on this important point, see George Joseph Seidel, O.S.B., *Heidegger and the Pre-Socratics* (Lincoln: University of Nebraska Press, 1964), esp. pp. 34-42.

11. Negation emerges as an ontological component in other contexts as well in Heidegger. One of the most suggestive occurs in Heidegger's treatment of evil. See the application of nothingness to evil in *S*, 117, 119, 125, and the assertion at *S*, 33 that evil must have being of some sort. Heidegger then develops this sense of evil as an ontological ground for human freedom, which he contends should be based on the possibility that humans are necessarily capable of both good *and* evil (*S*, 188-89). Presumably this is an instance illustrating how fundamental ontology exemplifies a morally neutral type of inquiry.

12. See also the preliminary illumination of the poet Georg Trakl's sense of "apartness" (*Abgeschiedenheit*) as developed in the chapter "*Die Sprache im Gedicht*" in *Unterwegs zur Sprache*, pp. 37-82. For commentary on this poetic evocation of nothingness as what is "apart" from something, see *HLP*, pp. 87-88, 173. And for an interesting application of Trakl's notion of apartness in the larger context of modern art in general, see Karsten Harries, "*Das befreite Nichts*," in *Durchblicke*, pp. 39-62.

## Chapter 3

1. An extensive literature exists on the Heideggerian notion of the "ontological difference," but as far as I know there has been relatively little work done on that sense of difference which serves as an ontological counterpart to sameness. The literature relevant to difference in the context of the ontological difference will therefore be cited, whenever appropriate, in the notes to chapter 7. For a development of Heidegger's notion of difference with a view toward Jacques Derrida, see Kenneth Itzkowitz, "Differance and Identity," *Research in Phenomenology* 8 (1978): 127-43.

2. For additional passages citing the empty formalism of identity understood in this sense, see *ID*, 125; *HE*, 213, 250, 371, 376.

## Chapter 4

1. For general (but uncritical) commentary on *Identität und Differenz*, see Joan Stambough's Introduction to her translation of *Identität und Differenz* in Martin Heidegger, *Identity and Difference*, trans. Joan Stambaugh (New York: Harper & Row, 1969), pp. 7-18; see also the section "*Identität, Differenz, Grund*" in Otto Pöggeler, *Der Denkweg Martin Heideggers* (Pfullingen: Neske, 1963), pp. 145-63.

2. *Identity and Difference*, p. 25. This edition is bilingual and contains an important emendation to the original German text introduced by the translator after conversation with Heidegger (p. 38). The German text is, as always, included in the body of the chapter whenever appropriate; the page references are to the original German as contained in the bilingual edition.

3. For additional passages asserting the ontologically informative character of the principle of identity, see *WD*, 99; *WM*, 37-38, 306.

4. For a well-documented account of relative identity and the principal differences between it and absolute identity, see Nicholas Griffin, *Relative Identity* (Oxford: Clarendon Press, 1977), pp. 1-21.

5. On the matter of identity understood as the ontological belonging together of difference, see *S*, 93, 104, 126, 152, 153; *MA*, 84.

6. See also the short article, "*Grundsätze des Denkens*," in which Heidegger examines the relation between history and the dialectical development of three "principles of thinking" (identity, contradiction, and excluded middle). Fichte and Hegel are briefly discussed in this context, and the article concludes with some observations on Marx. Martin Heidegger, "*Grundsätze des Denkens*," *Jahrbuch für Psychologie und Psychotherapie* 6 (1958): 33-41.

7. For critical comments on an earlier version of this interpretation, see Ted Klein, "What Has Identity to do With Appropriation? A Response to David A. White," *Southwestern Journal of Philosophy* 9 (1978): 65-72.

## Chapter 5

1. For a useful (although uncritical) review of Heidegger's various positions on thinghood, see Walter Biemel, "The Development of Heidegger's Concept of the Thing," *Southwestern Journal of Philosophy* 11 (1980): 47-66.

2. See also *FD*, 36, 130. For commentary on this point in the original Kantian

context in which it was introduced, see the analysis by Eugene T. Gendlin in the translation of *Die Frage nach dem Ding*: pp. 245-96.

3. Heidegger attempts to compel speculation on this issue by making such claims as "the word itself is the relation" between language as spoken and its referent (*US*, 170). It is not clear, however, how we are to think a part of the relation (i.e., between word and object). See *US*, 169, 185; *L*, 74; *GP*, 292-93; *HE*, 294, 328. For additional commentary on this difficult text, see *HLP*, pp. 23ff.

4. The almost pragmatic emphasis on the ontological sense of a being depending on its use rather than on, e.g., perception of its appearance was already part of Heidegger's thinking in *Sein und Zeit*. Cf. *SZ*, 67, 103; see also *HO*, 18ff, 24.

5. The earth-world dichotomy of the *Holzwege* essay "*Der Ursprung des Kunstwerkes*" has now been reformulated. World is no longer opposed to earth; rather, earth (and the other three sectors of the fourfold) are the constituents parts of the world. Therefore, when W. B. Macomber says that "the earth represents the density, enclosure, and darkness in the midst of which Dasein clears an opening and lays out the field in which decisions are possible," this designation refers to earth in the *Holzwege* sense and not to the fourfold sense of earth as introduced here. See W. B. Macomber, *The Anatomy of Disillusion* (Evanston: Northwestern University Press, 1976), p. 64.

6. For the major attempts to unearth the origin of the fourfold, see the following: William J. Richardson, *Heidegger through Phenomenology to Thought* (The Hague: Martinus Nijhoff, 1967), p. 572; Stanley Rosen, *Nihilism: A Philosophical Essay* (New Haven: Yale University Press, 1969), p. 132; Thomas Langan's hypothesis is in Etienne Gilson, Thomas Langan, and Armand A. Maurer, C.S.B., *Recent Philosophy: Hegel to the Present* (New York: Random House, 1966), p. 151. Additional speculation on the origin of the fourfold is in Dieter Sinn, "*Heideggers Spätphilosophie*," *Philosophische Rundschau* 14 (1967): 81-182, esp. p. 130. See also the response to these interpretations in *HLP*, pp. 31-33.

If one insists on locating a historical precedent for the fourness of the fourfold, I would suggest that the four cosmogonic elements of the pre-Socratics have a certain plausibility (although of course Heidegger has seen fit to alter their content). However, it could be that Heidegger named the four sectors as he did simply in virtue of reflection on a seminal poet. See in this regard the illumination of Hölderlin in *EH*, 17 where aspects of all four sectors are mentioned in close conjunction (although without the use of the word *Geviert* to name their unity). See also *EH*, 161 for additional evidence supporting this possibility. Otto Pöggeler concurs with this conjecture, but without locating a specific source in Heidegger's works on Hölderlin. Cf. Otto Pöggeler, *Der Denkweg Martin Heideggers* (Pfullingen: Neske, 1963), p. 248. Pöggeler's discussion of the fourfold is valuable (pp. 257-67).

7. For an early development of the near/far interplay in this ontological context, see *PG*, 308-26, 381. The notions of near and far also appear in *Sein und Zeit*: cf. 102, 105.

8. For more discussion on how mortals should comport themselves in order to "release" beings into thinghood, see Heidegger's important opusculum *Gelassenheit*. Many of the key technical terms introduced in this account of the fourfold are developed further in that work. It should be noted, however, that the problems to be raised in Section II of this chapter are not obviated by anything contained in *Gelassenheit*. For an extended commentary on *Gelassenheit*, see chapter 8, in *HLP*, "Thinking and Releasement (*Gelassenheit*)," pp. 168-89. See also John M. Anderson's Introduction to *Discourse on Thinking*, the translation of *Gelassenheit*, pp. 7-39.

218    NOTES

9. Additional commentary on the significance of the fourfold may be found in the following studies: James M. Demske, "Heidegger's Quadrate and the Revelation of Being," *Philosophy Today* 7 (1963): 245-57; Donald W. Cress, "Heidegger's Criticism of 'Entitative Metaphysics' in his Later Work," *International Philosophical Quarterly* 12 (1972): 69-86; Ysabel de Andia, *Présence et Eschatologie dans la Pensée de Martin Heidegger* (Paris: Editions Universitaires, 1975), pp. 233-38; and the Introduction by Albert Hofstadter to *Poetry, Language, Thought*, esp. pp. xiii-xxii.

10. For Heidegger's early views on perception, see *PG*, 49-54; *GP*, 445-48; and for other statements of the "not yet" and "no longer" aspect of perception, see *FD*, 111 and *NII*, 224.

11. Heidegger may have been influenced in this regard by the Leibnizian notion of the monad as a mirror of the universe. See *WM*, 393; *MA*, 120; and on the sense in which the Leibnizian monad incorporates the world (as does, in its own way, the Heideggerian thing), see *WM*, 385, 390-94; *MA*, 111, 119.

12. Heidegger is well aware of the need to address the problem of individuation. See, for example, his remarks on Schelling's "profound" contributions to this problem at *S*, 150; cf. also, *GP*, 414.

13. But see Heidegger's critique of the attempt to individuate two like things with respect to spatio-temporal position—thus, "insofar as each thing has its place, its time, and its time duration, there are never two same things" (cf. *FD*, 12-13, 14). See also Werner Marx's interpretation of Heidegger's notion of "particular whole" (*je Weilige*) as the source of individuation—Marx, p. 195.

14. Worthy of note in this regard is Heidegger's own discussion of nominalism at *GP*, 260.

15. See Heidegger's discussion of some of the many different senses "unity" may have at *HE*, 261-62; cf. also *HE*, 376; *KP*, 62-63; *ID*, 137. This diversification is not reflected in Heidegger's own appeals to unity in the context of the fourfold, or in the thinking on the temporality of presence (to be discussed in chapter 8).

# CHAPTER 6

1. For biographical information on Heidegger's early theological background, see Joseph Kockelmans, "Heidegger on Theology," *Southwestern Journal of Philosophy* (1973): 85-108, esp. 85-89. Also useful in this regard is Thomas Sheehan, "Heidegger's 'Introduction to the Phenomenology of Religion,' 1920-21," *Personalist* 60 (1979): 312-24.

2. Heidegger's explicit agnosticism was not, however, accepted as such by more than a few of his readers. Paul Tillich, writing in the mid 1930s, declared Heidegger's works to contain an "emphatic atheism" (quoted by Thomas F. O'Meara in "Tillich and Heidegger: A Structural Relationship," *Harvard Theological Review* 6 (1968): 249-61, esp. 258-59). Cf. also Maurice Corvez, "*La Place de Dieu dans l'ontologie de Martin Heidegger*," *Revue Thomiste* 61 (1953): 287-320; 62 (1954): 79-102, 559-83; 63 (1955): 377-90. This extended study begins with the following sentence: "The philosophy of Heidegger ignores God." Then, after presenting considerable background, drawn primarily from *Sein und Zeit*, Corvez concludes that (p. 385) "there is no place for God in the thinking of fundamental ontology." This study, written when it was, does not and of course could not take account of Heidegger's account of the fourfold. (I shall argue below that the fourfold virtually implies the real existence of deity.)

3. See also *EH,* 184; *EM,* 34; *HG,* 80, 95, 165. For commentary on the "flown gods," see Emerich Coreth, *"Auf der Spur der entflohenen Götter. Martin Heidegger und die Gottesfrage," Wort und Wahrheit* 9 (1954): 107-16.

4. For a discussion tracing the history of the death of God from Parmenides through Nietzsche, see Odette Laffoucriere, *Le Destin de la Pensée et "la Mort de Dieu" selon Heidegger* (The Hague: Martinus Nijhoff, 1968). Her conclusions (pp. 242-57) are very general and uncritical. See also James M. Edie, "The Absence of God," in *Christianity and Existentialism* (Evanston: Northwestern University Press, 1963), pp. 113-48. Edie takes *Sein und Zeit* to define the limits of Heidegger's position on God (cf. p. 124), although he does make brief references to several later works by Heidegger.

5. For a discussion of the possibility of proving God's existence in a Heideggerian context, see Franz-Maria Sladeczek, *Ist das Dasein Gottes Beweisbar? Wie steht die Existentialphilosophie Martin Heideggers zu dieser Frage?* (Wurzburg: K. Trilitisch, 1967). And for a parallel "blasphemy," as Heidegger sees it, i.e., construing God as a "value," see *L,* 84; *HO,* 239-40; *WM,* 179.

6. The affect of metaphysics on theology is frequently discussed in this regard: Cf. *HP,* 4, 141, 144, 183; *S,* 61, 79, 83, 175; *HO,* 179, 187; *ID,* 120-22; 128; *NII,* 349; *MA,* 211.

7. For commentary on the relation between language and thinking in this context, with particular reference to the development of Heidegger's thought by Heinrich Ott, see Eberhard Jüngel, *"Der Schritt Zurück: Eine Auseindersetzung mit der Heidegger-Deutung Heinrich Otts," Zeitschrift für Theologie und Kirche* 58 (1961): 104-22. Several scholars have denied the theism in Heidegger's later work. Thus, Robert Mason says that "Heidegger does not make the metaphysical move beyond Being to God because he believes that such a move originates from a radical misunderstanding of Being." But according to my reading of the fourfold, Being *demands* that that move to God be made in order that Being be preserved in its wholeness. See Robert Mason, "Rahner and Heidegger: Being, Hearing and God," *Thomist* 37 (1973): 455-88, esp. pp. 487-88. And for Arnold B. Come Heidegger "does not undertake to affirm or to deny the reality and knowability of God." See James M. Robinson and John B. Cobb (ed.), *The Later Heidegger and Theology,* vol. 1 (New York: Harper & Row, 1963), p. 102. Finally, Hans Jonas affirms with characteristic bluntness "the profoundly pagan character of Heidegger's thought." See his *The Phenomenon of Life: Toward a Philosophical Biology* (New York: Harper & Row, 1966), p. 248.

8. The notion of the divine as developed in the *Vorträge und Aufsätze* essays both extends and develops the notion of the holy *(das Heilige)* that appeared in several earlier essays. See the brief discussion of the holy in the "Letter on Humanism", and in *WM,* 182; *EH,* 161, 163; *HI,* 184-94. For commentary on the holy, see Karsten Harries, "Heidegger's Conception of the Holy," *Personalist* 47 (1966): 169-84.

9. The distinction between God or deity and the divine is correctly emphasized by Helmut Franz in his *"Das Denken Heideggers und die Theologie," Zeitschrift für Theologie und Kirche,* Beiheft 2 (1961): 81-118; the article is reprinted in Gerhard Noller (ed.), *Heidegger und die Theologie* (München: Chr. Kaiser Verlag, 1967): 249-89. James L. Perotti overlooks the distinction in his book *Heidegger on the Divine: The Thinker, the Poet, and God* (Athens: Ohio University Press, 1974), esp. p. 95. And for Charles E. Scott, "Heidegger has not laid down concrete requirements which God must meet, since he has made no theological commitments." Here again, however, the fact that God is the source of the divine, which in

turn is involved in continual contextual interplay with the other three sectors of the fourfold, seems to impose at least some "concrete requirements" for the being of deity. See Charles E. Scott, "Notes and Observations: Heidegger reconsidered. A Response to Professor Jonas," *Harvard Theological Review* 59 (1966): 175-85, esp. p. 184.

10. In the late essay "*Hölderlins Erde und Himmel*," originally given as a lecture and published in the fourth edition of *Erläuterungen zu Holderlins Dichtung*, Heidegger speaks of "the heavens, the earth, mankind, God" (*Der Himmel, die Erde, der Mensch, der Gott—EH,* 170). This usage of God instead of the divine is also repeated at *EH,* 175 and in *US,* 211, 214. By naming the distinctive being that defines each of the sectors of the fourfold, Heidegger comes as close to explicitly designating the reality of deity as he ever does, at least in the accounts dealing with the fourfold. Alfred Jäger has written that the fourfold does not have its truth in itself, but only as the goal of a long and extensive questioning. However, although it is usually sound to emphasize the provisional quality of Heidegger's thinking, it does not seem as though the existence of God is an issue requiring additional scrutiny. Thinking the nature of deity is, of course, another matter. See Alfred Jäger, *Gott: Nochmal Martin Heidegger* (Tübingen: Mohr, 1978), p. 144. For a summary of Heidegger's significance for theology according to Jäger, see pp. 443-44. For additional commentary on the significance of the fourfold with respect to theology, see Heinrich Ott, *Denken und Sein* (Zollikon: Evangelischer Verlag, 1959), esp. pp. 216-22.

11. For an extended discussion of Heidegger's commentary on Schelling, from a theological standpoint, see Jäger, pp. 161-333.

12. Additional discussion of the relation between deity and the "destiny of Being" may be found at *HO,* 41-42; *EH,* 40; and *NII,* 396. And for a benevolent exposition of the relation between deity and history, see John D. Caputo, "Heidegger's God and the Lord of History," *New Scholasticism* 57 (1983): 439-64.

13. For a vigorous critique of the theological implications in what Heidegger did, and did not, infer with respect to the nothing, see Karl Barth, "*Gott und das Nichtige*," in Noller, pp. 197-225.

14. For other passages concerning the hiddenness of God's presence (*Anwesenheit*), see *EH,* 166, 170, 173; *HG,* 232, 236. Karl Barth's formulation of the relation between God and eternity is also worth noting in this context: "God is the eternal Father so far as from eternity and in eternity He is the Father of the Son, who participates with Him, from eternity and in eternity, in the same essence." And Barth on time: "Time is distinguished from eternity by the fact that in it beginning, middle and end are distinct and even opposed as past, present and future. Eternity is just the duration which is lacking to time, as can be seen clearly at the middle point of time in the temporal present and in its relationship to the past and the future." The references: Karl Barth, *The Doctrine of the Word of God; Prolegomena to Church Dogmatics* (Edinburgh: T & T Clark, 1936), vol. 1, pt. 1, p. 452; vol. 2, pt. II, p. 608. Presumably Heidegger would levy the same metaphysical critique against Barth's notion of deity and temporality as he would against Augustine. For commentary comparing Barth and Heidegger, see S. Oshima, "Barth's *Analogia Relationis* and Heidegger's Ontological Difference," *Journal of Religion* 53 (1973): 176-94. It should be noted that Heinrich Ott denies that any of Heidegger's own thinking can be construed as "analogical" in any sense. See Ott, p. 145.

15. Cf. *HO,* 209; *WM,* 162, 169; *US,* 219; *NI,* 277, 322; *S,* 84; *KR,* 9; *P,* 162-74.

16. As Hans Jonas puts it, "But where the gods are, God cannot be" (Jonas, p. 248). In short, if Heidegger is ambiguous on whether there is one or many gods,

then Jonas infers that Heidegger's thought is necessarily "pagan." However, another Heidegger scholar has a quite different reaction to the same position: "When Heidegger speaks of 'alternatives' with regard to God or the gods, it is not in terms of his or their existence or non-existence but in terms of his or their presence or absence, and this presence and this absence do not exclude each other. Rather, they absolutely *belong* together." (Unfortunately, the author never clarifies how God or the gods can be both present and absent at the same time; one suspects that Jonas would accuse the above interpretation of internal inconsistency.) See Joan Stambaugh, "The Question of God in Heidegger's Thought," *Southwestern Journal of Philosophy* 10 (1979): 127-38, esp. p. 128. John Macquarrie strikes what might be understood as a middle course between the extremes set by Jonas and Stambaugh. Thus, God "is 'not yet' in Heidegger's thought, and therefore he had not passed beyond the first shock of despair which comes when the illusory and unauthentic character of an existence founded on the world is disclosed." See John Macquarrie, *An Existentialist Theology: A Comparison of Heidegger and Bultmann* (New York: Harper & Row, 1965), p. 136. For additional commentary on the relation between the divine and deity, see Helmut Danner, *Das Göttliche und der Gott bei Heidegger* (Meisenheim am Glan: A. Hain, 1971).

17. Hans Jonas counsels all who would embrace Heidegger's teaching in this regard that "the very least you buy is a doctrine of *permanent revelation*" (Jonas, p. 254—italics in text). He then develops the point by noting "implications such as these: that the revelation is unfinished and has an entirely open horizon for future advents of the word; that future revelations are not prejudged by past revelations, and no one revelation supplies an authoritative criterion by which others are to be judged. This does away with the possibility of, but equally with the need for, distinguishing between true doctrine and heresy—the very idea of a true doctrine disappears." Substantially the same point is made by Julius Bixler, who contends that it follows from Heidegger's position on the divine and the deity that "the creation itself is empty, and it is hard to distinguish the divinity who accompanies it from deviltry." See Julius Seelye Bixler, "The Failure of Martin Heidegger," *Harvard Theological Review* 56 (1963): 121-43, esp. p. 142. The various criticisms of Jonas have elicited two replies: the article by Charles E. Scott (see note 9 above) and William J. Richardson, "Heidegger and God—and Professor Jonas," *Thought* 40 (1965): 13-40.

18. In this regard Annemarie Gethmann-Seifert has concluded that Heidegger's assertions are "objectionable" (*austössig*) to a Christian theology, or even "must stand in contradiction to it." See Annemarie Gethmann-Seifert, *Das Verhältnis von Philosophie und Theologie im Denken Martin Heidegger* (Freiburg/München: Karl Alber, 1974), p. 121. For an extended discussion of Gethmann-Seifert's book, see Joseph J. Kockelmans's review in *Man and World* 8 (1975): 461-73.

19. A brief review of the spectrum of opinion on Heidegger's relevance to theology may prove useful at this point: Helmut Franz claims that in the end, Heidegger lets the relation between faith and God "in darkness" (although Heidegger himself never purports to analyze faith as such); see Franz, p. 114. Karl Löwith extends the same type of criticism by asserting that the relation between Denken and faith is left "ambiguous;" see Karl Löwith, "*Heideggers Auslegung des Ungesagten in Nietzsches Wort 'Gott ist tot',*" *Neue Rundschau* 64 (1953): 105-37, esp. pp. 123-24. On a more promising note, Gerhard Ebeling suggests that an appropriate theological analogue to the fundamental ontological distinction between Being and beings is that of the difference between "homo peccator" and "Deus iustificans." See Gerhard Ebeling, "*Verantworten des Glaubens in Begegnung mit dem Denken Martin Heidegger,*" *Zeitschrift für Theologie und Kirche,* Beiheft 2 (1961): 119-24,

esp. pp. 123-24. And, in a much broader but still generally favorable context, Alfred Jäger's lengthy study concludes with ten key theses concerning "the unthought God" (*Der ungedachte Gott*); cf. pp. 445-84. Finally, Hans Jonas challenges one of Heidegger's cardinal criticisms of metaphysics by affirming the theological relevance of the subject-object distinction. His contention is worth citing at some length (Jonas, p. 258—italics in text):

> Not Plato is responsible for it but the human condition, its limits and nobility under the order of creation. For far from being a deviation from Biblical truth, this setting of man over against the sum total of things, his subject-status and the object-status and mutual externality of things themselves, are posited in the very idea of creation and of man's position vis-a-vis nature determined by it: it is the condition of man *meant* in the Bible, imposed by his createdness, to be accepted, acted through—and transcended only in certain encounters with fellow beings and God, i.e., in existential relations of a very special kind.

In view of this broad spectrum of opinion, it seems fair to conclude that the significance and value of Heidegger's thinking with respect to theological considerations is still undecided. For general commentary on the relation between Heidegger and contemporary theology, see William J. Richardson, "Heidegger and Theology," *Theological Studies* 26 (1965): 86-100; and T. R. Williams, "Heidegger and the Theologians," *Heythrop Journal* 12 (1971): 258-80. See also Hans-Georg Gadamer, "The Religious Dimension in Heidegger," in *Transcendence and the Sacred*, ed. Alan M. Olson (Notre Dame: University of Notre Dame Press, 1981), pp. 193-207; and Bernhard Welte, "God in Heidegger's Thought," *Philosophy Today* 26 (1982): 85-100.

## Chapter 7

1. For additional commentary on the function of history in *Sein und Zeit*, see R. R. Rollin, "Heidegger's Philosophy of History in 'Being and Time'," *Modern Schoolman* 49 (1972): 97-112; also David C. Hoy, "History, Historicity, and Historiography in *Being and Time*," in *Heidegger and Modern Philosophy*, pp. 239-58.

2. For criticism of Heidegger's historicism, see Laurence Lampert, "On Heidegger and Historicism," *Phenomenology and Phenomenological Research* 34 (1974): 586-90; and Emil Fackenheim, "The Historicity and Transcendence of Philosophic Truth," *Inter-American Congress of Philosophy*, 7th, Laval University, Quebec (1967): 77-92. For a reply to Fackenheim, see *HLP*, pp. 196-97. And for a defense of Heidegger against historicism, see Otto Pöggeler, " 'Historicity' in Heidegger's Late Work," *Southwestern Journal of Philosophy* 4 (1973): 53-73. Marjorie Grene both develops and criticizes some of the apparent historicism in *Sein und Zeit* in "The Paradoxes of Historicism," *Review of Metaphysics* 32 (1978): 15-36. And for additional commentary, see Nathan Rotenstreich, "The Ontological Status of History," *American Philosophical Quarterly* 9 (1972): 49-58.

3. For a critical appraisal of Heidegger's interpretation of Plato, see David A. White, "Truth and Being: A Critique of Heidegger on Plato," *Man and World* 7 (1974): 118-34. For additional commentary see Robert Hahn, "Truth (Aletheia) in the context of Heidegger's critique of Plato and the Tradition," *Southwestern Philosophical Studies* 4 (1979): 51-57; Leon Rosenstein, "Heidegger and Plato and the Good," *Philosophy Today* 22 (1978): 332-54; and Hans Georg Gadamer, "Plato and Heidegger" in Mervyn Sprung, ed., *The Question of Being* (University Park: Pennsylvania State University Press, 1978), pp. 45-54.

4. Heidegger discusses the Aristotelian notion of *entelechia* as the "fulfillment" of Greek philosophy at *WM*, 352ff.

5. Cf. also *HO*, 76; *EH*, 175; *US*, 134.

6. It should be noted that in order for modernity to resurrect the Greek approach to things, Heidegger insists that the entire Greek culture must be exhumed—not just Plato and Aristotle (*FD*, 38). For a critical account of Heidegger on the early Greeks in this regard, see George Joseph Seidel, O.S.B., *Martin Heidegger and the pre-Socratics* (Lincoln: University of Nebraska Press, 1964), esp. pp. 34-49.

7. The status of the Middle Ages with respect to the epochal structure of metaphysics is difficult to determine. Heidegger's *Habilitationschrift* on Duns Scotus, published in his *Frühe Schriften*, is inconclusive on this point. Heidegger did, however, once set up a proportion in which he claimed that the Middle Ages were to Plato and Aristotle as Marx was to Hegel (*NII*, 132). The exact implications of this proportion are not made explicit, but it seems relatively safe to infer that the Middle Ages are intended to be seen as a derivative phase of thinking. For a study of Heidegger's relation to certain figures in mediaeval thought, see John N. Deely, *The Tradition via Heidegger* (The Hague: Martinus Nijhoff, 1971).

8. Although in some respect it is a completion still unthought. Thus, Heidegger says that "Leibniz" does not represent one seminal figure in modern philosophy, but rather a present aspect of Denken not yet fully understood—cf. *SG*, 65.

9. For additional discussion of the history of metaphysics in terms of the will, see *HE*, 384ff, and the various discussions of will contained in both Nietzsche volumes. And for a provocative critique of Heidegger's interpretation of Nietzsche, see Bernd Magnus, *Heidegger's Metahistory of Philosophy* (The Hague: Martinus Nijhoff, 1970), esp. 100, 114, 116-28, 134.

10. Cf. also *NII*, 226, 272. And for a discussion of the narrowness of "logic" on the inexhaustibility of the beginning of history, see *HA*, 15-16.

11. For a concise summary of Heidegger's position on nihilism, see *HO*, 201ff; also *WM*, 220.

12. In the same vein, Heidegger affirms that each thinker has his own way (*HO*, 194-95), with the apparent implication that no two ways are the same in all respects. It is worth pointing out at this juncture that the relativism characterizing the structure of metaphysics does not mean that there are no standards of correctness when one thinker judges another. For example, Heidegger says that Kant on time is "phenomenologically false" (*L*, 315). Furthermore, Heidegger also claims that (a) the Marburg school misunderstood Kant (*MA*, 209); (b) Bergson misunderstood Kant on time (*L*, 194), and (c) Hegel misunderstood Kant (*L*, 202). It is interesting to note that such evaluational comparisons seem to presuppose that the "ways" of the thinkers involved can be located on a common terrain.

13. For additional discussion of the ethical dimensions of history, esp. with respect to Heidegger's notion of a *Volk*, see *HO*, 63-64.

14. Cf. also *WD*, 62-63; *NI*, 464, 469.

15. See, as additional examples, Heidegger's discussion of J. S. Mill's interpretation of the copula (*GP*, 276); his analysis of Plato's Allegory of the Cave (*GP*, 402), and also his discussions of the methodological weaknesses of phenomenology (*PG*, 179).

16. For additional discussions of the notion of destiny in a variety of contexts, see *EM*, 99; *SG*, 120, 147, 160, 164; *WP*, 10; *HG*, 172, 173; *HO*, 311-12; *WD*, 71ff; *US*, 80; *ID*, 135ff; *NI*, 492; *HG*, 172-74, 176, 185, 228, 237. For commentary, see Karl Löwith, *Heidegger: Denker in dürftigen Zeit* (Göttingen: Vandenhoeck & Ru-

precht, 1965), esp. the section "*Geschichte, Geschichtlichkeit und Seinsgeschick,*" pp. 44-71.

17. The most concentrated single source developing Heidegger's views on technology are the two essays "*Die Frage nach der Technik*" and "*Die Kehre*" in *Die Technik und die Kehre*. However, the question of the meaning of technology is a common theme throughout much of Heidegger's middle and late work.

18. We have Heidegger's word that Descartes, Leibniz and Hume are all "planetary" philosophers (*NII*, 333) so presumably they are epochal as well. However, Kierkegaard is "no *Denker*" (*HO*, 230) and neither is Schopenhauer (*HE*, 20, 151). And since neither Husserl nor Sartre recognized the ontological significance of history (*WM*, 170), their status as thinkers must remain in doubt.

19. For additional commentary on the need to rethink the history of metaphysics, see Otto Pöggeler, "Metaphysics and Topology of Being in Heidegger," *Man and World* 8 (1975): 3-27; see also two articles by Calvin O. Schrag: "Re-Thinking Metaphysics" in Manfred S. Frings, *Heidegger and the Quest for Truth* (Chicago: Quadrangle Books, 1968), pp. 106-25, and "Heidegger on Repetition and Historical Understanding," *Philosophy East and West* 20 (1970): 287-95. Also, see the chapter "Historicality, Repetition, and Authentic Temporality" in Michael E. Zimmerman, *Eclipse of the Self; the Development of Heidegger's Concept of Authenticity* (Athens: Ohio University Press, 1981), pp. 119-32.

20. The critical approach developed here toward the historical factor of the ontological difference is not found, to my knowledge, in the principal literature available on the subject. See, for example, L. M. Vail, *Heidegger and Ontological Difference* (University Park: Pennsylvania State University Press, 1972), a work that, in general, does not adopt a critical attitude toward its subject. For a study that is indeed critical—but based on a questionable reading of the relevant Heideggerian texts—see Richard Rorty, "Overcoming the Tradition: Heidegger and Dewey," *The Review of Metaphysics* 30 (1976): 280-305. This article is reprinted in *Heidegger and Modern Philosophy*, pp. 239-58. See also in this regard a reply to Rorty's objections in David A. White, "On Historicism and Heidegger's Notion of Ontological Difference," *Monist* 64 (1981): 518-33. For another response to Rorty's position, see John D. Caputo, "The thought of Being and the Conversation of Mankind—The Case of Rorty and Heidegger," *Review of Metaphysics* 36 (1982/3): 661-85. A number of thoughtful objections are raised against Heidegger's development of the ontological difference in Van der Meulen's *Heidegger und Hegel*. See also Alberto Rosales, who criticizes Van der Meulen for not taking into account Heidegger's early views on the subject in his *Transzenden und Differenz; ein Beitrag zum Problem der ontologischen Differenz beim frühen Heidegger* (The Hague: Martinus Nijhoff, 1970), esp. pp. ix-x. This work concentrates on the ontological difference in *Sein und Zeit* and, to a lesser extent, in "*Was ist Metaphysik?*" For additional commentary on the subject of the ontological difference, see Alfredo Guzzoni, "*Ontologische Differenz und Nichts,*" in *Martin Heidegger zum Siebsigten Geburtstag*, pp. 35-48; Albert Dondeyne, "*La Difference Ontologique chez Martin Heidegger,*" *Revue Philosophique de Louvain* 56 (1958): 35-62, 251-93; Kurt Jürgen Huch, "*Zum Begriff der 'Ontologischen Differenz'* " in his *Philosophiegeschichtliche Voraussetzungen der Heideggerischen Ontologie* (Frankfurt am Main: Europäische Verlagsanstalt, 1967), pp. 21-43; and Fridolin Wiplinger, "*Die Ontologische Differenz als Horizont der Fragestellung,*" in his *Wahrheit und Geschichtlichkeit* (Freiburg/Munich: Karl Alber, 1961), pp. 91-146.

21. For example, "*Physis, logos, hen, idea, energeia,* substantiality, objectivity, subjectivity, the will, the will to power, the will to will" (*ID*, 66).

22. Thus, John D. Caputo asserts categorically, without benefit of argument, that there is no "why" to the sequence of epochs. See his *The Mystical Element in Heidegger's Thought* (Athens: Ohio University Press, 1978), p. 83. For a different approach to the relation between the epochs of metaphysics and Being, see Ysabel de Andria, *Présence et eschatologie dans la Pensée de Martin Heidegger* (Paris: Editions universitaires, 1975), pp. 63-68.

## CHAPTER 8

1. For additional commentary on the sense in which Being precedes beings, see *SZ*, 212, 325; *EM*, 61ff; *KP*, 20, 201; *GP*, 322.

2. The notion of showing (*Zeigen*) is developed in *Unterwegs zur Sprache*; for commentary and citation of appropriate texts, see *HLP*, 37, 62, 69, 127.

3. Cf. also *EM*, 33; *NII*, 211.

4. Heidegger consistently maintains throughout all his work that Being never fails to be understood in some sense: See *SZ*, 5, 183, 200; *EM*, 60ff; *KP*, 204; *NII*, 246-47; *PG*, 194; *GP*, 396, 398; *HE*, 60, 61, 341. Also, Heidegger at least once insisted that "one day, we know not when, Being will come into the word" (*HE*, 345).

5. For additional discussions in which Being is identified as presence, see *ID*, 94-95; *NII*, 217; *WM*, 230ff; *L*, 199; *HG*, 189. For other characteristics of Being, see *NII*, 250-53. In general, the approach toward Being in "*Zeit und Sein*" does not take earlier demarcations of Being into account.

6. Heidegger also discusses perceiving (*vernehmen*) in *PG*, 200, 220; *L*, 177, 351; *HE*, 178, 382, 391; on the relation between perceiving and representing (*vorstellen*), see *NII*, 295, 319-20.

7. Heidegger also admits that Being may not always be presence at *HO*, 142 and at *L*, 267.

8. The sameness of these two opposites is also maintained at *GP*, 433. See in addition *HE*, 33, where Heidegger interprets Heraclitus to be saying that light "is" darkness in its essence and vice versa, thus effectively denying that any opposition exists between the two, at least on the most basic ontological level. And for a discussion of the possibility of predicating a series of opposites of Being, see *GR*, 49-69.

9. For Heidegger's detailed discussion of Aristotle on time, see *GP*, 329-62; also, *L*, 259; *AM*, 156; *SZ*, 421ff. For commentary on Heidegger and Aristotle in this regard, see Ysabel de Audia's *Présence et Eschatologie*, esp. pp. 126-58. And for Heidegger's critique of Kant on time, see *Die Frage nach dem Ding*. Heidegger's interpretation of Kant is treated at length in Charles M. Sherover, *Heidegger, Kant & Time* (Bloomington: Indiana University Press, 1971). See also Ronald P. Morrison, "Kant, Husserl, and Heidegger on Time and the 'Unity of Consciousness'," *Philosophy and Phenomenological Research* 39 (1978): 182-98; and Otto Pöggeler, "Heidegger und das Problem der Zeit" in *L'heritage de Kant* (Paris: Beauchesne, 1982): 287-303.

10. The inauthentic character of the past-present-future division of time is discussed at *SZ*, 326; *GP*, 326; *WD*, 77-78; *MA*, 185-86; *GP*, 463; for an extensive early discussion of time, see *MA*, 256-84.

11. Heidegger also denies the identity of presence and duration at *WM*, 339ff. It is relevant to note the frequent but extremely brief references Heidegger makes to

Bergson: see *MA*, 138, 189; *L*, 249-50, 266, 267, 268; and for Heidegger's claim that Bergson on time is a "vulgar misunderstanding of Aristotle," see *GP*, 328; also, *GP*, 343, 345. For commentary, see J. Seyppel, "A Criticism of Heidegger's Time Concept with reference to Bergson's Durée," *Revue Internationale de Philosophie* 10 (1956): 503-8. And for other attempts to think temporality as "lasting," see the discussions of "lingering" at *HO*, 327, 339; *EH*, 106; *S*, 186.

12. In *Sein und Zeit*, Heidegger emphasized the importance of the notion of unity with respect to thinking the meaning of Being: cf. *SZ*, 232; also *NII*, 409; *WM*, 287; *MA*, 192; *EM*, 69; *H*, 37-46; and for temporality (*Zeitlichkeit*) as the fundamental unity of past, present, and future, see *GP*, 376, 388. For commentary, see Günter Wohlfart, "Der Augenblick. Zum Begriff der ekstatischen Einheit der Zeitlichkeit," *Allgemeine Zeitschrift für Philosophie* 7 (1982): 27-55.

13. By introducing this notion of the fourth dimension, Heidegger directs attention away from any one of the three classic divisions of time. He also apparently corrects his own earlier views; thus, the future was emphasized as the privileged dimension of time in *SZ*, 329; in *L*, 206, he says that true time must be understood from the standpoint of the present; and in *HO*, 72, he asserts that no point in time has preference over any other. In *Sein und Zeit*, Heidegger attempted to solve the problem of the unity of time by asserting that in every temporal ecstasis temporality is itself a whole (*SZ*, 350), although he did not address the problem of how to distinguish between that whole which was the present from that same whole which was, e.g., the future. See also the discussion of the authentic past (*Gewesenheit*) freeing the inauthentic past (*Vergangen—NII*, 9; *HG*, 107-8); and on the relation between the present and presence, see *L*, 403-4; on the relation between the now and the present, see *L*, 401, 404.

14. For further discussion of the dependency of time on man, see *EM*, 64; *WD*, 73 ff; and, with respect to the sense in which Being requires the preservation of human being, see *HE*, 373, 387; however, although Heidegger admits that Being needs human being, he insists that Being never depends on humanity—*NII*, 483 ff; *MA*, 194.

15. Additional commentary on the "It" of "It gives" may be found at *NII*, 377; *WM*, 167.

16. Heidegger also asserts that "time is time" is no tautology when thought according to Denken—*GP*, 341; see also the formulation "Time times" discussed at *US*, 213.

17. Heidegger asserts that the nature of Being cannot be deduced (*PG*, 198), and that words for Being can never be put into a definition (*SG*, 159). Heidegger himself hinted that even his own use of the word "Being" might be misleading as a name for *the* problem of Denken (*US*, 11). For an extended early discussion of the grammar and etymology of "*Sein*," see *EM*, 40-56.

18. For additional discussions of appropriation, see *US*, 258, 266ff; *NII*, 485ff, where Heidegger repeats that "appropriation appropriates;" Heidegger also said that temporality, just as appropriation, is "richer" than anything coming from it (*GP*, 438). It is perhaps useful to note that *Ereignis* was not always used in this technical sense; for examples where the context seems to require the sense of "event," see *NI*, 241, 254, 297, 435, 437; *NII*, 33, 401, 459; *EH*, 58, 107.

19. For a brief discussion of presence in the context of the fourfold, see *US*, 213. However, in *Sein und Zeit*, Heidegger warned that the primordial character of time may remain unknown (*SZ*, 408).

20. Otto Pöggeler's article "*Sein als Ereignis*" (Being as Appropriation) is an indispensable commentary. See *Zeitschrift für Philosophische Forschung* 13

(1959): 597-632; English translation by Ruediger Hermann Grimm, *Philosophy Today* 19 (1975): 16-42. See also Kenneth Maly, "Toward *Ereignis*," *Research in Phenomenology* 3 (1973): 63-93; John C. Caputo, "Time and Being in Heidegger," *Modern Schoolman* 50 (1973): 325-49; John McCumber, "Language and Appropriation; the Nature of Heideggerian Dialogue," *Personalist* 60 (1979): 384-96. And the discussion by Albert Hofstadter in the Introduction to *Poetry, Language, Thought* (pp. ix-xxii) should also be consulted.

21. It should be mentioned here that the protocol to a seminar concerning the lecture "*Zeit und Sein*," published in *Zur Sache des Denkens* (pp. 27-58), also does not discuss these issues. According to the publication notes provided at the end of *Zur Sache des Denkens*, Heidegger himself checked the text of this protocol and supplemented it in several places. The lines of thought contained in this protocol seldom interesect with the interpretive direction adopted toward "*Zeit und Sein*" in this chapter.

22. Werner Marx has pointed out that the self-concealing of Being in presence seems inconsistent with the mirror-play of Being as part of the doctrine of the fourfold. See Marx, p. 189. And Albert Hofstadter, focusing critical attention on the ontological aspects of Heidegger's thinking on works of art, accuses Heidegger of offering simply another version of "light metaphysics," but without any resident sense of rightness. See Albert Hofstadter, *Truth and Art* (New York: Columbia University Press, 1965), p. 197. In the same general vein, the lack of criteria for thinking about Being is also noted by Marx (p. 246) and in a much more polemical way by S. L. Bartky, "Originative Thinking in the Later Philosophy of Heidegger," *Philosophy and Phenomenological Research* 30 (1970): 368-91, esp. p. 378.

# Bibliography

This bibliography is divided into four parts. Part I lists primary sources by Heidegger; Part II provides the standard English translations of Heidegger currently available; Parts III and IV contain the secondary sources, book and articles respectively, either cited in or directly relevant to this study.

## I—Works by Heidegger

(A numeral after the title indicates that this work is part of the *Gesamtausgabe* series.)

*Aristotles, Metaphysik Theta 1-3 von Wesen und Wirklichkeit der Kraft* (33). Frankfurt am Main: Vittorio Klostermann, 1981.
*Aus der Erfahrung des Denkens.* 2d ed. Pfullingen: Neske, 1965.
*Einführung in die Metaphysik.* Tübingen: Max Niemeyer, 1953.
*Erläuterungen zu Hölderlins Dichtung.* 4th ed. Frankfurt am Main: Vittorio Klostermann, 1971.
*Die Frage nach dem Ding.* Tübingen: Max Niemeyer, 1962.
*Frühe Schriften.* Frankfurt am Main: Vittorio Klostermann, 1972.
*Gelassenheit.* Pfullingen: Neske, 1959.
*Grundbegriffe* (51). Frankfurt am Main: Vittorio Klostermann, 1981.
*Die Grundbegriffe der Metaphysik Welt-Endlichkeit-Einsamkeit* (29/30). Frankfurt am Main: Vittorio Klostermann, 1983
*Die Grundprobleme der Phänomenologie* (24). Frankfurt am Main: Vittorio Klostermann, 1975.
*Hebel der Hausfreund.* Pfullingen: Neske, 1957.
*Hegels Phänomenologie des Geistes* (32). Frankfurt am Main: Vittorio Klostermann, 1980.
*Heraklit* (with Eugen Fink). Frankfurt am Main: Vittorio Klostermann, 1970.
*Heraklit 1. Der Anfang des Abendländischen Denkens 2. Logik. Heraklits Lehre vom Logos* (55). Frankfurt am Main: Vittorio Klostermann, 1979.
*Hölderlins Hymne "Andenken"* (52). Frankfurt am Main: Vittorio Klostermann, 1982.
*Hölderlins Hymne "Der Ister"* (53). Frankfurt am Main: Vittorio Klostermann, 1984.
*Hölderlins Hymnen "Germanien" und "Der Rhein"* (39). Frankfurt am Main: Vittorio Klostermann, 1980.
*Holzwege.* Frankfurt am Main: Vittorio Klostermann, 1950.

*Identity and Difference.* Bilingual edition. Translated by Joan Stambaugh. New York: Harper & Row, 1969.

*Kant und das Problem der Metaphysik.* Frankfurt am Main: Vittorio Klostermann, 1951.

*Die Kunst und der Raum.* St. Gallen: Erker, 1969.

*Logik Die Frage nach der Wahrheit* (21). Frankfurt am Main: Vittorio Klostermann, 1976.

*Martin Heidegger zum 80. Geburstag.* Frankfurt am Main: Vittorio Klostermann, 1970.

*Metaphysische Anfangsgründe der Logik im Ausgang von Leibniz* (26). Frankfurt am Main: Vittorio Klostermann, 1978.

*Nietzsche I, II.* Pfullingen: Neske, 1961.

*Parmenides* (54). Frankfurt am Main: Vittorio Klostermann, 1982.

*Phänomenologie und Theologie.* Frankfurt am Main: Vittorio Klostermann, 1977.

*Phänomenologische Interpretation von Kants Kritik der Reinen Vernunft* (25). Frankfurt am Main: Vittorio Klostermann, 1977.

*Prolegomena zur Geschichte des Zeitbegriffs* (20). Frankfurt am Main: Vittorio Klostermann, 1979.

*Zur Sache des Denkens.* Tübingen: Max Niemeyer, 1969.

*Der Satz vom Grund.* Pfullingen: Neske, 1957.

*Schellings Abhandlung über das Wesen der Menschlichen Freiheit (1809).* Tübingen: Max Niemeyer, 1971.

*Sein und Zeit.* Tübingen: Max Niemeyer, 1963.

"Sprache und Heimat." In *Dauer im Wandel,* edited by Hermann Rinn and May Rychner. Munich: D. W. Callwey, 1961.

*Die Technik und die Kehre.* 2d ed. Pfullingen: Neske, 1962.

*Unterwegs zur Sprache.* Pfullingen: Neske, 1959.

*Vorträge und Aufsätze.* Pfullingen: Neske, 1954.

*Was Heisst Denken?* Tübingen: Max Niemeyer, 1961.

*Was ist das—Die Philosophie?* Pfullingen: Neske, 1956.

*Wegmarken.* Frankfurt am Main: Vittorio Klostermann, 1967.

## II—ENGLISH TRANSLATIONS OF HEIDEGGER

This part of the bibliography lists the standard English translations of Heidegger's works. The list is based on the "Heidegger Bibliography of English Translations" compiled by Keith Hoeller in the *Journal of the British Society for Phenomenology* 6 (1975): 206-8. Translations published since 1975 have been added to the list.

"Art and Space" (*Die Kunst und der Raum,* 1969). Translated by Charles H. Seibert. *Man and World* 6 (1973): 3-8.

*The Basic Problems of Phenomenology* (*Die Grundprobleme der Phänomenologie,* 1975). Translated by Albert Hofstadter. Bloomington: Indiana University Press, 1982.

*Basic Writings* (Introduction to *Sein und Zeit,* 1927—translated by Joan Stambaugh; "*Was ist Metaphysik?*" in *Wegmarken*—translated by David Farrell

Krell; "*Vom Wesen der Wahrheit*" in *Wegmarken*, 1967—translated by John Sallis; selections from "*Der Ursprung des Kunstwerkes*," in *Holzwege*, 1950; "*Brief über den 'Humanismus'* " in *Wegmarken*, 1967—translated by Frank A. Capuzzi; selections from *Die Frage nach dem Ding*, 1962; "*Die Frage nach der Technik*" in *Vorträge und Aufsätze*, 1954; selections from *Was Heisst Denken?*, 1954; "*Das Ende der Philosophie und die Aufgabe des Denkens*" in *Zur Sache des Denkens*, 1969. Edited by David Farrell Krell. New York: Harper & Row, 1977.

*Being and Time* (*Sein and Zeit*, 1927). Translated by John Macquarrie and Edward Robinson. New York: Harper & Row, 1962.

*Discourse on Thinking* (*Gelassenheit*, 1959). Translated by John M. Anderson and E. Hans Freund. New York: Harper & Row. 1966.

*Early Greek Thinking* ("*Der Spruch des Anaximander*," in *Holzwege*, 1950; "*Logos*," "*Moria*," and "*Aletheia*," in *Vorträge und Aufsätze*, 1954). Translated by David Farrell Krell and Frank Capuzzi. New York: Harper & Row, 1975.

*The End of Philosophy* ("*Uberwindung der Metaphysik*," in *Vorträge und Aufsätze*, 1954; "*Die Metaphysik als Geschichte des Seins*," "*Entwürfe zur Geschichte des Seins als Metaphysik*," and "*Die Erinnerung in die Metaphysik*," in *Nietzsche II*, 1961). Translated by Joan Stambaugh. New York: Harper & Row, 1973.

*The Essence of Reasons* (*Vom Wesen des Grundes*, 1929; also in *Wegmarken*, 1967). Bilingual edition. Translated by Terrence Malick. Evanston: Northwestern University Press, 1969.

*Existence and Being* (*Was ist Metaphysik?*, 1929; *Vom Wesen der Wahrheit*, 1943; both also in *Wegmarken*, 1967; "*Heimkunft / An die Verwandten*" and "*Hölderlin und das Wesen der Dichtung*," in *Erläuterungen zu Holderlins Dichtung*, 1971). Edited by Werner Brock. "What is Metaphysics?" and "On the Essence of Truth" translated by R. F. C. Hull and Alan Crick; "Remembrance of the Poet" and "Hölderlin and the Essence of Poetry" translated by Douglas Scott. Chicago: Regnery-Gateway, 1949.

"From the Last Marburg Lecture Course" ("*Aus der letzten Marburger Vorlesung*," in *Zeit und Geschichte*, Festschrift for Rudolph Bultmann, 1964). Translated by James M. Robinson. In *The Future of our Religious Past: Essays in Honor of Rudolph Bultmann*. Edited by James M. Robinson. New York: Harper & Row, 1971): 312-32.

Hegel's Concept of Experience ("*Hegels Begriff der Erfahrung*," in *Holzwege*, 1950). Edited by J. Glenn Gray. New York: Harper & Row, 1970.

*Identity and Difference* (*Identität und Differenz*, 1957). Bilingual edition. Translated by Joan Stambaugh. New York: Harper & Row, 1969.

*An Introduction to Metaphysics* (*Einführung in die Metaphysik*, 1953). Translated by Ralph Manheim. New Haven: Yale University Press, 1959.

*Kant and the Problem of Metaphysics* (*Kant und das Problem der Metaphysik*, 1929). Translated by James S. Churchill. Bloomington: Indiana University Press, 1962.

"Kant's Thesis about Being" (*Kants These über das Sein*, 1963; also in *Wegmarken*, 1967). Translated by Ted E. Klein and William E. Pohl. *Southwestern Journal of Philosophy* 6 (1973): 7-33.

"Letter on Humanism" ("*Brief über den 'Humanismus'*," in *Wegmarken*, 1967). Translated by Edgar Lohner in *Philosophy in the Twentieth Century*. Edited by

William Barrett and Henry D. Aiken. New York: Random House, 1962. Vol. 3: 271-302.

*Nietzsche Volume I: The Will to Power as Art* (*Nietzsche I*, 1961). Translated by David Farrell Krell. New York: Harper & Row, 1977.

*On the Way to Language* (*Unterwegs zur Sprache*, 1959). Translated by Peter D. Hertz and Joan Stambaugh. New York: Harper & Row, 1971. "*Die Sprache*," the first chapter in the German edition, appears in *Poetry, Language, Thought*.

On Time and Being (*Zur Sache des Denkens*, 1969). Translated by Joan Stambaugh. New York: Harper & Row, 1972.

"Only a God Can Save Us: *Der Spiegel's* interview with Martin Heidegger on September 23, 1966." Translated by Mario P. Alter and John D. Caputo. *Philosophy Today* 20 (1976): 193-219.

"The Pathway" (*Der Feldweg*, 1953; also in *Martin Heidegger zum 80. Geburtstag*). Bilingual edition. Translated by Thomas F. O'Meara (Revisions: Thomas J. Sheehan). *Listening* 9(1973): 32-9. An earlier translation by Thomas F. O'Meara appeared in *Listening* 2 (1967): 88-91.

*The Piety of Thinking* (includes *Phänomenologie und Theologie*, 1927; "*Grundsätze des Denkens*" in *Jahrbuch für Psychologie und Psychotherapie*, 1958). Translated by James G. Hart and John C. Maralda. Bloomington: Indiana University Press, 1976.

"Plato's Doctrine of Truth" ("*Platons Lehre von der Wahrheit*," in *Wegmarken*, 1967). Translated by John Barlow. In *Philosophy in the Twentieth Century*. Edited by William Barrett and Henry D. Aiken. New York: Random House, 1962. Vol. 3: 251-70.

*Poetry, Language, Thought* ("*Der Ursprung des Kunstwerkes*" and "*Wozu Dichter?*" in *Holzwege*, 1950; *Aus der Erfahrung des Denkens*, 1954; "*Bauen Wohnen Denken*," "*Das Ding*," and " . . . *dichterisch wohnt der Mensch* . . . ," in *Vorträge und Aufsätze*, 1954; "*Die Sprache*," in *Unterwegs zur Sprache*, 1959). Translated by Albert Hofstadter. New York: Harper & Row, 1971.

*The Question Concerning Technology* ("*Die Frage nach der Technik*" and "*Die Kehre*" in *Die Technik und die Kehre*, 1962; "*Nietzsches Wort 'Gott ist tot'* " and *Die Zeit des Weltbildes*" in *Holzwege*, 1950; "*Wissenschaft und Besinnung*" in *Vorträge und Aufsätze*, 1954). Translated by William Lovitt. New York: Harper & Row, 1977.

*The Question of Being* (*Zur Seinsfrage*, 1956; also in *Wegmarken*, Bilingual edition. Translated by William Kluback and Jean T. Wilde. New York: Twayne, 1958.

"The Way Back into the Ground of Metaphysics: ("*Der Rückgang in den Grund der Metaphysik—Einleitung zu: Was ist Metaphysik?*" in *Wegmarken*, 1967). Translated by Walter Kaufmann. In *Existentialism from Dostoevsky to Sartre*. Edited by Walter Kaufmann. New York: New American Library, 1957; revised and expanded edition, 1975: 265-79.

*What is a Thing?* (*Die Frage nach dem Ding*, 1962). Translated by W. B. Barton and Vera Deutsch. Chicago: Regnery, 1967.

*What is Called Thinking?* (*Was Heisst Denken?*, 1954). Translated by Fred W. Wieck and J. Glenn Gray. New York: Harper & Row, 1968.

*What is Philosophy?* (*Was ist das—die Philosophie?*, 1956). Bilingual edition. Translated by William Kluback and Jean T. Wilde. New York: Twayne, 1958.

"Who is Nietzsche's Zarathustra?" (*"Wer ist Nietzsches Zarathustra?"* in *Vorträge und Aufsätze*, 1954). Translated by Bernd Magnus. *The Review of Metaphysics* 20 (1967): 411-31.

## III—Secondary Sources: Books

Andia, Ysabel de. *Présence et Eschatologie dans la Pensée de Martin Heidegger.* Paris: Editions Universitaires, 1975.

Aristotle. *De Interpretatione*. Translated by E. M. Edghill. *Metaphysics*. Translated by W. D. Ross. In *Basic Works of Aristotle*. Edited by Richard McKeon. New York: Random House, 1941.

Augustine, Saint. *De Genesi ad litteram (Literal Commentary on Genesis)* In *Corpus Scriptorum Ecclesiasticorum Latinorum*. Vol. 28, Pt. 1. Vienna, 1984—.

Barth, Karl. *The Doctrine of the Word of God. Prolegomena to Church Dogmatics*. Vol. 1. Pt. 1 Edinburgh: T. & T. Clark, 1936.

Blitz, Mark. *Heidegger's Being and Time and the Possibility of Political Philosophy.* Ithaca: Cornell University Press, 1981.

Caputo, John. *The Mystical Element in Heidegger's Thought*. Athens: Ohio University Press, 1978.

Danner, Helmut. *Das Göttliche und der Gott bei Heidegger*. Meisenheim am Glan: A. Hain, 1971.

Deely, John N. *The Tradition via Heidegger*. The Hague: Martinus Nijhoff, 1971.

Fay, Thomas A. *Heidegger: The Critique of Logic*. The Hague: Martinus Nijhoff, 1977.

Gethmann-Seifert, Annemarie. *Das Verhältnis von Philosophie und und Theologie im Denken Martin Heideggers*. Freiburg/Munich: Karl Alber, 1974.

Gilson, Etienne, Thomas Langan, and Armand A. Maurer, C.S.B. *Recent Philosophy: Hegel to the Present* (New York: Random House, 1966).

Griffin, Nicholas. *Relative Identity*. Oxford: Clarendon Press, 1977.

Halliburton, David. *Poetic Thinking: An Approach to Heidegger*. Chicago: University of Chicago Press, 1982.

*Heidegger: The Man and the Thinker*. Edited by Thomas Sheehan. Chicago: Precedent Publications, 1981.

Hofstadter, Albert. *Truth and Art*. New York: Colombia University Press, 1965.

Huch, Kurt Jürgen. *Philosophiegeschichtliche Vorassetzungen der Heideggerschen Ontologie*. Frankfurt Am Main: Europäische Verlanganstalt, 1967.

Jäger, Alfred. *Gott: Nochmal Martin Heidegger*. Tübingen: Mohr, 1978.

Laffoucriere, Odette. *Le Destin de la Pensee et "La Mort de Dieu" selon Heidegger.* The Hague: Martinus Nijhoff, 1968.

Langan, Thomas. *The Meaning of Heidegger*. New York: Columbia University Press, 1959.

Löwith, Karl. *Heidegger: Denker in dürftigen Zeit*. Göttingen: Vandenhoeck, & Ruprecht, 1965.

Macomber, W. B. *The Anatomy of Disillusion*. Evanston: Northwestern University Press, 1967.

Macquarrie, John. *An Existentialist Theology: A Comparison of Heidegger and Bultmann*. New York: Harper & Row, 1965.

Magnus, Bernd. *Heidegger's Metahistory of Philosophy.* The Hague: Martinus Nifhoff, 1970.

Marx, Werner. *Heidegger und die Tradition.* Stuttgart: W. Kohlhammer, 1961. English translation *Heidegger and the Tradition.* Translated by Theodore Kisiel and Murray Greene. Evanston: Northwestern University Press, 1971.

Moehling, Karl. *Martin Heidegger and the Nazi Party: An Examination.* Dekalb, Illinois: Ph.D. Dissertation, 1972.

Murray, Michael, ed. *Heidegger and Modern Philosophy.* New Haven: Yale University Press, 1978.

Noller, Gerhard. *Heidegger und die Theologie; Beginn und Fortgang der Diskussion.* Munich: Chr. Kaiser Verlag, 1967.

Ott, Heinrich. *Denken und Sein: Der Weg Martin Heideggers und der Weg der Theologie.* Zollikon: Evangelischer Verlag, 1959.

Perotti, James L. *Heidegger on the Divine; The Thinker, the Poet, and God.* Athens: Ohio University Press, 1974.

Plato. *The Sophist.* Translated by F. M. Cornford. In *Collected Dialogues.* Edited by Edith Hamilton and Huntington Cairns. New York: Bollingen, 1963.

Pöggeler, Otto. *Der Denkweg Martin Heideggers.* Pfullingen: Neske, 1963.

—, ed. *Heidegger: Perspektiven zur Deutung seines Werks.* Cologne: Kiepenhauer & Witsch, 1970.

—. *Philosophie und Politik bei Heidegger.* Freiburg im Breisgau: 1972.

Richardson, William J. *Heidegger through Phenomenology to Thought* 2d ed. The Hague: Martinus Nijhoff, 1967.

Robinson, James M. and Cobb, John B. eds. *The later Heidegger and Theology.* Vol. 1. New Frontiers in Theology. New York: Harper & Row, 1963.

Rosales, Alberto. *Transzenden und Differenz; ein Beitrag zum Problem der Ontologischen Differenz beim frühen Heidegger.* The Hague: Martinus Nijhoff, 1970.

Rosen, Stanley. *Nihilism: A Philosophical Essay.* New Haven: Yale University Press, 1969.

Sallis, John, ed. *Heidegger and the Path of Thinking.* Pittsburgh: Duquesne University Press, 1970.

Schwan, Alexander. *Politische Philosophie im Denken Heideggers.* Cologne: Westdeutscher Verlag, 1965.

Seidel, George Joseph, O.S.B. *Martin Heidegger and the Pre-Socratics.* Lincoln: University of Nebraska Press, 1964.

Sherover, Charles M. *Heidegger, Kant & Time.* Bloomington: Indiana University Press, 1971.

Sladeczek, Franz-Maria. *Ist das Dasein Gottes Beweisbar? Wie Steht die Existentialphilosophie Martin Heideggers zu dieser Frage?* Wurzberg: K. Trilitisch, 1967.

Starr, David E. *Entity and Existence: An Ontological Investigation of Aristotle and Heidegger.* New York: Burt Franklin & Co., 1975.

Strawson, P. F. *Introduction to Logical Theory.* London: Methuen & Co. Ltd., 1952.

Tauxe, Henri Charles. *La Notion de Finitude dans la Philosophie de Martin Heidegger.* Lausanne: Editions L'Age d'homme, 1971.

Thomas Aquinas, Saint. *The Summa Contra Gentiles.* Translated by the English Dominican fathers. London: Burns, Oates & Washbourne, 1923—.

Tragesser, Robert S. *Phenomenology and Logic.* Ithaca: Cornell University Press, 1977.
Tugendhat, Ernst. *Der Wahrheitsbegriff bei Husserl and Heidegger.* 2d ed. Berlin: Walter de Gruyter & Co., 1970.
Van der Meulen, Ja. *Heidegger und Hegel, oder Widerstreit und Widerspruch.* Meisenheim am Glan: A. Hain, 1953.
Veatch, Henry B. *Two Logics; The Conflict between Classical and Neo-Analytic Philosophy.* Evanston: Northwestern University Press, 1969.
Versenyi, Laszlo. *Heidegger, Being and Truth.* New Haven: Yale University Press, 1965.
Vycinas, Vincent. *Earth and Gods: An Introduction to the Philosophy of Martin Heidegger.* The Hague: Martinus Nijhoff, 1961.
White, David A. *Heidegger and the Language of Poetry.* Lincoln: University of Nebraska Press, 1978.
Wiplinger, Fridolin. *Wahrheit und Geschichtlichkeit.* Freiburg/Munich: Karl Alber, 1961.
Zimmerman, Michael E. *Eclipse of the Self: The Development of Heidegger's Concept of Authenticity.* Athens: Ohio University Press, 1981.

## IV—SECONDARY SOURCES: ARTICLES

Apel, Karl-Otto. *"Wittgenstein und Heidegger: Die Frage nach dem Sinn von Sein und der Sinnlosigkeitsverdacht gegen alle Metaphysik."* *Philosophisches Jahrbuch* 75 (1967): 56-94.
Barth, Karl. *"Gott und das Nichtige."* In Noller, *Heidegger und die Theologie*: 197-225.
Bartky, S. L. "Originative Thinking in the Later Philosophy of Heidegger." *Philosophy and Phenomenological Research* 30 (1970): 368-91.
Biemel, Walter. "The Development of Heidegger's Concept of the Thing." *Southwestern Journal of Philosophy* 2 (1980): 47-66.
Birault, Henri. *"De l'Etre, du Divin, et des Dieux Heideggers l'Existence de Dieu."* *Cahiers de l'actualite religieuse* 16 (1961): 49-76.
Bixler, Julius Seelye. "The Failure of Martin Heidegger." *Harvard Theological Review* 56 (1963): 121-43.
Borgmann, Albert. "Heidegger and Symbolic Logic." In Manfred S. Frings, ed. *Heidegger and the Quest for Truth.* Chicago: Quadrangle Books, 1968: 139-62.
Bröcker, Walter. *"Heidegger und die Logik."* *Philosophische Rundschau* 1 (1953-54): 48-56.
Caputo, John D. "Heidegger's God and the Lord of History." *New Scholasticism* 57 (1983): 439-64.
―――. "The Thought of Being and the Conversation of Mankind—The Case of Heidegger and Rorty." *Review of Metaphysics* 36 (1982/3): 661-85.
―――. "Time and Being in Heidegger." *Modern Schoolman* 50 (1973): 325-49.
―――. Review of David A. White's *Heidegger and the Language of Poetry. Review of Metaphysics* 33 (1980): 811-13.
Coreth, Emerich. *"Auf der Spur der entflohenen Götter. Martin Heidegger und die Gottesfrage."* *Wort und Wahrheit* 9 (1954): 107-16.

Corvez, Maurice. "*La Place de Dieu dans l'ontologie de Martin Heidegger.*" *Revue Thomiste* 61 (1953): 287-320; 62 (1954): 79-102; 559-83; 63 (1955): 377-90.

Cress, Donald W. "*Heidegger's Criticism of 'Entitative Metaphysics' in his later work.*" *International Philosophical Quarterly* 12 (1972): 69-86.

Dondeyne, Albert. "*La Difference Ontologique chez M. Heidegger.*" *Revue Philosophique de Louvain* 56 (1958): 35-62, 251-93.

Demske, James M. "Heidegger's Quadrate and Revelation of Being." *Philosophy Today* 7 (1963): 245-57.

Ebeling, Gerhard. "*Verantworten des Glaubens in Begegnung mit dem Denken Martin Heideggers.*" *Zeitschrift für Theologie und Kirche Beiheft* 2 (1961): 119-24.

Edie, James M. "The Absence of God." In *Christianity and Existentialism*. Evanston: Northwestern University Press, 1963.

Fackenheim, Emil L. "The Historicity and Transcendence of Philosophic Truth." *Inter-American Congress of Philosophy*, 7th, Laval University, Quebec (1967): 77-92.

Franz, Helmut. "*Das Denken Heideggers und Die Theologie.*" *Zeitschrift für Theologie und Kirche*. Beiheft 2 (1961): 81-118.

Gadamer, Hans Georg. "Plato and Heidegger." In Sprung, Mervyn, ed. *The Question of Being*. University Park: Penn State University Press, 1978.

⸻⸻. "The Religious Dimension in Heidegger." In *Transcendence and the Sacred*. Edited by Alan M. Olson. Notre Dame: University of Notre Dame Press, 1981.

Gray, J. Glenn. "Splendor of the Simple." *Philosophy East and West* 20 (1970): 227-40.

Grene, Marjorie. "The Paradoxes of Historicity." *Review of Metaphysics* 32 (1978): 15-36.

Guzzoni, Alfredo. "*Ontologische Differenz und Nichts.*" In *Martin Heidegger zum Siebsigsten Geburtstag*. Pfullingen: Neske, 1959.

Hahn, Robert. "Truth (Aletheia) in the Context of Heidegger's Critique of Plato and the Tradition." *Southwest Philosophical Studies* 4 (1979): 51-57.

Harries, Karsten. "*Das befreite Nichts.*" In *Durchblicke Martin Heidegger zum 80. Geburtstag*. Frankfurt am Main: Vittorio Klostermann, 1970.

⸻⸻. "Heidegger as a Political Thinker." *Review of Metaphysics* 29 (1976): 642-49.

⸻⸻. "Heidegger's Conception of the Holy." *Personalist* 47 (1966): 169-84.

⸻⸻. Review of David A. White's *Heidegger and the Language of Poetry*. *Philosophy and Literature* 4 (1980): 132-33.

Hermann, Rolf-Dieter. "Heidegger and Logic." *Sophia* 29 (1961): 353-57.

Hinnees, Richard C. "Being and God in Heidegger's Philosophy." *Proceedings of the American Catholic Philosophical Association* 31 (1957): 157-62.

Hoeller, Keith. "Heidegger Bibliography of English Translations." *Journal of the British Society for Phenomenology* 6 (1975): 206-8.

Hoy, David C. "History, Historicity, and Historiography in *Being and Time*." In Murray, *Heidegger and Modern Philosophy*.

Itzkowitz, Kenneth. "Differance and Identity." *Research in Phenomenology* 8 (1978): 127-43.

Jonas, Hans. "Heidegger and Theology." In *The Phenomenon of Life*. New York: Harper & Row, 1966.

Jüngel, Eberhard. "*Der Schritt Zurück: Eine Auseinandersetzung mit der Heidegger-Deutung Heinrich Otts.*" Zeitschrift für Theologie und Kirche 58 (1961): 104-22.

Kates, Carol A. "An Intentional Analysis of the Law of Contradiction." *Research in Phenomenology* 9 (1979): 108-26.

Klein, Ted. "What has Identity to do with Appropriation? A Response to David A. White." *Southwestern Journal of Philosophy* 9 (1978): 65-72.

Köchler, H. "*Das Gottesproblem im Denken Heideggers.*" Zeitschrift für Katholische Theologie 95 (1973): 61-90.

Kockelmans, Joseph. "Heidegger on Theology." *Southwestern Journal of Philosophy* 4 (1973): 85-108.

_____ Review of Annemarie Gethmann-Siefert's *Das Verhältnis von Philosophie und Theologie im Denken Martin Heideggers*. Man and World 8 (1975): 461-73.

Kreeft, Peter. "Zen in Heidegger's *Gelassenheit.*" International Philosophical Quarterly 11 (1971): 521-45.

Lampert, Laurence. "On Heidegger and Historicism." *Philosophy and Phenomenological Research* 34 (1974): 586-90.

Löwith, Karl. "*Heidegger's Auslegung des Ungesagten in Wort 'Gott ist tot'.*" Die Neue Rundschau 64 (1953): 105-37.

McCumber, John. "Language and Appropriation: The Nature of Heideggerian Dialogue." *Personalist* 60 (1979): 384-96.

Maly, Kenneth. "Toward *Ereignis.*" Research in Phenomenology 3 (1973): 63-93.

Mason, Robert. "Rahner and Heidegger: Being, Hearing and God." *Thomist* 37 (1973): 455-88.

Mohanty, J. N. Review of Thomas A. Fay's *Heidegger: The Critique of Logic*. Southwestern Journal of Philosophy 11 (1980): 174-79.

Morrison, Ronald P. "Kant, Husserl, and Heidegger on Time and the Unity of 'Consciousness'." *Philosophy and Phenomenological Research* 39 (1978): 182-98.

Nagel, Ernest. "Logic Without Ontology." In Yervant Hovhannes Krikorian, ed. *Naturalism And The Human Spirit*. New York: Columbia University Press, 1944.

O'Meara, Thomas F. "Tillich and Heidegger: A Structural Relationship." *Harvard Theological Review* 61 (1968): 249-61.

Oshima, S. "Barth's *Analogia Relationis* and Heidegger's Ontological Difference." *Journal of Religion* 53 (1973); 176-94.

Ott, Heinrich. "*Die Bedeutung von Martin Heidegger's Denken für die Methode der Theologie.*" In *Durchblicke*: 27-38.

Pöggeler, Otto. "*Sein als Ereignis.*" Zeitschrift für Philosophische Forschung 13 (1959): 597-632. English translation "Being as Appropriation." Translated by Ruediger Hermann Grimm. *Philosophy Today* 19 (1975): 16-42.

_____ "Heidegger Today." In Edward G. Ballard and Charles E. Scott, eds. *Martin Heidegger: In Europe and America* (The Hague: Martinus Nijhoff, 1973).

_____ "*Heidegger und das Problem der Zeit.*" In *L'heritage de Kant*. Paris: Beauchesne, 1982.

_____ " 'Historicity' in Heidegger's Late Work." Translated by J. N. Mohanty. *Southwestern Journal of Philosophy* 4 (1973): 53-73.

_____ "Metaphysics and Topology of Being in Heidegger." *Man and World* 8 (1975): 3-27.

Richardson, William J. "Heidegger and God—and Professor Jonas." *Thought* 40 (1965): 13-40.

———. "Heidegger and Theology." *Theological Studies* 26 (1965):

Richey, Clarence. "On the Intentional Ambiguity of Heidegger's Metaphysics." *Journal of Philosophy* 55 (1958): 1144-8.

Rollin, R. E. "Heidegger's Philosophy of History in 'Being and Time'." *Modern Schoolman* 49 (1972): 97-112.

Rorty, Richard. "Overcoming the Tradition: Heidegger and Dewey." *Review of Metaphysics* 30 (1976): 280-305. Reprinted in Murray, *Heidegger and Modern Philosophy*: 239-58.

Rosen, Stanley. "Thinking about Nothing." In Murray, *Heidegger and Modern Philosophy*: 116-33.

Rosenstein, Leon. "Heidegger and Plato and the Good." *Philosophy Today* 22 (1978): 332-54.

———. "Mysticism as Preontology: A Note on the Heideggerian Connection." *Philosophy and Phenomenological Research* 39 (1978): 57-73.

Rotenstreich, Nathan. "The Ontological Status of History." *Philosophical Quarterly* 9 (1972): 49-58.

Schrag, Calvin O. "Heidegger on Repetition and Historical Understanding." *Philosophy East and West* 20 (1970): 287-95.

———. "Re-Thinking Metaphysics." In Frings, *Heidegger and the Quest for Truth*. Truth.

Schultz, Walter. "God of the Philosophers in Modern Metaphysics." Translated by Parvis Emad. *Man and World* 6 (1971): 353-71.

Scott, Charles R. "Notes and Observations: Heidegger Reconsidered. A Response to Professor Jonas." *Harvard Theological Review* 59 (1966): 175-85.

Seidl, Horst. "*Zur Seinsfrage bei Aristoteles und Heidegger.*" *Zeitschrift für Philosophische Forschung* 30 (1976): 203-26.

Seyppel, J. "A Criticism of Heidegger's Time Concept with Reference to Bergson's Duree." *Revue Internationale de Philosophie* 10 (1956): 503-8.

Sheehan, Thomas. "Heidegger's 'Introduction to the Phenomenology of Religion', 1920-21." *Personalist* 60 (1979): 312-24.

Sinn, Dieter. "*Heideggers Spätphilosophie.*" *Philosophische Rundschau* 14 (1967): 81-182.

Smith, Christopher. "Heidegger, Hegel, and the Problem of *das Nichts*." *International Philosophical Quarterly* 8 (1968): 379-405.

Stambaugh, Joan. "The Question of God in Heidegger's Thought." *Southwestern Journal of Philosophy* 10 (1979): 127-38.

Tugendhat, Ernst. "*Das Sein und das Nichts.*" In *Durchblicke*: 132-61.

Vater, Michael. "Heidegger and Schelling: The Finitude of Being." *Idealistic Studies* 5 (1975): 20-58.

Volkmann-Schluck, Karl Heinz. "*Der Satz vom Widerspruch als Anfang der Philosophie.*" In *Martin Heidegger zum Siebigsten Geburtstag*. Pfullingen: Neske, 1959: 134-50.

Welte, Bernhard. "God in Heidegger's Thought." *Philosophy Today* 26 (1982): 85-100.

White, David A. "Heidegger on Sameness and Difference." *Southwestern Journal of Philosophy* 11 (1980): 107-26.

———. "On Being and Unity in Heidegger." *Tulane Studies in Philosophy* 32 (1984): 87-93.
———. "On Historicism and Heidegger's Notion of Ontological Difference." *Monist* 64 (1981): 518-33.
———. "Truth and Being: A Critique of Heidegger on Plato." *Man and World* 7 (1974): 118-34.
———. "Two Premises in Heidegger's Analysis of Identity." *Southwestern Journal of Philosophy* 9 (1978): 51-64.
Williams, T. R. "Heidegger and the Theologians." *Heythrop Journal* 12 (1971): 258-80.
Wohlfart, Günter. *"Der Augenblick. Zum Begriff der ecstatischen der Zeitlichkeit bei Heidegger." Allgemeine Zeitschrift für Philosophie* 7 (1982): 27-55.
Zimmerman, Michael E. "Heidegger, Ethics, and National Socialism." *Southwestern Journal of Philosophy* 5 (1974): 97-106.
———. "Heidegger's 'Completion' of *Sein und Zeit*." *Philosophy and Phenomenological Research* 39 (1979): 537-60.
———. "Some Important Themes in Current Heidegger Research." *Research in Phenomenology* 7 (1977): 259-81.

# Index

Anaximander: as "originary" thinker, 52; and sameness, 69

*Angst* (see Anxiety)

*Anwesen* (see Presence)

Anxiety: and negation, 47, 50-52, 57-59, 63-66; and sameness, 77

*Aristoteles, Metaphysik Theta 1-3 von Wesen und Wirklichkeit der Kraft*: 97, 111, 113, 121, 157, 194

Appearance: and deity, 138, 141-42, 143; and thinghood, 113-14, 117

Appropriation (*Ereignis*): and fourfold, 110, and metaphysics, 176; and presence, 179, 186-87, 188-89, 190-91; and principle of identity, 93; and sameness, 85-86, and thinghood, 110. *See also* Being; Time

Aristotle: 14-15; and Being, 191; Heidegger's critique of, 32-34, 39-40, 42; and metaphysics, 153, 155, 157, 161, 162-63; and negation, 47-48; and origin of logic, 23, 31, 203; and principle of contradiction, 30, 38; and sameness, 69; on time, 225

Artifact: and fourfold, 112, 120-22; perception of, 113-14; and presence, 117, 181; and thinghood, 117, 125

Augustine, St.: on God, 141; on time, 220

Barth, Karl: and eternity, 220n

*Bauen* (see Building)

Being (*Sein*): and beings, 42, 52, 55, 66, 71-72, 74-79, 113, 165, 193-203; concept of, 177, 186; and deity, 133, 138, 140, 144, 148; forgetting of, 152, 165; and fourfold, 137, and history, 3, 101, 159; and logic, 12-13; and *logos*, 32; meaning of, 11, 83, 105, 124, 182; and metaphysics, 96-99, 155-57, 167; and negation, 53, 56, 63, 190, 195-99; as presence, 94-95, 176-87, 191-93; and principle of contradiction, 30; and principle of identity, 164; and sameness, 69, 70, 86; and the thinking of, 69, 170, 172, 187. *See also* Presence

Bergson, Henri: and time, 223, 226

Building (*Bauen*): and fourfold, 112-13; "rules" for, 112

Christianity: and deity, 141, 143

Concept: of Being, 177, 186; of God, 132; and types, 120-21

Concern (*Sorge*): as name in Heidegger, 16

Continuum: and deity, 146; and historicism, 169; and structure of presence, 199-200

Contradiction: principle of: in Aristotle, 29-34, 38-40, 42; and correctness in logic, 25, 30, 37; Heidegger's critique of, 22, 30-31, 33-36; and language, 28, 34-35; and *logos*, 34; in metaphysics, 29-30; multiple senses of in Heidegger, 26-27; and negation, 36-37; and principle of identity, 26

Dasein: and anxiety, 50-51, 57-59; and death, 129; and deity, 133; and feeling, 51-52, 214; and history, 150; and logic, 27-28; and negation, 51-52. *See also* Mortals

Death: and Dasein, 129

Deity: and destiny, 137; and divine, 134-35, 145-46, 219-20; nature of, 113; and presence, 140-41; and thinking, 132-33; and Yahweh, 142-43; and Zeus, 132, 142-43, 144. *See also* Divine; God

*Denken* (see Thinking)

Descartes, Rene: as "planetary" thinker, 224; and sameness, 68

Destiny (*Geschick*): and Being, 153, 159, 163, 167, 171, 183; and deity, 138-39; and epochs in metaphysics, 153, 160, 164; and history, 158-60; and metaphysics, 183; and thinghood, 115

Determination: and metaphysics, 159; and presence, 195-96

*Dichten* (see Poetizing)

Difference: as degree and kind, 76-77; and negation, 56; and presence, 198. *See also* Sameness

*Ding* (see Thinghood)

Divine: and appearances of deity, 131; and deity, 131, 144-47; and thinghood, 109, 144-47. *See also* Deity; God

Duration: and presence, 202

Dwelling (*Wohnen*): in fourfold, 111-12; as near and far, 112

Earth: in fourfold, 108-9, 217

*Einführung in die Metaphysik*: 12, 15, 23-25, 31-32, 44, 69, 108, 149-51, 154, 156

Epoch: in Being, 149, 169-72, 173, 206; and history of metaphysics, 153, 156-58, 164, 180; and necessity, 172; and possibility, 161; and presence, 193; and principle of contradiction, 29; and principle of identity, 93-94; and sameness, 82, 84; sequence of, in metaphysics, 166-68

*Ereignis* (see Appropriation)

*Erläuterungen zu Hölderlins Dichtung*: 26, 68, 120, 130, 138, 158
Essence: of divine, 134-35; and thinghood, 120, 123. *See also* Nature
Eternity: and God, 136-37; in Karl Barth, 220; and laws of logic, 27-28
Evil: Heidegger's notion of, 215; and negation, 215

Falsehood: and negation, 48-49. *See also* Truth
Fay, Thomas: on Heidegger and logic, 10-12
Feeling: as anxiety, 51, 57, 62; as courage, 51-52, 58; and negation, 49-50, 61-62
Fichte, Johan G.: and laws of logic, 216; and principle of identity, 92
Fourfold (*Geviert*): and Being, 106, 114, 124-26, 133; and deity, 109, 128, 133-34; and destiny, 115; and divine, 109, 134, 143-44, 146-47; and dwelling, 111; and earth, 108-9, 217; and heavens, 109; and individuation of things, 116-24; and *logos*, 119-20; and mortals, 111, 119, 137; and place, 112, 117; and presence, 110, 117; and thinghood, 107-8, 110. *See also* Thinghood
*Die Frage nach dem Ding*: 22, 67, 107, 111, 115, 121, 130, 132, 157
Future: as part of presence, 184, 196-97; in *Sein und Zeit*, 226

*Gegenwart* (see Present)
*Gelassenheit*: 120, 217
German Idealism: and history of metaphysics, 155; and principle of identity, 92, 98
*Geschehen* (see Historizing)
*Geschick* (see Destiny)
*Geviert* (see Fourfold)
God: appearances of, 109; and eternity, 136-37; and gods, 129-30, 134, 145; in Hölderlin, 132; lack of, 130, 135-42; and logic, 27; and mortals, 132; proofs of existence for, 131. *See also* Deity, Divine
Grammar: and language, 8, 76; and logic, 7, 8, 31
Greeks: and deity, 130, 132, 143; and history of Being, 152-53, 156, 158, 223; language of the, and presence, 108, 205; and sameness, 72, 74, 82
*Die Grundprobleme der Phänomenologie*: 191, 199

Heavens: in fourfold, 109
Hegel, Georg: and metaphysics, 156, 179, 223; and principle of contradiction, 29, 213; and principle of identity, 92-93, 95, 98, 99
*Hegels Phänomenologie des Geistes*: 21, 113, 157, 178
Heidegger, Martin: as agnostic, 129; "meaning" of, 7, 15; and mysticism, 8; and Nazism, 20, 212; as philosopher, 9, 21, 206; and theological background, 128
Heraclitus: as "originary" thinker, 152; and sameness, 69
*Heraklit 1. Der Anfang des abendländischen Denkens 2. Logik. Heraklits Lehre vom Logos*: 24, 31, 33, 51-52, 65, 107-8, 113, 119, 148, 152-53, 155-58, 177
*Heraklit Seminar Wintersemester 1966/67*: 158
Historicism: and Being, 168, 171-223; and Dasein, 151; and sameness, 82-83, 85
Historizing (*Geschehen*): beginning of, 150, 154; and Dasein, 150-51; and destiny, 153, 158, 159, 163; and metaphysics, 155-58, 160, 162; and sameness, 157; and thinking, 152-53, 159, 160, 165, 170; and time, 159. *See also*: History
History: and Being, 149, 157; and logic, 155; and nature of deity, 144, 147; and ontological difference, 149, 164-65, 168-69; origin of, 154; as possibility, 160-62. *See also*: Historizing
Hölderlin, Friedrich: and God, 132; and origin of fourfold, 217
*Hölderlins Hymnen "Germanien" and "Der Rhein"*: 154, 158, 182
Holy: in Heidegger, 219
*Holzwege*: 69, 72, 106, 108, 115, 120, 129-30, 140, 145; 151-54, 156-58
Human nature: change in, 17; and logic, 17; and presence, 191; and time, 209, 226
Hume, David: as "planetary" thinker, 224
Husserl, Edmund: as "planetary" thinker, 224

*Identität und Differenz*: 9, 69, 71, 89-95, 97, 131, 133, 148, 158, 165, 171-73
Identity, principle of: and history of metaphysics, 92-93, 97-100; and principle of contradiction, 91; and sameness, 88-89; and sequence of epochs in metaphysics, 95-98; and thinking, 90, 92, 100-101; and time, 94-95, 100; and unity, 89-90
Individuation: problem of, 107, 116-26; and presence, 117-18; and thinghood, 106, 108, 114; and types, 116, 118, 120, 124
Interpretation: principles of, for Heidegger, 3-21; and representational thinking, 13-14

Jesus Christ: and nature of deity, 141-42
Judaism: and nature of deity, 141, 143

Kant, Immanuel: as epochal thinker, 162; and principle of contradiction, 213; and thinghood, 105, 107, 130; and time, 183, 223
*Kant und das Problem der Metaphysik*: 213

Kierkegaard, Søren: as "planetary" thinker, 224; and principle of contradiction, 213

Language: in Aristotle, 34; and Being, 11, 168, 173; as gesture, 8; and grammar, 8-9, 33; and *logos*, 34, 107; in metaphysics, 6; and presence, 176-77; and sameness, 70, 73, 78; and saying, 25, 133; as silence, 36; and thinghood, 108; and thinking, 5-8; and time, 36, 179; as unsaid, 65. *See also* Logic; *Logos*

Leibniz, Gottfried W.: 29, 30; and logic, 67; and metaphysics, 154, 223; and sameness, 69

Lingering (*Weilen*): and presence, 192, 200; and thinghood, 110, 118

Logic: and Being, 25-26, 32, 39, 42, 63, 83, 177-78, 186-87, 204-5, 206, 208; and grammar, 8; laws of, 13, 24, 27-28; and *logos*, 12, 23-25, 31-32, 34-35, 107; and metaphysics, vi-vii, 20, 29, 46, 52, 92-96, 101; and negation, 36, 45-53, 59; and principle of contradiction, 26, 29-42, 44; and principle of identity, 26, 72, 82, 88-91; presuppositions in, 25, 33-35; and rightness, 10, 12, 25, 37, 41, 48; and sameness, 68-74, 124; as symbolic, 23, 41; and thinking, 10-12. *See also* Language; *Logos*

*Logik Die Frage nach der Wahrheit*: 24-26, 34, 40, 48, 107, 152

*Logos*: and origin of logic, 12, 31-32; as proposition, 34-35; and saying, 25; and thinghood, 119. *See also* Language; Logic

Marx, Karl: and laws of logic, 216; and metaphysics, 223

Meaning: of Being, 11, 83, 105, 124, 182; and negation, 48; of proposition, 225

Metaphysics: and Being, 17-18, 99, 163, 179-80, 192; and deity, 129-30; as epochal, 152-58, 160-61, 164-65, 166-67, 170-71; and interpreting Heidegger, 4-6, 13, 17-20; and logic, vi, 13, 23, 28, 35; and negation, 46, 48, 52, 54, 59-60, 177; overcoming of, 18-19, 207; and presence, 94-95, 176, 187, 189, 203; and principle of contradiction, 29, 35; and principle of identity, 90, 92-100; and sameness, 69, 71, 157; and technology, 69, 161, 180; and thinghood, 14, 105, 108, 118; and thinking, 3, 7, 19-20, 149, 169-70

*Metaphysische Anfangsgründe Logik im Ausgang von Leibniz*: 25, 67, 133, 177, 183

Middle Ages: in history of metaphysics, 223

Mill, John S.: and the copula, 223

Mirroring: and Being, 227; and Leibniz, 218; and thinghood, 110, 114, 117, 119

Modernity: 223; and epochs of metaphysics, 154-55; and Heidegger, 206; and sameness, 82

Mood: and anxiety, 49; and negation, 47-50, 58-59, 64

Mortals: and deity, 137; and fourfold, 109, 111. *See also*: Dasein

Mysticism: and Heidegger, 8

Nature (*Wesen*): of deity, 13, 137; in fourfold, 116; of thinghood, 122. *See also* Essence

Nazism: and Heidegger, 20, 212

Near and far: and presence, 185; and sequence of epochs, 157; and thinghood, 112, 117

Necessity: and history of metaphysics, 167; and laws of logic, 28, 33; and principle of identity, 91, 96; and sequence of epochs, 172

Negation (*Nichts*): and anxiety, 47, 50-52, 57-59, 63-66; and Being, 52, 53, 56, 66, 165, 190; and Dasein, 50-51; and falsehood, 48-49; and logic, 36, 45-53, 59; and metaphysics, 46, 52, 54, 59-60; and Plato, 55, 62-64; and presence, 177, 185, 189, 195-96, 198-99; and principle of contradiction, 36-37, 44; and principle of identity, 26, 100; and thinghood, 65, 125-26; and thinking, 45, 47; and Whitehead, 60-62

Newton, Isaac: and laws as true, 27; and sameness, 68

*Nichts* (see Negation)

Nietzsche, Friedrich: 29, 30; and death of God, 129-30, 132; and history of metaphysics, 154-58, 162, 219; and nihilism, 158; and sameness, 68, 69

*Nietzsche I*: 30, 36, 49, 68-69, 72, 131, 153-54, 156, 158, 164

*Nietzsche II*: 29, 65, 68, 72, 148, 154-56, 158-59

Nihilism: and history of metaphysics, 155-56; and Nietzsche, 158

Nominalism: and thinghood, 121, 125

Noun: in Aristotle, 31, 39-40; in Plato, 214; and time, 39

Ontological difference: and Being, 56; and deity, 133; and fourfold, 124-25; and history, 149, 224; and metaphysics, 42, 79, 164; and negation, 56, 66, 195-99; and perception, 113; and presence, 176, 193-95; and principle of contradiction, 42; and principle of identity, 94; and sameness, 71-72, 74, 76, 81-82, 216; and simultaneity, 199-202; and thinghood, 105-6, 119; and thinking, 165, 169-70; and unity, 194-95. *See also* Being; Presence

Ontology: as name, 15, 16

Pantheism: and deity, 144, 146, 147
Parmenides: 32; and history of metaphysics, 161, 219; and presence, 182; and principle of contradiction, 30; and principle of identity, 92-93, 95, 97-98, 101; and sameness, 69, 71; as thinker, 152
Particularity: and negation, 55; and sameness, 74, 76; and thinghood, 123-24
Past: and deity, 140; and history of metaphysics, 169, 171; as part of presence, 184, 196-97, 199, 226
Perception: and appearances, 113-14; ontological status of, 113-14, 218; and presence, 181-82, 186, 225
*Phänomenologische Interpretation von Kants Kritik der reinen Vernunft*: 24
Philosophy: and God, 131, 148; "greatness" in, 192; Heidegger's place in, 206-7; and presence, 203, and science, 46
Place: and appropriation, 186; and fourfold, 112; and space, 112
Plato: and deity, 132; and metaphysics, 153-55, 156, 163; and negation, 47-48, 55; and origin of logic, 23, 30, 155; and principle of contradiction, 30; and sameness, 69; and unity, 123, 203
Poetizing (*Dichten*): and sameness, 68, and thinking, 8, 68
Possibility: and history, 160-62; and logic, 27; and metaphysics, 154, 156-58, 163; and negation, 57
Presence (*Anwesen*): and appropriation, 179, 186, 190-91; and deity, 130, 134, 139-41; 147; and language, 173, 176; and *logos*, 39, 119, 203; and negation, 66, 177, 189, 198; and possibility, 182; and preserving, 119, 192; and principle of identity, 94; and propositions, 7-8, 40; and sameness, 74-75, 86; and thinghood, 106, 110, 117-18, 181; and thinking, 106, 126, 148, 164, 170, 175-76, 187; and unity, 194-95. *See also* Being; Time
Present (*Gegenwart*): and God, 139, 141; as part of presence, 195-200
Preserving: and presence, 119, 192
*Prolegomenon zur Geschichte des Zeitbegriffs*: 9, 50, 107, 133
Proposition: as affirmative and negative, 40; and Being, 34; and negation, 53-54, 62-63; ontological limits of, 23-24; and presence, 188; and showing, 7; and thinghood, 107. *See also* Statement

Rahner, Karl: and Heidegger on God, 219
*Raum* (see Space)
Realism: and thinghood, 125
Reference: and negation, 48; and proposition, 70

Relation: and ontological difference, 81; and presence, 179
Relativism: and logic, 25
Representation: 13; and history of metaphysics, 16
Rightness: in logic, 12, 13

*Zur Sache des Denkens*: 7, 16, 86, 175-86
*Sagen* (see Saying)
Sameness: and appropriation, 85-86; and Being, 69, 70, 86; and destiny of Being, 183; and historicism, 82-83, 85; and history of metaphysics, 72, 74, 82; and language, 68, 73, 76; and negation, 76, 77; and ontological difference, 71-72, 74, 76, 81-82, 216; and part/whole, 73-74; and presence, 74-75, 86; and principle of identity, 71-72, 78, 88-89; and skepticism, 84-85; and thinghood, 107, 124, 126; and thinking, 74, 84, 124-25. *See also* Difference
Sartre, Jean-Paul: as "planetary" thinker, 224
*Der Satz vom Grund*: 26, 69, 71, 76, 130, 153, 157-59, 183
Saying (*Sagen*): and God, 133; and *logos*, 25
Schelling, Friedrich W. J.: and deity, 136, 220; and individuation, 218; and principle of identity, 92
*Schellings Abhandlung über das Wesen der menschlichen Freiheit (1809)*: 26-27, 136, 145, 154-55
Schopenhauer, Arthur: as "planetary" thinker, 224
Science: and logic, 22; and philosophy, 46
*Sein* (see Being)
*Sein und Zeit*: 8-9, 25, 27, 31-34, 40, 50, 129, 150-51, 157, 165, 177
Self-reference: in presence, 178, 184, 200
Showing: and Being, 176; and meaning of propositions, 225
Simultaneity: and presence, 184, 187-89, 193, 199-201; and principle of contradiction, 37, 38, 41, 44-45
Skepticism: and sameness, 84-85
Socrates: and metaphysics, 203; and thinking, 153, 154, 163, 210
*Sorge* (see Concern)
Space (*Raum*): and destiny, 159; and near and far, 117; as place, 112; and presence, 184
Spinoza, Benedictus: 162
Statement: and *logos*, 32. *See also* Proposition
"Step back": and thinking the ontological difference, 165-66
Strawson, P. F.: and principle of contradiction, 35-37, 38

*Die Technik und die Kehre*: 133, 148
Technology: and logic, 23; and metaphysics, 69, 161, 180; and presence, 224
Theology: and Being, 148; and dogma, 138, 142, 144; and fourfold, 132; and Heidegger, 128; and logic, 131, 132; and mortals, 137; and revelation, 145, 221. *See also* Deity; God
Thinghood (*Ding*): as artifact, 117, 125; and deity, 144-47; and destiny, 115; and fourfold, 109-13; in Kant, 105, 107, 130; and metaphysics, 105, 108, 118; and mortals, 109, 111; natures in, 120, 122-23; in Plato and Aristotle, 107; and possibility, 124; and sameness, 75-79, 125-26; and space-time, 117; and thinking, 106-7, 112, 124-25; and types, 116, 118; and wisdom, 119-20
Thinking (*Denken*): and Being, 16, 69, 170, 172, 187; and deity, 132-33, 142, 147-48; and language, 5-8, 34-35, 36; and logic, 10-12, 25; and metaphysics, 3, 7, 17, 19-20, 149, 169-70; and negation, 45, 47, 57, 66; and ontological difference, 165, 169-70; and poetizing, 18, 68; and presence, 106, 126, 148, 164, 170, 175-76, 187; and principle of contradiction, 28, 35, 41, 42; and principle of identity, 90, 92, 100-101; refutation of, 20-21; and rightness, 21, 24, 37, 41; and sameness, 69, 74, 84, 124-25; and thinghood, 106-7, 112, 124-25; and wisdom, 175
Thomas Aquinas, St.: and God, 136
Tillich, Paul: and Heidegger, 218
Time (*Zeit*): as Being, 177-78; and deity, 135, 136, 139, 147; as divisible into moments, 38-39; as four-dimensional, 185-86; and history, 150; and logic, 28-39, 94-95, 185; as past, present, future, 95, 101, 184, 195, 196-97. *See also* Being; Presence
Totality: and beings, 48; and negation, 48-49, 55, 57; and thinghood, 114, 126
Trakl, Georg: 125; and negation, 215

Truth: in Aristotle, 31, 40; and falsehood, 5; and interpreting Heidegger, 5, 9; and propositions, 23, 33; and untruth, 65. *See also* Falsehood
Type: concept of, 120-21; and deity, 139, 145; in fourfold, 116, 118; and problem of individuation, 116-25

Unity: 17, 218; and deity, 146, 148; and fourfold, 110, 123; and metaphysics, 163; and presence, 184-89, 192-94, 201; and principle of contradiction, 37; and principle of identity, 89-92, 99, 100
Universal: and thinghood, 120
*Unterwegs zur Sprache*: 16, 26, 32, 68, 110, 128, 132

Verb: in Aristotle, 31, 39; and grammar, 31; in Plato, 214
*Vorträge und Aufsätze*: 32, 68-69, 71, 108-12, 115-16, 119, 134, 139, 141, 145

*Was Heisst Denken?*: 23, 26, 32, 65, 68, 132, 157-59, 187, 196
*Was ist das—die Philosophie?*: 31-32, 154, 157
*Wegmarken*: 9-10, 15-17, 20, 23, 25, 46-53, 55-58, 65-66, 112, 129, 133-34, 155, 158-59, 176
*Weilen* (see Lingering)
*Welt* (see World)
*Wesen* (see Nature)
Whitehead, Alfred North: and negation, 60-62, 64
Wisdom: and thinghood, 119-20; and thinking, 175
*Wohnen* (see Dwelling)
World (*Welt*): and fourfold, 110, 217

*Zeit* (see Time)
Zeus: and Greeks, 143; and nature of deity, 130, 132, 142-43, 144